Rantings of the Loon Pant King

Rantings of the Loon Pant King

Tex Austin

The Book Guild Ltd

First published in Great Britain in 2023 by
The Book Guild Ltd
Unit E2 Airfield Business Park,
Harrison Road, Market Harborough,
Leicestershire. LE16 7UL
Tel: 0116 2792299
www.bookguild.co.uk
Email: info@bookguild.co.uk
Twitter: @bookguild

Copyright © 2023 Tex Austin

The right of Tex Austin to be identified as the author of this
work has been asserted by them in accordance with the
Copyright, Design and Patents Act 1988.

All rights reserved. No part of this publication may be
reproduced, transmitted, or stored in a retrieval system, in any form or by any means,
without permission in writing from the publisher, nor be otherwise circulated in
any form of binding or cover other than that in which it is published and without
a similar condition being imposed on the subsequent purchaser.

Typeset in 12pt Minion Pro

Printed and bound in the UK by TJ Books LTD, Padstow, Cornwall

ISBN 978 1915122 919

British Library Cataloguing in Publication Data.
A catalogue record for this book is available from the British Library.

About the Author

Tex Austin was born in England during the post-war period of austerity and rationing at the end of the 1940s. He discovered rock 'n' roll in the 1950s and started making records for Decca and Elektra in the 1960s. He then quit the music biz and became famous as the Loon Pant King at London's Kensington Market during the 70s. Many rants and escapades later he wrote this book to share his loony 'madventures'.

Tex Austin Website: www.tex-austin.co.uk
www.facebook.com/tex.austin.rantings

Contents

Foreword		xi
Introduction		xiii
1:	Let's Take it from the Top	1
2:	Our Gang	5
3:	School Days	9
4:	Broads and 1960s Beat Groups	13
5:	Topless	18
6:	Juvenile Delinquents	24
7:	Our First Live Gig	27
8:	YMCA	30
9:	Car Crazy /Belle Vue	34
10:	Action Van	37
11:	London Calling	40
12:	Soho Street Life	43
13:	Hitching Home	46
14:	The Imps (1963–1965)	50
15:	The Dimples (1965–1967)	55
16:	Lincoln Pop Festival	59
17:	Dimps vs Pink Floyd	63

18:	Cornwall, 1966	67
19:	Let's Rumble	71
20:	Party Time	78
21:	Don Arden / Galaxy Entertainments	83
22:	Decca Records	86
23:	Mad Geoff	90
24:	Gospel Garden (1967–1968)	95
25:	Pete Stringfellow / Camp Records	100
26:	Groupies	105
27:	Methuselah (1968–1969)	110
28:	Romantic Interlude	114
29:	Elektra Records	118
30:	Distant Jim (1969)	122
31:	Cosmarama / LSD	126
32:	Tripping	129
33:	Freak Out	133
34:	Bell-bottom Blues	138
35:	Loon Pants / Isle of White Festival 1970	142
36:	Kensington Market / Loondon Showroom	146
37:	Hebden Bridge	150
38:	Luckie Mucklebackit's Experimental Clothing Laboratory	154
39:	Cologne Exhibition / Wuppertal Monorail	158
40:	Into Europe	162
41:	Typical Day at Kensington Market	167
42:	Release / The Beast	172
43:	Shit or Bust	178
44:	Hong Kong Pong	182
45:	Hampton Court Daze	187
46:	Taggs Island	191
47:	Dingwall's	194

48:	Musical Chairs	198
49:	Upcerne Downcerne	203
50:	Asterix	207
51:	Greece / Poros	212
52:	Punk Scene	215
53:	Alice Pollock / Circus	218
54:	Dave Gilmour / Alice Pollock Fashion Show	222
55:	John Conteh / John Bindon / Ossie Clark	227
56:	New York, New York	231
57:	New Orleans / Cajun Country	235
58:	Los Angeles	239
59:	San Francisco / Marin County	242
60:	Morroco / Marrakech / Agadir	245
61:	Putney / Incredible String Band	248
62:	Islington / Hope and Anchor / Pogues	252
63:	Ranelagh Yacht Club	256
64:	Pepperdines Sarsaparilla	261
65:	Free Drinks	265
66:	Busking In London	270
67:	Gigging In Munich	275
68:	Demon Records / Muswell Hill Murders	278
69:	Tex's Royal Connection	281
70:	Sooterkin	286
71:	Samoir Django Festival	291
72:	Sam Miguels	295
73:	'60s Megabash	299
74:	A Bonfire of The Vanities	304
75:	Conspiracy Theory Or Fact?	308
76:	Final Curtain	312
77:	Appendicitis	316

Foreword

Touch wood I'm not quite ready for the old Brompton cocktail just yet, but as the years roll by, one's awareness of the importance of social history tends to become more acute. Memories and reminiscences turn into valuable currency as our familiar world is vandalised in the name of progress.

Amongst all the mundane and trivial mental images floating about in the ether, there are countless little gems out there that should be cherished and captured for posterity before it's too late. Often more interesting than great battles, royal weddings or grand state occasions are the weird and wonderful tales of ordinary folk. Hopefully my small contribution to this archive hits the spot.

The stories are loosely chronological and mainly factual, though mildly censored in an attempt to protect the innocent and guilty alike. Here then is a flippant, irreverent and tongue-in-cheek account of the years spent playing in various aspiring 1960s beat groups and of my rag trade experiences as a fashion designer and 'King of the Loon Pants' during the early 1970s glam rock period to punk and beyond. As I say, all that's written here is true-ish and a reasonably accurate slice of late twentieth-century life as I see it.

What instigated the actual writing of this volume was a request for anecdotes by Ray Moody, author of *Nearly Famous* (A–Z of '60s East Coast UK Rock Groups). I jotted down a small selection of short stories for him about life on the road and found the process most enjoyable, proving both cathartic and therapeutic.

Although more comfortable writing than public speaking and not by nature a raconteur, I have on occasion as the mood has taken me and, much to my own surprise, held a small but appreciative audience spellbound with some personal horror story or another and many times people have told me that I ought to write a book. I don't know if they just meant instead of boring them to death with long-winded stories, but I've chosen to accept it as a compliment in the spirit that I hope it was intended. In any event I have acted on their advice and trust that the final result isn't too disappointing.

I dedicate this load of old baloney and 'Tales of Derring-Don't' to Josie, my long-suffering other half. Also to my mum and dad for all the grief I've put them through over the years, and all the relatives and friends that have bailed me out from time to time. I'm sure they all know who they are. Well, here goes…

DISCLAIMER. It needs to be stressed that this book has been over thirty years in the writing and should be recognised as a work of its time. Please be warned that these memoirs contain colourful colloquialisms and ideologies dating back to the '50s, '60s and '70s, and strongly reflect the values and norms of the era. As an experiment, I thought it maybe more interesting and accessible to have lots of bite-sized chapters to randomly dip into at any point, making each one almost a mini story in itself.

Introduction

Loon Pants

'Loon Pants' were designed, manufactured and marketed by my trading company Craig Stuart Fashions Ltd during the early 1970s.

People have often asked me how I feel about being the man who invented 'Loon Pants'. Well, admittedly it's a rather dubious claim to fame, but to be fair they were extremely trendy between 1970 and 1975.

What exactly are they, some of you may be thinking? Loon Pants were 27" flared, semi-hipster, unisex trousers in cotton drill with a zip and a button but no pockets or proper waistband. That's it. They were flattering, easy to make, dirt cheap and sold by the truckload.

Regardless of the fact that they are now thought of as a bit of a joke, almost everybody was wearing them at the time and a lot of people made a great deal of money from good old Loons. The first pair ever sold was from the back of a minivan at the infamous 1970 Isle of White Festival featuring

Jimi Hendrix, ELP and the Who, etc. We started with 250 pairs that sold out within a couple of days, so it soon became apparent how popular they were destined to be.

After that I punted them around Kensington Market, which had now taken over from Carnaby Street and King's Road as the world's top fashion Mecca. It was without doubt *the* place to be and, our first customers were Lionel Avery at Pam Todd's stall and Ian Grieg at Flarewear / Whispering Kite. These outrageous bell-bottoms took off immediately and were called Elephant Flares to start with but soon became known as Loon Pants. This name obviously struck a chord with the public.

As word got out we even started selling them from my parents' house. The front room was turned into a thriving retail outlet and my dear old mum was kept busy with a constant stream of eager customers turning up all day. She loved it, especially when footballer Kevin Keegan, who lived just round the corner, kept popping round for a new pair every couple of weeks.

Sales went stratospheric at Kensington Market and then started flying off the shelves nationwide. Available in every conceivable colour and fabric they became iconic throughout the UK as part of the 'post hippie' uniform, usually worn together with tank tops and stack-heeled platform boots. Or alternatively with frog fronts or tie-dye granddad shirts. Amazingly 'Loons' stayed in style for half a decade, until Falmers, Baggies, South Sea Bubble and the punk scene took over.

Even the V&A requested a pair for permanent display at the museum together with a matching Loon jacket. So to answer the question, I guess that I do feel quite proud in a surreal kind of way that Craig Stuart Loons became a small part of rag trade history.

1

Let's Take it from the Top

It's a well-worn cliché that most people declare a single defining moment as the one that irrevocably changed their lives forever. Exactly the same thing happened to me the day I heard Elvis Presley in 1956. It was a blinding revelation, an almost religious experience which I remember as clearly as yesterday. I can picture it now. All of us kids sitting in the school hall dining room, scoffing our gruel. Just another monotonous day of incarceration at Colditz Junior Boys when one of the teachers, Paddy Patterson, who was feared for his liberal use of 'the slipper', was testing the assembly hall PA sound system for the forthcoming Christmas play. Then suddenly, 'Hound Dog' came blasting out of the loudspeakers, the most amazing sound I ever heard.

A split second later, jitterbugging juveniles were involuntarily leaping about on tables with food flying everywhere, jiving around to this fantastic new noise. After having spent several years of excruciatingly boring classical piano lessons and suffering a BBC diet of 'How Much Is That Doggy in the Window' and 'Oh Mien Papa', I had almost developed a pathological hatred of music. But this was something different. In an instant I was like a child possessed, strutting about, posing with an imaginary air guitar, miming to unknown and indecipherable lyrics in a manner totally out of character with an otherwise ordinary nine-year-old boy.

Momentarily, mayhem ensued, but almost as soon as the fun had started it was all over. The disruptive cacophony was rapidly unplugged by the headmaster, who no doubt gave poor old Paddy a good bollocking, but by then it was too late and the damage done. The die was cast. I wanna be a rock 'n' roller. Cheers, Paddy!

But let's not get ahead ourselves. Long before I dreamt of becoming a 'Teen Idol' or the 'Loon Pant King' there were plenty of other adventures to mention first, so let's just take it from the top. Or we can take it from the bottom, where, let's face it, the bulk of this effluent will emanate. So just to set the scene, my first memory at around the age of three was getting almost pecked to death by a jealous cockerel who found me in the hen house snuggled up asleep with his pretty prize pullet. I lived to tell the tale only because my old man intervened and drop-kicked the vicious bastard clean over the rooftops to that great big KFC in the sky.

My second memory was helping a neighbour to dismantle a Rolls-Royce limousine that was his pride and joy. I say help loosely because he'd taken the engine to pieces ready for repair and went in for his dinner, leaving all the bits neatly and systematically spread out on his garage floor ready for reassembly. In his absence (as you may already have guessed), I sneaked in and obligingly rearranged all the various components whilst borrowing a few especially choice items for my own private collection. Upon his return all hell broke wind and I got the distinct impression that my invaluable assistance wasn't fully appreciated. Many such calamitous and ill-fated incidents set the pattern of much of my life to come.

To paraphrase Spike Milligan, I was born at a very early age having been conceived in Scarborough. Nine months later I was sprogged in Scunthorpe, a bleak northern steel town and butt of cheap music hall jokes much like Penistone and Cockermouth. Yeah, I know, I can hardly believe my incredible good fortune either. 'Twas in this unholy place my parents branded* me Craig 'Nick' Austin, though I've been called a lot worse. Being half Scottish on my mother's side might explain why I was called Craig, but it remains a mystery as to why my old pappy was the only one that ever called me Nick. I'm not sure if that was meant to be Saint Nick or Old Nick. Probably the latter, for even as a toddler I was always a mischievous little devil, forever running away, hiding out and getting into bother. By the way, I wasn't tagged as Tex until much later in life.

---

*   (This footnote might seem slightly complicated at first, but stick with it because it is *extremely* interesting.)
     I use the phrase 'branded' advisedly because it's a little-known fact that our original birth certificate is basically a warehouse receipt under Uniform Commercial Code as defined by Black's Law Dictionary. In other words we are human collateral used as a security traded on the stock exchange and our own birth certificates are just copies.
     From every birth certificate issued, a legal personality (or legal fiction), otherwise known as a strawman, is created with the same name. Confused? Well, that's the general idea so as to fool and bamboozle. When government officials, court clerks or police often appear to be speaking English they are actually speaking 'legalese' designed to make you agree to verbal and written contracts without you even knowing it. The most common example is that when someone is being cautioned, the cops will say, 'do you understand?' as in 'do you comprehend?'. However, what this actually means in legalese is 'do you stand under my authority?'. As soon as you say yes, it creates a verbal contract.

Whenever you 'register' something it amounts to handing over title, be it a car (where you become the registered keeper) or a newly born child. When a parent notifies on their baby by signing a birth certificate, the child becomes a ward of the state that is theoretically allowed to take the child away at any time or for any reason.

Or whenever you receive a 'bill' it is sent to you but actually belongs to your strawman, not you. All fines, summons and legal documents, etc., that start with Mr, Mrs or Miss written in capital letters again belongs to your strawman, not you. Unless you know better, when you go to court you are representing your strawman, and as a result, you, the human, take on any fines or taxes, etc., on behalf of the strawman.

In other words, the 'human you' in Common Law (not Maritime, Admiralty or Statute Law) does not need to pay, but because you made a contract with the court by appearing on behalf of your strawman you then become liable. So by creating this corporate fiction with the same name, a registered birth certificate can be used to denote ownership and be monetised as financial futures or shares in the stock market.

Wikipedia and various legal and government sources deny this is correct, but they would, wouldn't they? However, if it is true, each certificate could be worth millions, so as you can imagine, the implications are simply mind-zapping.

Austin family photo.

2

Our Gang

The end of the Second World War was a period of severe austerity and rationing when chocolate and bananas were still classed as luxury items. However, Horlicks and Ovaltine were easily available, and as a result I was often sick as a dog after devouring a whole container in one sitting, stupid prat.

To subsidise the meagre rations, my parents kept poultry and grew cabbages and various other fruit and veg in our large back garden. Then one day, because the authorities wanted to turn our orchard into a public park, we were shifted from a big old rambling house to a little shoebox on a hideous modern council estate.

Our new 'sterile living unit' in the middle of this grim reservation was so cold that throughout winter the bedroom windows were permanently iced up, even on the inside. The only good thing was there were loads of other kids in the neighbourhood to mess about with and we soon formed our own little gang of reprobates.

My best pal was Mick West, even though we scrapped much of the time when he kept pinching my dinky toy cars. At around the age of four I did (just the once) manage to beat the crap out of him in front of a large crowd of cheering onlookers before he was whisked off to the doctors for emergency treatment. For me it was a proud moment considering that 'Westy' was later to become a notorious local hardcase with a formidable reputation.

In front of our row of houses there was a big overgrown derelict field where all the lads built a maze of trenches and dens covered in tin sheeting. Occasionally we'd kidnap some poor little sod from the estate and hold them prisoner for a few hours till their parents sent out a search party. Equally disturbing and for some abstruse anthropological reason known only to the likes of Sir David Attenborough, we would just spontaneously squat down and shit in opposite corners of our dugout pit. Perhaps it was some weird kind of subconscious tribal or territorial type thing? QI, though, don't you think?

As well as playing cowboys and injuns, chicken and block (similar to tag), one of our favourite escapades was digging up grass sods and piling them up across the adjoining road to stop the traffic getting through. On one occasion we even managed to up-skittle a grocery van, the same one selling the cream cakes that I used to poke my fingers into when no one was looking.

A particularly curious fetish I had was that every morning I'd tip the leftover contents of the teapot onto hot embers left in the fire grate. I just loved to hear the sound of sizzling tea leaves and watch a pool of sticky brown gunge spread pleasingly over the hearth. No matter how often I got a rollicking I just carried on doing it, leaving my poor old mum to mop up the treacly mess on a daily basis. Dear Marje, is this considered normal behaviour?

Before we ever got our own telly I'd go to my grandparents' house to watch *Andy Pandy* and later *Bill and Ben the Flowerpot Men* on their magic lantern. Whilst at the house I'd secretly root around in cupboards and drawers searching for sweeties. The choccy bars I somehow always managed to sniff out were in fact 'Chocolax', a laxative chocolate that delivered a whole new confectionary experience. After wolfing the lot down in one go, it wasn't long before the purge began and Montezuma proceeded to extract his spiteful revenge. Even though this tiresome folly was repeated on a regular basis I never seemed to learn. Every week they'd try and hide the stuff away, but I'd always manage to find it again next time.

It was much the same with my granddad's asthma cigarettes, which intrigued me greatly. At a glance they looked like regular fags but were in fact just a white tube with what I assumed was a small tobacco pellet at one end. One by one I'd work my way through the packet and briefly pretended to smoke them before blasting out the pellets like a pea shooter. As usual I'd be given a thick ear, but it never stopped me doing it over and over again. My granddad needed these medicinal ciggys for bronchial problems after being gassed in the First World War. Medicinal asthma cigarettes might sound like a contradiction in terms, but as I later discovered they were in fact herbal, not tobacco, and were all the rage before the invention of inhalers.

As a child I obviously never realised which specific herbs they contained and even now it's quite hard to believe what was actually in them. The ingredient list reads like a medieval witch's flying-brew. There was a potent mixture of delirium-inducing narcotics including Datura (loco-weed), Belladonna (deadly nightshade) and a highly poisonous psychoactive anaesthetic known as Henbane. On top of this euphoric concoction were added various hallucinogenic substances such as opium and cannabis plus hemlock and mandrake that are both lethal if consumed to excess. Wow, no wonder my old grandpappy loved his super snout so much.

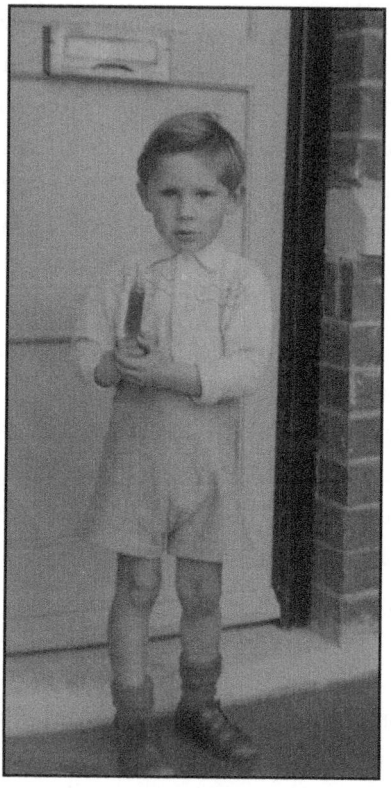

A young Tex.

3

School Days

After five years of seemingly endless summers, gallivanting free as a flea, the diabolical school system finally imposed itself and then proceeded to mercilessly quash our natural spirit, filling our heads with what's laughingly called education. Admittedly, within months we were learning the basic three Rs which I concede as being quite useful, but thereafter I personally absorbed very little of real value apart from through my own private studies. To me school was no more than a glorified borstal and a waste of potentially the best ten years of our young lives. Imagine travelling the world at that age instead of being stuck in a sausage machine churning out fodder for factories that no longer even exist.

The only good thing about school was being severely spanked by strict middle-aged ladies, although I didn't fully appreciate it at the time. Believe it or not I was actually quite bright but detested the institutional regimentation from day one with its rigid rules and silly uniforms. Instinctively I always loathed school caps, shiny shoes and wearing socks unless permanently rolled down like a street urchin.

The year 1953 was the coronation of Queen Elizabeth, and if you can swallow this, they taught everybody, including all the boys, how to curtsey, for Christ's sake. Humiliating or what? There was a big celebration party where we were all given a day off and a special gift from the new queen. I was looking forward to mine, fully expecting to receive a Meccano Set, which was my favourite toy at the time. However, instead I got some crappy piece of tat which out of spite I threw on the floor and stamped on in front of the whole civic gathering.

Yes, admittedly I was a bit of a problem child to start out with, but slowly over time my wayward behaviour did improve… marginally. I have a theory that *The Beano* comic was responsible for much of this rebellious conduct. It's not surprising when our role models were Dennis the Menace, Roger the Dodger and the Bash Street Kids. Even Minnie the Minx and Beryl the Peril from other rival comics were girly versions of Dennis the Menace. I was known as Craig the Plague, by the way.

The tail end of the '50s and early '60s just drifted by with eleven-plus exams, new schools, canings, suspensions and a fanatical obsession with train-spotting (yes, afraid so!). However, I must add in vigorous defence of the much-maligned 'railway enthusiasts' of the glorious steam era, that we were nothing like the nerdy anoraks of today.

Even at such a tender age we loved rock 'n' roll and had a certain style, if only as apprentice tearaways sneaking round loco sheds and running wild all over the country for days on end. Even on our meagre pocket money we could still afford the cheap excursion and rover tickets available back then in the good old days of British Railways. We would giggle uncontrollably while asking for a three and nine ticket, the cost of a day return to Doncaster that we knew was the same price as a packet of Durex. We'd survive on a diet of Lubbly Jubblys, Nux bars and crisps, all washed down with a bottle of Vimto.

It would probably be unthinkable now, but without supervision or a care in the world, we'd be off trawling the back-street slums of Liverpool and Glasgow in our relentless quest for more and more engine numbers. It was partly a form of addiction, I suppose, but was mainly just one long, continuous, exciting childhood adventure, where no one knew who we were or what mischief we were up to. It was exhilarating and gave us a taste of complete freedom away from the usual restraints of home, school and authority. Then eventually we'd run out of funds and return back to normality, exhausted and covered from head to toe in soot and grime.

Just for the record and for any other saddos out there, my own local motive power depot was Frodingham with its shed code 36C, home of WD Vulcan 90732. But as they say, all good things must come to an end. As much fun as it had been, when the hormones finally kicked in, our little train-spotting hobby was soon replaced with a much greater fascination for 'Girls, Girls, Girls'.

It was at this point that the phrase 36C acquired an entirely different connotation after all the lads suddenly started taking an unhealthy interest in the girls' netball team. At first I was quite shy but soon got the hang of it and somehow, without wishing to brag, ended up with my very own fan club and Valentine's galore. At school my nickname was 'Crag' and my best mate at the time was a guy called 'Logger' who was also a bit of a heartthrob. He too had a similar fan club. All the girls were either in his fan club or mine and no one else really got a look in.

Then very unfairly, we were given six of the best (thrashed mercilessly with a cane) by 'Rastass', the psycho headmaster, for something that wasn't really our fault. This happened after things got out of hand when both fan clubs started a mass graffiti campaign all over the school walls, scrawling 'I LOVE CRAG' or 'I LOVE LOGGER' absolutely everywhere. It was much like Beatlemania before it was even invented. Quite phenomenal, really, but we just took our good fortune for granted and perhaps never really cashed in to best advantage. If only I knew then what I know now!

4

Broads and 1960s Beat Groups

Whilst in our final interminable year at school, we formed a small clique, calling ourselves the Maverick Gang, modelled on the popular TV series starring our hero James Garner as the frock-coated gambler Bret Maverick. Each of us chose what we thought were hardcase names mainly beginning with the letter B, such as Butch, Bluto, Brutus and Brick, though there was also a Duke (pronounced Dook) which was deemed acceptably tough. We'd be up to all the usual horseplay, terrorising the younger kids by sticking their heads down the toilet bowl and giving them dead legs or Chinese burns.

Although school uniforms were compulsory, the Mavericks would flout the rules as much as possible. My dear old granny would taper my standard-issue grey flannel trousers into skin-tight drainpipes and school ties would be worn thin side forward, thus transforming them into trendy 'Slim Jims'. Streaks of lightening or spiky maces would be drawn onto shirt collars and pink dots painted on shoes. These would usually be either Denson 'winkle pickers' or crepe sole Stylo Stomper 'beetle crushers'.

By now I was heartily sick of school but somehow fluked a handful of 'mock' GCEs. However, by the time it came to taking the real ones I'd had enough. At this point I just ditched all my books before taking off on a week's holiday to the Norfolk Broads with a couple of mates who also didn't give a toss about exams. We hired a cabin cruiser from Hoseasons who must have been mad letting us loose with any of their boats. Having said that, it wasn't exactly one of their luxury models so maybe they guessed we might be trouble.

After a few initial minor collisions in the rusty old tub, we eventually got the hang of it and became quite expert sailors by the end of the week. It was great just to get away from any thoughts of revising for boring 'O' Levels and we just got on with the business of exploring the labyrinth of picturesque East Anglian waterways. The furthest we ventured was to Great Yarmouth, where the boat was almost dragged out by the current into the North Sea, which was quite scary to say the least.

In the evenings we'd moor up and find the nearest pub, obviously. Even though all three of us were underage, we usually got away with being served without any problems. After a skinful we'd then head for some village dance or record hop to eye up the local talent. For some strange reason their yobby yokel boyfriends didn't take too kindly to this and most nights we'd end up running for our lives to avoid a kicking.

During the day we'd sober up and have a bit of fun with lads from some of the other boats. It was like being pirates attacking and sabotaging each other's ships. Our best revenge attack came after we filled up several huge 'Rubber Johnny' condom bombs with water before lobbing them at our rival's boat, totally drenching them and their vessel into submission.

Back home after our little marine adventure we were all obsessively into rock 'n' roll, and like everybody else at the time I was glued to Radio Luxembourg every night. Between songs there were non-stop adverts for Horace Batchelor and his 'famous infra-draw method', whatever the hell that was. All I do know is being indelibly brainwashed that his address was in Keynsham, spelt K-E-Y-N-S-H-A-M. Keynsham. Bristol.

Anyway Radio Luxembourg, '208' on the medium waveband, gave us all that Auntie Beeb (BBC Light Programme) couldn't or wouldn't. Names that became legends like Bill Haley, Elvis Presley, Buddy Holly, Little Richard, Jerry Lee Lewis, Eddie Cochran, the Everly Brothers, Gene Vincent, Chuck Berry and Pat Boone (no, only kidding).

It wasn't long before I acquired my very own record player, a Ferguson 'Elizabethan' Stereo, together with the first record I ever bought, 'Love Potion No. 9' by The Clovers. From then on our gang would skive off school and spend half our lives hanging around in record shops, ferreting out more and more obscure US-imported titles to impress our friends.

By this time there were also some quite respectable British rock acts around such as Cliff Richard and The Drifters and later Hank Marvin with The Shadows, who inspired a whole generation of young guitar players. My three personal favourites were Nero and the Gladiators, Krew Kats and The Cresters. Also popular were:

- Billy Fury and the Tornados.
- Johnny Kidd and the Pirates.
- Mike Berry and the Outlaws.

- Joe Brown and the Bruvvers.
- Dave Berry and the Cruisers.
- Marty Wild and the Wildcats.
- Adam Faith and the Roulettes.
- Peter Jay and the Jay Walkers.
- Shane Fenton and the Fentones.
- Tommy Bruce and the Bruisers.
- Screaming Lord Sutch and the Savages.

Most of these acts played the local 'Scunny Baths' ballroom on a Saturday and also on Thursday night, which was payday. The place would be heaving with drunken brawling steelworkers and teddy boys kicking the shit out of each other.

Before my crowd were really old enough to go into pubs, we'd each polish off a whole bottle of cheap QC or RSVP sherry down some back alley in less than five minutes and then stagger around the dancehall completely rat-arsed for the rest of the night. To this day as a consequence, I cannot stomach the smell of sherry or port without wanting to retch.

Once inside the venue, they'd always have some corny dance band on first, which everybody merely tolerated. In those days rock music was still such a novelty that everyone would go totally ape when the beat group finally took to the stage. It's quite amusing that the drummer in almost every group I ever saw at the Baths Hall managed to bang their head on the low balcony at some point during their performance.

The funniest one was Honey of the Honeycombs, who caught a serious whack that sent her flying 'arse over tit' right off the back of the stage. The audience gasped as she vanished from sight before re-appearing moments later in a flood of tears, dazed and dishevelled. This humiliating fall from grace was by far the best bit of their show but the poor girl was in such a state that she had to be replaced by a stand-in drummer for the rest of the set. Apart from that they were rubbish and the worst group I ever saw at the old Baths Ballroom. On the other hand, even some of the lesser-name outfits of that period are worthy of mention:

- The Lizards.
- The Puppets.
- The Jaybirds.
- The Cheynes.
- The Beatmen.
- The Redcaps.
- The Marauders.
- Beat Merchants.
- Mighty Avengers.
- The Flee-Reckkers.
- Bern Elliot and the Fenmen.
- Denny Lane and the Diplomats.

The whole scene of course changed with the arrival of The Beatles and the sound of Merseybeat. It was around this time I was given my first guitar for Christmas, so thanks for that, Nana Nora. It was a blond Hofner Senator, which by today's standards was a primitive box with a high action, no cutaway and a real dog to play. But to me at the time, it felt like the guitar equivalent of a Stradivarius. Within weeks I'd worn my fingers to the bone learning Chuck Berry licks and three chords from Bert Weedon's 'Play in a Day' tutorial. In no time I was putting a band together with a few pals and organising our first rehearsal.

5

Topless

For our first rehearsal, a friend generously offered us the use of his father's garage. Conveniently it was part of a large detached house with no immediate neighbours and hence no nasty noise problems. Unfortunately, the only nasty noise problem was the one we created ourselves. To say it was a bleedin' awful racket would be a gross understatement.

The vocalist was tone-deaf and the drummer was a reject from the boys' brigade with only one single, solitary snare drum. The guitarists, including myself, were rubbish and we barely hit a right note between us during the whole session. It was a demeaning shambles and we were left wallowing in self-pity that our naive dreams of being famous by teatime had been cruelly shattered. What a bunch of chumps! Back to the drawing board.

By the second rehearsal, after replacing the useless singer, things were starting to get slightly more organised and beginning to come together. I was now working as an apprentice 'printer's devil' which conveniently provided finance for a modest RSC amplifier with a couple of cheapo Fane loudspeakers. Everyone began buying items of new equipment and we more or less carried on for a while in a state of blind optimism. Then things generally started to shape up with a vague feeling of anticipation that something was in the air. We didn't know quite what but were soon to find out.

This was the summer of 1963 and though I was now working, the rest of the lads were still at school or sixth form college. In the afternoons and evenings, everyone would just hang out at the rehearsal room doing homework or be sitting around strumming guitars and playing records.

Like I said, we knew something was afoot when lo and behold there appeared at the door this new housekeeper that we'd never seen before. She had obviously been employed to look after the property and keep her eye on us lot while our friend's dad was away on business. Naturally we were slightly concerned whether this new set of domestic arrangements would jeopardise the status quo, as we more or less had the run of the place with rarely any adults around.

Upon her arrival we cautiously gave each other the once-over, and to be honest, she wasn't really my type, though she seemed very pleasant and slightly resembled Morticia from the Addams Family. She must have been in her mid-thirties, I guess, and quite attractive in the more mature womanly kind of way, bearing in mind, of course, that we were only just turning sixteen at the time.

A couple of days went by and there didn't appear to be any problems, in fact quite the reverse. At first she would kindly bring in trays of delicious ice-cold drinks and platters of freshly cut sandwiches, which was all very nice. Then she happened to mention she was a bit of an artist and could she paint a picture of the band? Yeah, sure, no problem, and with this she set to, sketching a huge wall-sized mural which was to take a week or so to complete. We were quite flattered and looked forward to viewing the finished product in due course. Anyway, life carried on as normal for a few more days until suddenly, things definitely started hotting up.

During the rehearsal, a rumour went flying round that she was sunbathing in the back garden, *topless*! Nah, it couldn't be. What, here in England? Such a thing was unheard of in 1963. Of course, in a flash we were all up at the window checking, just in case. Sure enough, there she was as promised wearing only the bottom half of a very skimpy bikini, her ample assets exposed for all the world to see. By now, our noses were pressing hard against the glass as the lads fell about like sniggering buffoons, pushing, shoving and tumbling over each other for a better view. At the same time we were trying not to make too much din so as not to disturb her and make her cover up. Quite obviously she must have heard us but just pretended she hadn't, knowing full well what we were up to. Wow, this was way more exciting than the occasional sneaky peek at mucky photos in *Health and Efficiency* magazine. From here on in, things began to get distinctly raunchy!

The topless sessions became a regular feature and the novelty beginning to wear off when events took a new twist. Upon my arrival at rehearsals after work, one of the lads (no names, no pack drill) looked like the cat that had got the cream. With a self-satisfied smirk, he proudly announced that he'd given the housekeeper one. This was confirmed with barely concealed squeals of delight by another unnamed third party who, rather unchivalrously, boasted that he too had performed the dirty deed. I still didn't really believe them, assuming it was just a wind-up, when she appeared round the door dressed only in a see-through negligee, provocatively announcing that she had something to show us. My mind was now working overtime as she beckoned us through the house. What on earth was going to happen next?

As it transpired, she had finally finished the group portrait and this was preview time. The painting, large as life was a garish, brightly coloured depiction of all the boys in the band with grinning faces, leering and lecherous. All of us were distinctly recognisable and, although fully clothed, had grotesquely exaggerated features and huge great bulges and lumps in the fronts of our trousers. It was genuinely shocking and debauched, but we just thought it was hilarious. Hardly a great masterpiece but definitely 'interesting'. However, all the evidence was stacking up and began to confirm the truth of the other guys' earlier revelations. I had an eerie sense of foreboding that, although I didn't really fancy her, it was only a matter of time before my turn came to succumb and join the rest of the flock. Like a lamb to the slaughter.

In the early '60s it was trendy for every man and his dog to want to be the next Brian Epstein. Somehow we acquired one such misguided chancer who thought he'd try for a piece of the action and he became our manager. He was a few years older than us and claimed to be a journalist, which we figured would be handy for a bit of free PR. Plus he also had the added attraction of owning a van, useful in the unlikely event that we might ever be good enough to play a gig.

As it turned out, he was a bit of a 'Jack the Lad' and in no time at all had acquainted himself with the housekeeper and was taking full advantage of the situation. Also by now, the rest of the band, including myself, had finally submitted to her overwhelming powers of seduction and were becoming old hands at the game. At first I declined, but she got very angry and stormed out of the room, returning with a bowl of ice cream which was thrust in my face. "This is what you should have given me," she screamed hysterically. If she didn't get her own way she'd go berserk as if possessed. Then, in the twinkle of an eye, she could instantly change from a mad woman into a sweet, alluring temptress with a completely different personality. In the end there was no point in trying to resist.

She was totally manipulative and it was like being entangled in a black widow spider's web and getting devoured. We were just young male bodies to be simply chewed up and spat out. It was as if she could cast spells and charms, luring her innocent victims into doing exactly whatever she wanted. I don't know if it was something she put in the drinks, but she had all sorts of aphrodisiac pills and potions by her bed. I shall never forget my first time. She actually lured me up to her room with the immortal words: "Would you like to come up and see my etchings?" Truly. I mean, how could anyone possibly fall for a line like that without having first been drugged or something.

The whole situation was starting to get out of hand. The truancy officer must have been starting to smell a rat after we began bringing loads of mates down from the school so they too could get their wicked way. There was always a mountain of bikes permanently parked up against the side of the house as the lads queued up to take it in turns to service the boiler. It was like a station waiting room. The word was spreading like wildfire. Roll up, roll up. Raving nymphomaniac. Come and get it. Soon, total strangers were turning up unannounced for a bite of the cherry. Cars would be arriving all hours of day and night. It was getting ridiculous. She of course loved every minute of it and was insatiable.

Any thoughts of music had taken a back seat, as it was impossible to get any work done with all the distractions going on. It was chaos and things couldn't possibly go on like this for much longer. The final straw came when our manager, 'Jack the Lad', took it upon himself to start charging Norwegian sailors from nearby Gunness Wharf £5 a time for her services. They'd turn up mob-handed in full nautical uniform, sou'westers, rubber wading boots, the lot, to queue up in the lounge and wait their turn. I don't think she was seeing any of the money or was even bothered about it. She was just having the time of her life.

Then suddenly the bubble burst. Our friend's father who owned the house finally got wind of what was going on, and all the fun and games came to an abrupt halt. The housekeeper was dismissed and swiftly dispatched back from whence she came. We in turn were given our marching orders and unfortunately lost the rehearsal room into the bargain. And that was that.

6

Juvenile Delinquents

After this setback, a brief period in limbo ensued where we amused ourselves with various irresponsible delinquent pranks and temporary diversions. We'd taken to driving around in the manager's van, dressed up in cloaks and masks staging mock murders, stabbings and abductions around the town centre. Half the fun was observing the reaction of any passing witness to these elaborate charades. A bit sick, I know, but who can fathom the workings of the bored and deranged teenage mind?

Another game was the escaped lunatic routine. A couple of us would dress up in white doctor's coats and sit in the front of the van while a 'mental patient', locked in the back, would be acting demented, screaming and banging wildly on the inside of the vehicle trying to attract attention. Once we'd gathered a decent crowd of onlookers, the lunatic, looking suitably bonkers in striped pyjamas, would escape through the back doors and make a run for it. The men in white coats would set off in frantic pursuit, shouting to the bystanders, "Stop the Mad Axeman"... as if.

Eventually they'd catch the escapee and drag him back kicking and struggling, then bundle him into the back of the van before driving off at high speed, supposedly to the asylum. These antics would always prompt the desired results and were a good giggle, but I'm sure nobody watching actually took any of it seriously. They probably just thought it some kind of perverse publicity stunt or a bunch of jerks making a 'hammy' horror movie. Whatever, we'd probably get arrested these days for such activity.

Also, don't ask me why, but late at night we would drive down to this rough doss house called Santon Hostel with the sole intention of waking up all the sleeping Irish labourers with the loudest boat foghorn you've ever heard in your life. It was driven by compressed air and could be heard a mile away. The racket was awesome. We'd race in, skidding round in the van on the gravel in front of the hostel, yelling, banging and creating a terrible din with this foghorn, trying to provoke these poor sods who'd been flogging their guts out all day on some building site. Of course they rushed out to give chase but were always half-drunk, half-dressed or half-asleep and were never quite quick enough to catch us. For no apparent good reason whatsoever we'd be there, hanging out the back of the van, taunting and gesticulating at a bunch of totally irate, vengeful navvies with murder in their hearts, who were right on our tails. Looking back now, I can only assume we must have had a death wish.

Whilst on the subject of death wishes, around this time I had become obsessed with motorbikes in the misguided belief I was cut out to be a Hells Angel. The fantasy was to be a 'ton up' boy on a classic 1,000cc Vincent Black Shadow with the wind in my hair and the freedom of the road. This was, of course, pre skid-lids. The reality was a clapped-out 200cc Triumph Tiger Cub, which would virtually rattle itself to pieces at anything approaching 40mph. The gearbox leaked oil and by rights should have seized up at any moment, though I didn't have an inkling regarding such mundane mechanical matters.

Because of my lack of even the most basic concept of motorcycle maintenance, it was no time at all before the clutch cable snapped and the bike found itself climbing up a tree. Luckily I was thrown off at the initial lurch before the bike gathered maximum momentum. Somehow it stuck on full throttle and the bike took on a life of its own with wheels spinning, kicking mud and crap everywhere as it shot skywards in an incredible aerial display. My life flashed before me and in an instant any further desire to be astride any form of motorised two-wheeled transport was gone forever.

This close encounter suddenly put things back in some kind of perspective. Fannying around having a laugh was all very well, but time was a-wasting. Band rehearsals resumed in earnest and the manager was told to get his arse into gear. We're back on course.

7

Our First Live Gig

Desperate by now for a booking, the group's big break finally came in the winter of 1963. Billed as The Countdowns, our first-ever public performance was at the 'Iron and Steel', a dog-rough working men's club in Scunthorpe that was definitely on the wrong side of the tracks. Even by the standards of the day, this was particularly bad example of the type of shit-hole that most rock groups soon grew to hate, loathe and detest. Bingo ruled and the bands were called 'turns'.

Music was merely an unwelcome intrusion to the ubiquitous tombola and was always too loud for the punters. All we ever heard was, "Tone it down a couple of notches, lads, or tha'll be paid off by t'committee." This threat was always delivered in a 'reet' broad and wildly exaggerated northern accent and often accompanied by a barrage of missiles. Hence the witty phrase 'No turn unstoned'. God knows why they ever booked the bands in the first place.

The only venues worse than working men's clubs were miners' welfares. Names that still make the blood run cold – Greasebrough, Grimethorpe, Thurnscoe, Moorends, Goldthorpe and Clay Cross. Grim colliery towns where Neanderthal pitmen with fists the size of hams would at the drop of a hat and, without any hint of finesse or decorum, simply pull the plug halfway through a number. They were a law unto themselves. Whether it was too loud or if you ran over your allotted spot by a couple of seconds they'd just bring down the curtain in the middle of a song. Unbelievable!

There was no way you could even argue against their extreme fascist actions without being maimed. We would just end up standing there like lemons in total silence and sheer disbelief at the insensitivity and crassness, not to mention complete lack of professionalism of these morons. Obviously, one's bitter personal opinion of them was never expressed directly to their faces from fear of retribution. We'd be plotting to exact some hideous revenge but never quite summoned up enough courage to actually do anything and then just end up being happy to get out alive.

Blissfully unaware at this point of these particular depressing facts of life, we arrived all starry-eyed and ready to knock 'em dead at this wretched smoke-filled snake pit known as the Iron and Steel Club. Just from the name you can imagine what the place was like. After setting up our distinctly underwhelming array of musical equipment, we promptly proceeded to get well and truly bladdered in the company of the motley crew of assorted misfits masquerading as patrons.

The comforting alcohol soon induced a state of euphoria and tingling excitement which gradually replaced the mixture of fear and apprehension that always precedes a live gig. This, however, rapidly evaporated when at five minutes to showtime we got word that our drummer, 'Mr Ultra Unreliable Useless Bastard', was on some poxy night-school course and hence unable to make the first set. Nice one, arsehole! Time for a quick prayer. Embarrassed and panicking, we found ourselves almost surreally asking the audience, "Is there a drummer in the house?" Amazingly enough some heroic drunk volunteered and we snapped his hand off. Any port in a storm. As useless as he was he managed to save the day, though how we struggled through that first half without being lynched I'll never know. It was like a bad dream.

The final humiliation was when our own proper drummer finally turned up for the second set and played even worse than the drunken stand-in. Why do we put ourselves through this torture? After all this, you may think, never again. However, from such a shaky start, things must have picked up as the rest of the evening wore on. The only song I can remember singing that night was Little Richard's 'Ooh My Soul', which to my astonishment went down a storm.

It was my first taste of being in the limelight and felt great. By the end of the night some nutter in the crowd even offered us a recording deal. We declined, sacked the drummer and all staggered home worse for wear but happy in the knowledge that we had at last broken our duck. Welcome to the glamorous world of showbiz.

8

YMCA

After a series of different band names and personnel changes, there were now four of us in our embryonic rock group but currently without a drummer, having ditched the last one.

Hopefully, without being too boring and just for the record, I'll quickly mention who's who in the line-up. On rhythm guitar was the good guy of the group Bill Harley Gibson, which is a cool name if you're into iconic Yank motorsickles and geetars. Next up was John 'Boot' Ancliffe* on bass who was the serial piss-taker and joker. Third was vocalist Fred Havercroft, an extremely amusing fella and Paul McCartney lookalike who always fancied himself as a ladies' man.

Finally, myself on lead guitar. Modesty of course forbids me, but suffice to say, whereas most people are afflicted with a myriad of annoying peculiarities and bad habits, I could be described as being the human barometer of normality, reasonableness and good sense, though obviously I'm not one to brag.

The Imps at YMCA Rehearsal Room

Now with a gig under our belt, the search was on for a new drummer and somewhere permanent to rehearse. As luck would have it, Fred the singer came up trumps on both counts with ace percussionist Chris Ellerton and a practice room at the YMCA. The Young Men's Christian Association? What, us lot? Who would ever believe it?

As you can gather, the YMCA wasn't exactly our scene, but beggars can't be choosers and it was for free, well, sort of. Not unreasonably, we were expected to play a few freebie gigs for the YM in lieu of rent, which was cheap at the price and an excellent opportunity to gain more experience and play to a new audience. So, everyone a coconut. In true YMCA fashion, the chap who ran the place was gay, though that wasn't quite the vernacular we used at the time. He seemed a decent sort but I think he must have fancied us which is probably why he let us use the room in the first place.

Typical of the irresponsible little shits we were, the place was soon like a tip with rubbish and equipment strewn everywhere. It was also a serious fire hazard with us just sticking bare electrical wires from the amplifiers into sockets with pencils and matchsticks instead of using proper plugs. Considering the terrible din and mess we made, I'll never understand how the long-suffering bloke actually put up with us. In fact I suppose we really owe the guy a belated apology and an eternal debt of gratitude, so I take my 'hat' off to him. Plus the amazing thing is, in all the time we rehearsed there, nothing ever got broken or stolen, even though there was no lock on the door and the room was eventually stacked with hundreds, probably thousands of pounds' worth of musical equipment. No lock? We must have been fucking insane!

Chris the new drummer was the catalyst we needed. He was mean and moody with a black leather jacket and a chip on both shoulders. As well as being 'difficult', he was also a badass on the kit and injected energy, attitude and aggression into his playing. He brought with him fresh influences such as The Hollies and Cliff Bennett's Rebel Rousers, and in no time the music came on in leaps and bounds.

So much so, that at the next youth club gig I gamely attempted a spontaneous rendition of 'Czardas', possibly the fastest and most difficult piece of instrumental music ever written short of 'Bum of the Flightle Bee'. I think the words 'over-ambitious' might be deemed appropriate, and after untangling my lacerated and bleeding fingers trapped underneath the guitar strings, we quickly reverted back to our regular set list. Even after fifty years I've still not learned how to play it properly.

Soon, bookings were coming thick and fast, and we'd started investing in new equipment. Just like the Shadows and The Beatles it was Vox amps and Reslo microphones all round. Boot got himself a violin bass. Freddy bought a new Carlsbro PA system, though the loudspeakers were just strung up naked in a corner 'Heath Robinson-style' and not even in any proper cabinets. Chris had a full 'Rodgers' drum kit, although Bill and I still had to struggle along with a pair of primitive Hofner Senator guitars. Decent axes such as Fender and Gibson were still hard to come by and out of our price range for the time being. Then, finally, after a few more gigs using various group names such as The Countdowns and the Chevrolets, we decided the band's new moniker was – 'THE IMPS'.

* In later life after moving to Australia, John 'Boot' Ancliffe has suffered from motor neurone disease. He successfully led the 'Dying with Dignity Queensland' campaign for the Voluntary Assisted Dying bill that was passed in 2021. Good on ya, cobber. About time it was legal in the UK.

9

Car Crazy / Belle Vue

I was now almost seventeen, mad on cars and desperate to pass my driving test as soon as possible. Bill Gibson, The Imps' rhythm guitarist was also car-crazy and in a moment of madness we bought a Jaguar XK120 soft-top sports car, minus the engine for a fiver (yes just £5, believe it or not) from a local doctor before either of us could even drive.

We had to tow it home with a rope, but without the weight of an engine, the front end had risen way up in the air and made it impossible to see where the hell we were going. Though extremely dangerous and no doubt illegal, the only way to actually steer it was for me to stand up on tiptoes whilst peering over the long bonnet/hood and aim it best I could.

In the end it proved an over-ambitious restoration project that never happened and the car just stood gathering dust in Bill's front garden for a year. After several warnings to shift it, his mother finally lost patience and demanded that the damn thing be removed immediately. As a result it ended up at the scrapyard and I'm not sure we even got our initial outlay of a fiver back. Little did we know it would be worth £100,000 or more today.

Incidentally, Bill later went on to form Zytek Engineering that developed Formula One's first fully electronic engine management system in the Toleman-Hart car driven by a young Ayrton Senna in 1984. His company also supplied systems for Rolls-Royce, Aston Martin, Jaguar and Bentley, etc., as well designing racing-car engines that finished first, second and third at the gruelling Le Mans 24 Hours. Wow, what a guy. He eventually sold Zytek and in 2014 formed Gibson Technology that continues to remain at the forefront of the motorsport world.

Even after the XK120 fiasco we still hadn't learnt our lesson. Wild enthusiasm continued to override any common sense in our blind pursuit of crazy motors. At weekends we'd trek around on our push bikes to salvage yards and old garages sniffing out interesting motors. Amongst the shortlist was an ancient double-deck Rolls-Royce hearse and a sleek single-deck Jaguar Mk 7 hearse, plus a fleet of huge gangster-style Packard limos from my cousin's firm of undertakers in Lincoln. I don't know what the attraction was, but we certainly seemed to have a morbid fascination with funeral cars.

My favourite was a superb, thirty-foot-long, left-hand drive American 1940s Cadillac Fleetwood limousine for sale at £25. Alas, but probably just as well, somebody beat us to it, though deep down I've always regretted missing the chance of such a fine specimen. Christ knows where we could have parked or maintained these monstrosities, but they were the stuff of dreams.

Stock car racing was something else we were all loopy about. The roar of those old un-silenced Yankee V8s was incredibly exciting, fuelling teenage fantasies of being hell-drivers ourselves someday. A memorable stock car experience for me was an outing to Wimbledon Stadium, near to where my old school chum 'Godders' lived after moving to London. I stayed with him for a few days at his parents', who owned a newsagent's shop and proudly boasted that Paul McCartney was one of their regular customers.

Whilst there we had several other special treats, the first being a trip to the original theatre stage-show version of *Behind the Fridge* starring Peter Cook and Dudley Moore. Next was seeing Ken Dodd & the Diddy Men 'Live' at the London Palladium and thirdly was to catch the Moody Blues at Wimbledon Palais with their original 'Go Now' line-up featuring Denny Lane. Not a bad few days' worth of entertainment.

Quite often a gang of us would take a rail excursion to see the Demolition Derby's at Belle Vue Speedway Stadium in Manchester. These Belle Vue day trips were usually combined with a massive piss-up plus all the fun of the fair, including the flea circus and a huge bone-shaking wooden rollercoaster called 'The Bobs'. The train journey home would mainly be spent being sick, setting off jumping crackers and chucking light bulbs out the window. All of which was quite tricky to explain away when the guard came round and found us in total darkness, surrounded by empty firework carcasses and smelling of puke. Cretins.

10

Action Van

Jack the Lad, The Imps' manager, had mysteriously disappeared from the scene and moved on, probably at Her Majesty's pleasure. Without his van, transport to gigs was becoming a major problem, so we started using a bloke called Stan at Decoy Taxis to ferry us around. As a stop gap it was a lifesaver, but what we really needed was our own vehicle, so I started taking driving lessons.

Within a couple of weeks of my seventeenth birthday after an intensive course at Dougie May's driving school, the feared test was passed. Then, following frenzied celebrations, I acquired a rusty but trusty old Bedford Dormobile with sliding doors and column gear change. The group name was boldly printed on each side of the van together with a painting of an imp, which is a mischievous cross-legged demon. Unfortunately I don't have any photos of the van, but it was soon covered in lipstick and multi-coloured graffiti courtesy of our legion of adoring female fans. Most of the messages were quite flattering apart from one that said 'Pretentious Crap', which we left on anyway even though it was now a complete eyesore.

We got no end of complaints from the neighbours. One chap in particular, an unfeasibly tall, barking-mad Scottish architect who always reeked of garlic, just went berserk one day. He became so incensed that he leapt on the side of the van in an uncontrolled rage as we drove down the road. All we could do to save ourselves was just punch and kick him till he fell off. In the end he finally realised he couldn't win and just gave up in despair. The eyesore remained.

By now, I was certainly beginning to discover some of the joys of vehicle ownership. The expression 'Passion Wagon' could have been invented for the old Bedford as it rapidly transformed itself into a mobile mattress over the following months. The expense of running this 'Action Van' was another matter. Everyone else was skint so it was always muggins who ended up paying the bills. I was often so broke myself that if I drove from my house to the Co-op filling station for two bobs' worth of petrol it was just about enough to get me back home again. It was ridiculous. More than once, the pump attendant felt so sorry for me that she gave me back a tanner for a bag of chips.

Anyway, I thought of a really good way to subsidise my meagre income by breeding and selling homing pigeons. Initially I'd buy the birds from my mate Johnny Milner, keep them in my loft for a while and then flog 'em off to some mug punter. The sucker, would more often than not, let the birds out too early and they'd just fly straight back to me. Then I'd flog them on to somebody else and the cycle would continue. However, I digress.

Quite a few of the other local groups also had vans. Most had Dormobiles or Ford Thames, though rival band

The Dimples had a peculiar-looking flat-fronted Morris Commercial and The Chechakos had a very desirable Commer Minibus that all the other bands jealously coveted. One bunch of clowns even had a handcart with their name down the side that they pushed to gigs.

The Imps' van was made to look cool with a strategically placed but otherwise useless roof rack and had a few strange idiosyncrasies. The window wipers only worked by frequently slamming the sliding door shut, and in winter the windscreen would ice up if not rubbed with a raw potato. Having no indicators, the only way to signal was manually. The sliding doors were so lethal that you risked slicing an arm off every time you braked for a corner.

There were only two front seats, so any extra passengers had to squat precariously in the back on assorted pews and rickety stools. They weren't fixed to the floor so would be slithering around the van in all directions at every bend or bump in the road. It was a similar situation when the gear was packed in the van. It was never secured properly and consequently if you had to brake sharply, pieces of equipment and cymbals would fly forward, skimming past your head and virtually decapitating anyone who didn't duck out the way in time.

11

London Calling

In 1965, out of nowhere, a mysterious and irresistible voice loudly beckoned as Fred and I clearly heard the sound of London calling. On the spur of the moment, ill prepared and with inadequate funds, we decided to just take off and head for the bright lights like moths to a flame. Hitch-hiking was our only viable option, so with no choice but to stick out our thumbs we took to the highway. Travelling light, we were on our way without a plan or a clue and heading south. A few lucky lifts later we were dropped at the North London suburb of Hendon, literally with only the clothes we stood up in.

After several hours on the road we'd arrived, starving hungry and unable to resist the temptation of an Oriental feast at the first Chinese restaurant we could find. Though satiated after a good meal and a couple of beers, blowing most of our money in one fell swoop probably wasn't really such a sensible idea in view of our already stretched financial circumstances. But what the hell, let the devil take the hindmost. We were just out to have fun and didn't have a care about such trivialities.

Next stop Soho. This was to be our base for the following week and first port of call was 'Le Macabre', a popular beatnik hangout with decor something akin to Madame Tussaud's Chamber of Horrors. It was a cross between a dungeon and a ghost train, with garrotted heads, skulls and luminous skeletons in cages hanging from the walls. Very tasteful. Freddy and I were always pratting about, and so after being 'asked to leave' we moved on down Wardour Street to 'The Ship' pub for a few pints and then finished off at the Marquee Club.

There wasn't much happening at the Marquee that particular evening except a folk and poetry event, which wasn't really our scene. However, although the entertainment proved disappointing, we did manage to get friendly with a couple of girls and had a bit of a snog and a grope in a dimly lit corner. We were hoping this might lead to a bed for the night, but it was not to be. The girls had to catch the last tube home to Mummy and Daddy, so we said our goodbyes and arranged to meet them later in the week.

With that, we went off in search of alternative sleeping arrangements. Not being able to afford a hotel, we settled for a neon-lit twenty-four-hour Top Rank Bowling Alley just off Piccadilly Circus and after finding a couple of seats decided to get our heads down. No sooner had we drifted off than an ugly-looking bouncer rudely interrupted our slumber, reminding us in no uncertain terms that sleeping was not allowed on the premises. This policy was obviously to discourage every bum and dosser in town from taking up residence, though we still couldn't help feeling outraged and indignant at the gross unfairness of it. But there was nothing we could do, and with nowhere else to go, we had to take it in turns to sneak forty winks while the other acted as lookout.

A long, uncomfortable night followed and it was a blessed relief when dawn finally broke. At least we could get out into the fresh air, stretch our legs and find ourselves a cheap and cheerful breakfast. The rest of the day was spent sightseeing and aimlessly hanging round in cafés. Though largely unaffected by the vice and sleaze surrounding us in this particular location, I suppose in passing we did derive a certain perverse pleasure observing some of the saucy 'goings-on' whilst pondering the question of where we might be spending the night. Definitely not the bowling alley again, that's for sure.

As darkness fell we figured a bench in Regent's Park would be our best bet. With an eye out for the police and park rangers, over the railings we went. Though by no means the Ritz, at least there wouldn't be any Top Rank heavies rousing us every five minutes. Snuggling down on a royal bench apiece at the end of a very long and tiring day, we were soon dead to the world.

Being summertime it was scorching hot in the day and we'd brought only the lightest of clothing with no thought of sleeping bags or topcoats. However, by three in the morning we awoke bolt upright, chilled to the bone, freezing and shivering, believing we must have been transmuted to Siberia in the night. Totally unprepared and previously inexperienced at sleeping rough, we had to learn fast. The next night we gathered together old newspapers to use as blankets, which was marginally better, but even so we still woke with teeth chattering and huge imaginary icicles on the end of our noses. We were certainly discovering the hard way that the streets of London are indeed paved with cold.

12

Soho Street Life

Three days and nights on a park bench without any proper sleep or a square meal inevitably starts to take its toll, and by the fourth morning we had terrible bags under our eyes and were starting to hallucinate. We were filthy dirty and hadn't washed, shaved, combed our hair or worst of all brushed our teeth since arriving. The soles of our shoes were worn out from miles of walking and our clothes were becoming increasingly grubby, ragged and creased. We were in fact starting to look like a couple of tramps. It was alarming to keep catching the reflection of these two grungy deadbeats in shop windows and thinking we were being followed.

By now hunger and thirst were driving us to desperate measures as we took to half-inching bottles of milk off doorsteps and rifling through bins for scraps of food. Through necessity we soon found ourselves shamelessly begging in the streets, trying to cobble together enough money for a cheap night out and a few drinks.

Looking back, it's hard to believe how soon we had to resort to such tactics in such a short period of time, but it was simply a matter of survival. The transformation was rapid, like an instinct lurking just below the surface of normally accepted behaviour, ready to spring into action when circumstances dictate. And with it came a curious liberation and certain boldness. A loss of self, where no one knows you, allowing you to fearlessly say and do whatever you feel like.

Houses and property start to take on uncanny human qualities, appearing hostile and alien as you increasingly feel more and more the outsider. Buildings seemed to point and jeer, saying, "Get back onto the streets where you belong, scum." Ordinary people transform into wraith-like facades, strait-jacketed with a constricted air of conformity, conditioned like zombies going through the motions, trapped and somehow unable to break out of the mould.

A strange dichotomy exists. This new loss of ego inspires a precise and clear knowledge of who you are, juxtaposing the illusion of who you merely think you are. A feeling of great freedom and power is bestowed upon you. Like a rare stage performance on really good night when the audience is in the palm of your hand and you can do no wrong. Something clicks and then you hit the 'zone'. A natural high, perfect, beautiful, simple. As I mentioned, we'd already started hallucinating earlier in the day and with these kinds of thoughts buzzing round our heads, we were obviously now completely delirious.

We wandered around purposelessly, grabbing much-needed shut-eye in the warm sunshine amongst the pigeons in Trafalgar Square. Eventually we stirred, looking forward to our date with the girls who we had arranged to meet at the Marquee again that night. The entertainment this time was the Graham Bond Organisation, a jazzy blues band featuring Dick Heckstall Smith plus a pre-Cream Jack Bruce and Ginger Baker. We met the girls, had a few drinks and a canoodle, then fixed a further assignation the following day at a funfair on Hampstead Heath.

However, since that first meeting, our physical appearance had undergone a dramatic decline and we probably weren't at all the same two charming heartthrobs they remembered falling for on the previous occasion. The fact we must have stunk something rotten and resembled a pair of down-and-outs may have had some bearing as to why they never showed up next day. So, having been jilted, we gave Hampstead the once-over and after a quick twirl on the waltzers, found a nice shady nook and snatched a snooze on the Heath.

13

Hitching Home

So, after being stood up by a couple of dolly birds on Hampstead Heath, Fred and I headed back 'up west' for another stint of purgatory. However, upon arrival we realised we could stand it no more: enough was enough. No one in their right mind would attempt to start hitching from Leicester Square at midnight, but all I can say is it seemed like a good idea at the time. At first all went well. A rock group van picked us up almost immediately but then dropped us off in no-man's land between Wembley and Staples Corner on the North Circular Road with no choice left but to pound the pavement.

An hour or so dragged by without a sniff of a lift and we were manic. Rest was now so badly needed that we seriously considered climbing onto a factory roof up a two hundred-foot ladder just for somewhere to lay our heads. Fred had to physically restrain me from just crashing on someone's front lawn. I just didn't care anymore, that's how desperate we were. With great relief, we hit upon a playing field with an unlocked park keeper's hut and promptly flaked out till early morning.

Daylight brought better prospects and a Sunbeam Rapier took us up to Stevenage. It was a glorious morning and as we walked towards Baldock along the old A1 road there was a slight mist, which added to the atmosphere and raised our spirits. It was like England as you imagine it should be and for a brief moment it felt good to be alive. Despair, however, soon began to set in again after another hour or so when we found ourselves on the tarmac, kneeling in prayer, pleading for cars to stop.

We had almost given up when an old banger pulled over and in we got. I immediately sprawled out on the back seat feeling like I was in seventh heaven. Fred sat in the front, slightly paranoid that the guy might be a bit fruity, but as I nodded off I could vaguely hear the comforting murmur of conversation as the car chugged along. My reverie, however, was short-lived when a few miles up the road we juddered to a halt as the car ran out of petrol. I'll never forgive Fred for his next few words. I could not believe my ears, as I heard him volunteering to fetch a can of fuel for this otiose waste of effin' space.

We were in the middle of nowhere, it was still early morning, nowhere was open and the nearest garage was probably miles away. My mood was such that I could have gladly killed the pair of them. The driver for being so stupid and inefficient and Fred for being so obliging and helpful. I know it was totally selfish, but I couldn't help myself. I was just so tired and past it that I didn't want to face the thought of walking one more step.

But now I had no choice and off we staggered. As it happened, we found a garage less than a couple of miles up the road, but it felt more like a hundred. I was literally dying and virtually in tears. All I can remember is Fred dragging me along the road at the end a scarf he'd picked up somewhere, with me carrying the can, so to speak. Somehow we crawled back, filled her up with gas and collapsed into the car to continue the next leg of journey without further incident.

After being dropped off we were almost immediately picked up by fine fellow in a luxurious Rover three-litre Coupe saying he could take us as far as Doncaster. We jumped in and sank into the sumptuous leather-bound seats and were whisked off up the Great North Road at a constant 115mph, though we did slow down a smidge to drive through the lovely old historic town of Stamford. Then he stepped back on the gas as we stormed on past 'highwayman' Dick Turpin's local pub, the famous Ram Jam Inn, to reach our destination in no time. Sadly I've recently heard that property developers now want to demolish the Ram Jam Inn and build some ghastly shopping centre. Bloody philistines.

Anyway, having arrived refreshed at Doncaster, it wasn't long before a rather pungent fishmonger's van on its way to Grimsby provided us with wheels for the last lap. The driver was a good old boy with an amazing twiddly whistling style the likes of which I'd never heard before. Eat your heart out, Roger Whittaker. The guy was so impressive and professional that in a fleeting moment of fantasy we almost offered him a management contract.

Anyway, not before time, journey's end. The nightmare was over. We were dropped literally on the doorstep and I can honestly say I've never been so glad to get back home. I didn't think I would ever admit such a thing about Sunny Scunny, as it's often called, a place with which I've always had a love-hate relationship.

My parents must have been quite shocked to see this grimy, skeletal figure standing on their doorstep as they greeted me with, "Hello, son, how did you get on in London?"

Almost farcically I heard myself uttering the most ludicrous reply. "Oh absolutely brilliantly, thanks, I've had the best time of my life ever." Still not quite believing what drivel had just spewed forth from my lips, I hosed myself down, scrubbed off all the muck with a stiff yard brush and spent the rest of the week in a nice, crisp, warm bed… Bliss.

14

The Imps
(1963-1965)

Out of all the bands I've worked with over the years, I always had a soft spot for The Imps. It was my first real group and everything was such a buzz. It was all so new, fresh and exciting, like finding your true identity for the first time. Nothing else mattered and the group became all-important and all-consuming with true commitment and dedication. Also it was such a happy, uncomplicated time, no cares and no worries. Well, apart from the Cuban Missile Crisis. That was a bit hairy.

    Everything was looking up and life was sweet. My poor old mum had been seriously ill but was thankfully now more or less recovered. I'd left school behind, which, as you might have already gathered, I'd hated. Working as a 'printer's devil' was a drag but at least provided the wherewithal to buy all the latest new equipment for the band, plus flash new suits and Denson winkle pickers every couple of months. I'd got some wheels, girls galore and the '60s were starting to swing.

The Imps (1963-1965)

Fashions were hot and the music scene healthier than at any time before or since.

The band had plenty of work locally, with our favourite venue being the Jazz Workshop, a small dark cellar similar to Liverpool's famous Cavern Club. This trendy hangout started life as a trad jazz den, but rock, pop and the onslaught of the British Beat Boom had now replaced Acker Bilk and Humphrey Littleton on the bandstand. Two or three nights a week the place would be heaving with sweating, gyrating mods grooving to the latest, loudest sounds. The atmosphere was electric. Like *Ready Steady Go!* – the weekend starts here. We had a residency playing every other week, alternating with other favourites like the Chechakos, Badd Ladds, Southlanders, Ian King and the Classics, and the Dimples.

Between sets our drummer Chris Ellerton would nip over the road to the Brown Cow pub for few drinks and would often be late back. We were always threatening him with the sack for his unpunctuality and for being, how can I put this politely... er, 'challenging', and this was the perfect opportunity to wind him up, good style. In his absence and just to keep him on his toes, we'd invite our mate 'Squelch' as substitute drummer to sit in with us. At the best of times Chris was always a bit touchy and irascible, but when he'd arrive back from the pub to find us steaming away and thrashing it out without him, he'd go ballistic. He'd work himself up into such a lather and become so angry that he would storm on stage to claim his rightful place and end up playing absolutely brilliantly for the rest of the night just to prove a point.

There was never really much trouble at Jazz Workshop but there was one incident when Nick Cole, a music journalist from the *Steelbeat* gossip column, collapsed in a drunken stupor in the middle of the dance floor. For some reason I took it upon myself to revive him by emptying the contents of a beer bottle on his head. He obviously took offence and got up and slugged me straight in the gob, rendering me speechless. My lip immediately swelled up, turning black and blue in the process, and left me looking (even more) like a hideous orangutan for the next few weeks. We soon got over our little tiff, though, and many years later Nick was still giving us good reviews in the local press. Sadly, Jazz Workshop was demolished not long after, making way for some dismal housing development.

A big day for us was making our first ever demo-disc at a studio in Leeds. We recorded Doris Troy's 'What'cha Gonna Do About It' and a Hollies cover for posterity, and the five of us took home one vinyl copy each. I managed to lose mine along the way and wonder how many of these discs actually survived.

For the next year or so during this golden age, every ballroom, youth club and church hall in the country was promoting 'beat nights'. Seven nights a week there was something exciting happening and groups were working flat-out. Imp-mania exploded as we rapidly gained a reputation as the coolest cats in town. At least we thought so. Especially after a junior matinee gig at the local bug hutch, when screaming fans pursued us along the High Street and into Woolworth's, ripping off our clothes and yanking out great chunks of hair. With no means of escape it was scary but very exciting and rather disappointingly the only time we were mobbed like this on such a dramatic scale.

The group were constantly improving, honing our craft, developing harmony skills and starting to get more and more bookings slightly further afield at such places as Woodhall Spa, Malton and Stamford, where we supported Sandra and the Boyfriends. Or was it Dawn and the DJs? Anyway, whichever one it was, I fell instantly in love with Sandra, or was it Dawn? But alas, after the gig I never saw either of them again.

Then came really bad news when Fred the singer decided he was leaving the band to become an estate agent. An estate agent? My God, that really is bad news. Boom boom. Luckily Ian Macdonald, later known as Iain Matthews of 'Matthews Southern Comfort' fame, came to the rescue and briefly replaced Fred on vocals. Iain subsequently had a massive No. 1 UK hit in 1970 with 'Woodstock' after spending a few years with Pyramid and Fairport Convention. At the time of writing he was living in San Antone, Texas, and touring with Plainsong, though I recently heard he's now in Holland and back with MSC.

Unfortunately things never really worked out with Iain, although he and Bill from The Imps later formed 'The Moderation' with guitarist Rick Laughton. Although I only saw them perform once at a gig in Kirton Lindsey village hall, they were seriously impressive. Plus I pulled, so all in all a very satisfactory evening.

Then bass player 'Boot' dropped his bombshell. He was leaving the band and transferring allegiance to our arch-rivals 'The Dimples'. It was a blow, but we decided to carry on with me switching to bass and bringing in Greg Tomlinson on guitar from the recently disbanded Chechakos. So after a shuffle-about we decided to carry on as a four piece and change our name to The Craze.

A lot of promoters daren't book us because they thought we were something to do with the Krays and half-expected Ronnie and Reggie to turn up with a team of East End villains. By now we were losing momentum and the final straw was when Bill announced he was off to university. We had almost decided to call it a day when, as fate would have it, Boot left The Dimples to marry his girlfriend Lynn, and

Greg and I were immediately drafted in as replacements. Great! Everything was falling into place nicely. The Dimples was to be a whole new ballgame.

IMPS – John (Boot) Ancliffe, Chris Ellerton, Craig Austin, Bill Gibson, Fred Havercroft.

The Imps.

15

The Dimples (1965-1967)

So, after playing guitar with The Imps and bass with The Craze I was invited to join The Dimples in 1965. The Dimples were, if you like, the new kids on the block, put together by John Gladwin and Terry Wincott (later Amazing Blondel) with Stu Smith on drums. As the name implies, the 'Dimples' played blues in the style of John Lee Hooker and Muddy Waters rather than rock but with a fresh, modern approach both musically and visually.

John and Terry were both ex-pupils of De Aston* boarding school for posh brats in Market Rasen. Amusingly, someone once said that most English 'public' schools are places where parents send their odious offspring rather than have them clutter up the house, ha ha. Anyway, the two of them were referred to simply as Gladwin and Wincott, though their profile wasn't as straight-laced or stuffy as one might imagine. Whereas most bands of the time still wore shiny 'Shadows' suits, these boys had all the latest trendy Carnaby

Street mod gear, plus a certain something that made them stand out from the crowd.

With Boot now gone, Greg and I settled in nicely and things soon began to happen. For starters I handed in my notice at the council office where I worked in order to go full time with the band. It was a job I'd drifted into as an apprentice 'printer's devil', learning skills that didn't interested me. My time was spent guillotining endless reams of paper or processing metal printing plates. Mostly, though, I'd be churning out reports on an offset-litho machine, which was the most mind-numbingly boring occupation in the world.

So, apart from wages, the only good thing about the job was an abundance of sexy secretaries to gawp at all day long. The borough council, in typical pervy fashion, always managed to employ a high percentage of very attractive girls, which sometimes made it difficult to concentrate on the task in hand. Speaking of which, I did occasionally manage to entice a couple of willing 'assistants' into the darkroom for a quick fumble whenever a batch of film needed developing. Still, without a second thought I resigned and was off like a shot to embrace my new career as a Teenage Idol.

Apart from previously being cruelly exploited as a paperboy delivering the Daily Drivel six days a week for peanuts in hail, rain and snow, working as a printer was the only 'proper' job I've ever had in my life. OK, I've been self-employed numerous times but vowed never again to graft for anyone else as a wage slave or be part of the existing system. It's doubtful my contribution to society is in any way worthwhile compared to doctors, nurses, farmers, engineers and tradesfolk, etc., but for better or worse this crazy mixed-up alternative lifestyle was to become my destiny for a while, and would at least allow me to try and turn the world onto some half decent music and fashion.

The Dimples (1965-1967)

Soon the Vox and Selmer amps were replaced with a trio of huge hundred-watt Sound City stacks and a massive new PA system. Stuart beefed up his drum kit, Greg had a lovely blond cutaway Guild guitar, Wincott a Rickenbacker and me a Fender Precision Bass. With the rest of us on three-part harmony backing, Gladwin took over lead vocals as razzle-dazzle frontman, where he fancied himself as a ranch hand from the High Chaparral. At gigs he started wearing a bum-freezer waiter's jacket and smothering himself from head to toe in talcum powder like it was trail dust. Admittedly this sounds a little oddball, though at the time it seemed quite normal with all the other goofiness going on all around. Tamla, R&B and rare soul songs gradually replaced the old blues-based repertoire and it was all systems go. Even the once-coveted 'Chechakos' Commer minibus became ours after the demise of the Morris J4 in a lucky escape at Doncaster when a front wheel sheared off, just one of many near misses over the next few years.

Whilst travelling endlessly round the country, no one was spared or excluded from mercilessly mickey-taking at all times by the rest of the band. It kept you on your toes and sharpened you up for life on the road. Five guys in each other's pockets twenty-four hours a day, year in year out, was like living under a microscope and a series of escalating 'in' jokes, elaborate rituals and bizarre social practices gradually began to establish themselves.

Everyone took turns in being the butt of each other's jokes, and though often cruel and scathing, it was usually taken in good spirit and as part of the fun. There was always a whole array of subject matter to be continually exploited, and although the themes were often tedious, repetitive and frequently annoying, there would always be some new, inventive way of squeezing a smirk out of any situation, no matter how dire.

As you can imagine, I have a vast catalogue of juicy tales and examples of brainless, infantile and deviant behaviour pertaining to all the various band members over the years. Obviously I'd love to share the gruesome details, but to spare their blushes and also for fear of potential legal ramifications, I'd best just keep schtum.

---

*   Two other notable musical De Aston pupils were Bernie Taupin, lyricist for Elton John, and Rod Temperton from Heatwave ('Boogie Nights'), who wrote the hits for Michael Jackson's *Thriller* album. Must be something in the water.

THE DIMPLES – (L to R) Craig 'Tex' Austin, Terry Wincott, John Gladwin, Stu Smith, Greg Tomlinson.

The Dimples.

16

Lincoln Pop Festival

Probably the biggest gig The Dimples ever did was a huge open-air pop festival on 30 May 1966 at Lincoln City football ground, Sincil Bank. It was a hot Whit Monday and the weather was perfect. This must have been one of the UK's earliest open-air rock festivals on such a grand scale and drew a large crowd that filled the pitch as well as the stands. I've no idea how many were there, but it was almost certainly the best gate they had all season.

Headlining was The Who and they performed brilliantly. I've seen them plenty of times but never as good as on this occasion. Townsend and Daltrey were bickering as usual, but no matter, when Pete threw his pork-pie hat out into the audience at the end of the set, the crowd went totally mental trying to grab hold of it for a keepsake.

Also on the star-studded bill were The Kinks, Small Faces, Georgie Fame, Yardbirds, Screaming Lord Sutch, Creation, Koobas, She Trinity, Crispian St Peters, Barron Knights, Ivy

League, Alan Price Set, The Children, The Brotherhud, Dave Dee, Dozy, Beaky, Mick, Titch and Uncle Tom Cobley, and all. MCs and DJs on the day were Keith Fordyce, Ray Nortrop and necrophiliac pedo-perv Jimmy Savile.

The club shower and changing facilities doubled as dressing rooms, which all the bands quite happily shared throughout the proceedings without too many pop primadonnas throwing temper tantrums. Various different stages were scattered around the pitch but were a considerable distance away from the dressing room, so the groups would have had to run the gauntlet right through the middle of crowd to reach the performance areas. To alleviate this problem and stop the bands getting mobbed, a weird-looking wire-mesh tunnel had been constructed down from the dressing rooms, across the turf and along to the stages.

Unlike today there were no massive sound systems so the various groups just used equipment typically consisting of two or three piddling little thirty-watt amplifiers. In the open air this was pathetically inadequate and a miracle that anybody could hear the music at all. Only The Who had anywhere enough gear to be heard properly, with several hundred-watt stacks filling the stage. Obviously Keith Moon played his drums so loud he never needed any extra volume anyway.

The Dimples were third on the bill and hit the stage around 1.30 in the afternoon wearing hipster trousers, desert boots and some insanely heavy gambler-style frockcoats so were sweating buckets in the eighty-degree heat. Despite this dumb fashion faux pas, we went down pretty well, or at least didn't get booed off. After our set we just hung around happily watching all the other acts until ten o'clock-ish that evening.

The two outstanding bands for me were The Koobas from Liverpool and Creation, who did a couple of songs called

'Painter Man' and 'Makin' Time' which featured the guitarist playing with a violin bow. This was four or five years before Jimmy page used the same gimmick with Led Zeppelin, so they were well ahead of their time. All in all, a truly pioneering event. Nice one Lincoln City FC (The Imps) and *The Lincolnshire Chronicle*, who helped sponsor the gig.

Later as we headed for home on the way out of Lincoln, Wincott and I fancied fish and chips so asked our roadie to pull up outside the next chippy that was still open. The rest of the guys were really moaning and complaining about having to stop, but we insisted. When we got back outside with our take-away they'd just buggered off and left us stranded. The bastards. We couldn't believe it. At first we thought they were just hiding round the corner and would be back any minute to pick us up, but there was no sign of them. We finished off the last of our chips and silently contemplated what the hell to do next and where we might doss for the night.

Apart from being virtually penniless, it was too late for public transport, so we reluctantly resorted to huddling together in a dank and very smelly telephone box. That lasted all of two minutes. Then we asked a passing rozzer if we could kip down at the cop shop. Not a chance, but he suggested we check and see if anyone had forgotten to lock their car doors, would you believe?

Finally, after wandering around for a while we came across the Lincolnshire Roadcar bus depot and sneaked in the back of an old apple-green double-decker. Refuge at last. With no other option, we lay down our weary heads for the night and dozed off best we could whilst plotting our revenge on the rest of the band.

Morning arrived and we awoke shivering and even more furious that we'd been deliberately marooned. Without actually killing them, the only way we could think of getting our own back was to head home by taxi and charge the full fare plus a hefty tip to the double-crossing dickheads. Anyway, they must have felt guilty 'cos without any fuss they stumped up what at the time was best part of a week's wages. Twats.

17

Dimps vs Pink Floyd

Another memorable gig was at Hull Skyline Ballroom on 28 September 1967 supporting Pink Floyd alongside Mick Ronson's 'Rats' and Prof's band 'Disturbance'. We always enjoyed the Skyline and had a sizable following, especially with all the lovely Hammond's department store girls as fans. It was shortly before Guy Fawkes Bonfire Night and for some nefarious purpose we had a box of fireworks stashed in the van. After the gig we packed away the gear as usual and set off for home along the A63 dual carriageway out of the city when we found ourselves racing side by side with the Pink Floyd van.

Next thing we knew after some initial banter, hectoring and shouting, a full-scale conflict spontaneously erupted between the two bands. Occupants of both rival Ford Transits were suddenly locked in mortal combat as a massive barrage of bangers, pyrotechnic stage props and other assorted incendiary was launched indiscriminately at each other's speeding vehicles. Bloodcurdling screams of terror and pain could be heard through the open windows and doors of the vans, as flaming missiles ignited hair and flesh of the cowering victims within. As we napalmed each other's battlewagons, the almighty rumble continued the full length of the carriageway with no regard whatsoever for the sanctity of human life or the plight of any innocent road users caught in the crossfire. The action eventually receded as ammo was spent and a cease-fire declared.

OK, I might be exaggerating slightly, but in the end all parties survived relatively unscathed. Former adversaries then stopped off at Norman's tranny caff to share a 'peace pipe', very popular at the time, followed by a fry-up to quell the resulting munchies. Norman's greasy spoon was a disgraceful abomination situated near Goole but was the only joint still open so late into the night. The place was filthy and disgusting beyond belief and by rights should have been condemned. For example, to pass the time whilst sitting there in squalor waiting for our meal, we'd hold the world championship 'blue bottle swatting' competition. Without a word of a lie, you could squish two or three hundred in a matter of minutes before any scran was even slopped up.

Then when the grub did finally arrive we'd always make our roadie 'Piggy' Jackson laugh in mid-swallow, forcing him to project tea, chips, beans and lumps of sausage out through his nose. This remarkable party piece peculiar to Piggy could be produced almost on cue and went down a treat at whichever pit-stop we happened to be in at the time. All this was fairly typical of the adolescent and irresponsible behaviour of the era, though hopefully we've all grown up and matured since. Mind you, when we all get back together again it sometimes makes me wonder.

We also did another gig with Pink Floyd at the Ritz Ballroom, Kings Heath in Birmingham later that year on 16 December 1967. It was one of their first appearances in the Midlands shortly after the release of the second single 'See Emily Play'. On the same bill that night was 'The Rare Breed' featuring Ozzy Osbourne and Geezer Butler, who would later find fame and fortune as members of Black Sabbath. Also DJ Dave Terry and of course The Dimples, who had now changed their name to Gospel Garden. As I remember it there can't have been more than a dozen or so people in the audience all evening. A very strange gig indeed.

Because of the expense, hotels were a rare luxury. We would regularly travel two hundred miles to a town, play the gig and then travel straight back afterwards, arriving home at five o'clock in the morning. Once in the depths of winter we were about to head back from a London gig in the old red Commer minibus. One of the band, in a childish strop, slammed the front door really hard to prove some ridiculous point and the front window cracked. Oh, shit. We set off hoping for the best but as we hit the A1 North the glass just disintegrated and fell to pieces. Gerald 'Tax' McGillycuddy, the roadie, was driving and luckily wearing leather gloves. To his credit he had the wit and wherewithal to instantly punch out what was left of the screen by now lethally obscuring the view. We were all in shock as the van lurched to and fro across the carriageway before regaining control.

With no front windscreen on the coldest night of the century, our only option was to make it back best we could. This meant freezing our bollocks off and within minutes it was unbearable. Tax (short for Taxi) was the only one left in the front. The rest of us had crawled into the back seats and were huddled up like members of Shackleton's expedition, trying to keep the sub-zero temperatures at bay. It was impossible. It maybe wasn't quite as bad for me as I was wearing a thick hooded Dracula cape I'd picked up earlier that day from Kleptomania in Soho. It was wrapped around me snug as a bug, but I was still frozen stiff.

We even had the engine cover off, which was situated inside the van giving off a modicum of heat, but not enough to keep out the arctic cold. The only way to survive and revive ourselves was pull in at every transport café on the road back. At each one we'd drink hot tea to thaw out and as you can imagine we made a lot of stops that night. It took friggin' hours of torment and agony to get home. It is without doubt the longest and most unpleasant journey I can ever remember. Yet it must have been so much worse for Tax, who sat up front on his ownsome, facing the freezing blast head on. He did brilliantly and didn't complain one bit. He just got on with it. What a guy.

18

Cornwall, 1966

At the height of the glorious summer of '66, The Dimps combined a holiday in Cornwall with a gig at St Austell Town Hall. Our destination was Port Melon near Mevagissy, where Gladwin's parents owned a holiday cottage and the rental apartment where we were staying. After loading the trusty old Commer van with all the gear plus some suntan lotion we took off for the West Country towing John's speed boat behind us.

It was a long haul down from Lincolnshire and upon arrival we asked the gatekeeper chap directions to our apartment. He pointed the way with a doom-laden warning that the place was haunted, which was a very reassuring way to start our vacation. As there were five of us in the band plus Tax the roadie, we had to work out sleeping arrangements before settling in. The apartment had one room with four single bunks and another room with a big double bed. Wincott and I drew the short straws and had to share the double bed, Morecambe and Wise style.

As we climbed into the king size one night we heard a spooky tapping coming from the window. Being two floors up we were slightly concerned what the strange noise might be, when all of a sudden the curtains started flapping wildly. Instantly we remembered the gatekeeper's ghoulish warning and realised we were being attacked by poltergeists. Scared half to death, we pulled the bedcover over our heads for what good it would do and lay there frozen with fear.

After what felt like a lifetime, we could hear the sounds of muffled laughter behind the door and suddenly twigged it was a bloody wind-up. Bastards. They were all in on it and had tapped the window from the adjoining room with a couple of broom handles tied together. They had also managed to rig up an elaborate pulley system made of string and bent coat hangers so the curtains would rise up in a ghostly fashion. Very ingenious. Nice try, lads, almost had us going for a couple of minutes.

Being curry addicts, we were suffering serious withdrawals and gagging for an Indian meal after eating nothing but chips and ice cream for the past few days. There was a big neon sign that we'd spotted in Mevagissy that read 'RAB ALAD' restaurant so we all headed down there one evening eagerly anticipating some lovely hot spicy vindaloo and a big stack of poppadoms. Just imagine our bitter disappointment when we got there only to discover that the neon sign should actually have read 'Crab Salad' but the letters 'C' and 'S' had fallen off and never been replaced. Not only that but the restaurant was shut and we couldn't even get a bloody crab salad either.

Next day we were looking forward to a bit of posing in the speed boat and took it out for a spin round the bay. Boating sounds so much fun and looks so glamorous in the movies but the reality was truly awful. It was the first and last time I shall ever be tempted to be bumped, battered and bruised at fifty knots on a rock-hard seat that fractures your spine whilst being sea-sick and soaked to the skin in the perishing cold. Or am I missing something?

After that I should have known better, but having brought my trunks I felt grudgingly obliged to venture into the sea, which admittedly looked deceptively inviting on a hot summer's afternoon. However, I'm shit-scared of water and can't swim so had to settle for a modest paddle and ventured in. Trust me, even on the hottest day the sea is freezing. By the time the water had reached chest level my genitals had shrivelled to zero and I was gasping for breath, having never experienced such cold before in my life. Inexplicably the others were merrily splashing about having fun as I hung on for grim death trying to get back to dry land as soon as possible to thaw out.

As you have may have gathered I'm not particularly keen on water-based activities. Our roadie 'Tax' (not to be confused with Tex) on the other hand loved to swim and even had a life-saving certificate. I wasn't really aware of his aquatic skills at the time, but he was soon to prove his prowess. A huge storm was brewing and before long the raging sea was hurling huge boulders over the roofs of houses at the foot of the bay. I'd noticed earlier that all the windows had heavy shutters and now I could understand why. Never have I seen such massive waves and even cars were being swept away in the tsunami.

There was a large crowd gathering to watch the tempest when a couple of surfer types jumped into the maelstrom. It seemed inevitable they would be dashed onto rocks, but they just bobbed about no problem and were having an absolute ball. Next thing I knew Tax was in there with them. At first I thought he'd gone in to save their lives, but he'd just jumped in for the hell of it like the other two. They put on a spectacular show for everybody, who clapped and cheered when they eventually re-emerged from the huge breakers.

Very stupid but most impressive all the same. Afterwards at the Rising Sun pub he was feted like a hero and the entire band were very happy just to bask in his reflected glory.

I must just say that over the years we had some ace road crew serve their apprenticeships with us and then go on to work with top big-name bands. Jerry 'Tax' McGillycuddy went to the Small Faces. Chris Adamson to Pink Floyd and Tom Petty. Pete Burke to the Stones, The Who, Elton John and Grateful Dead. Nigs Hudson to Osibisa. Mick West and John Donoghue to Amazing Blondel, etc. Most of them were as daft as brushes and always going on about pepper-birds and bread-beetles. Don't ask.

Dimples Commer Van and speedboat.

Tex, Stu Smith and John Gladwin in Cornwall 1966.

19

Let's Rumble

It was John Gladwin who did all the graft getting gigs and dealing with agents, contracts and other boring problems. Also, his father financed all the band's equipment, rehearsal room and a brand-new six-wheel transit van with reclining aircraft seats, so they both deserved considerable credit. Because the band was his baby, John usually wanted his own way and consequently there were occasional minor disputes and dissension in the ranks. However, when push came to shove we'd always work as a team to forge a formidable united front against the rest of the world. I suppose it's what they call bonding nowadays, though I really hate that expression.

We were always on the road, continuously working a gruelling schedule of dates the length and breadth of the country. The Go-Go in Newcastle, Oscars in Ilford, Golden Torch at Tunstall, Sheffield City Hall, The Marquee in London, Lincoln Co-op, Twisted Wheel at Manchester, Nottingham Boat Clubs, Boston Gliderdrome, Broken Wheel at Newark, The Kirk at Middlesbrough, California Ballroom Luton, The Place at Hanley, Quay Club in Newcastle, plus endless Meccas, Top Ranks and Locanos till we hardly knew what day it was.

Interspersed with these relatively prestigious venues, we were filling in spare dates at some right shit holes. These were the dreaded working men's clubs, miners' welfares and squaddie camps, all of which spelt trouble. Up until this time, apart from a few minor skirmishes, we hadn't really been involved in any serious punch-ups. In any case, apart from being professional cowards, musicians in the '60s were into 'peace and love' and not really into pain if it could possibly be avoided. We needed functioning fingers to earn a living so tried not to risk physical injury, even though self-inflicted drug-induced brain damage was deemed perfectly acceptable. Sometimes, though, fights were inescapable.

The first major incident occurred at a back-street dive in Darnell, a slum district of Sheffield, and for the usual reason. Women! The evening had started ominously when a plain-clothes detective from CID came into our dressing room just before the show asking some really bizarre questions. No one had a clue what he was on about and eventually he disappeared. Anyway, we thought no more of it and got up on stage for our first set, by now well pissed and acting cocky. We really should have known better in a place like this than to start eyeballing the local totty. It soon became apparent that we'd upset quite a few of the resident yobs and could sense trouble brewing as the crowd started getting restless.

Things finally reached fever pitch, and with the sad inevitability of a Greek tragedy, the ugly mob stormed the stage baying for blood. We ran for our lives, this way and that, cowering behind the piano and ducking a volley of broken bottles. While attempting to barricade ourselves in the dressing-room toilets, it was as if time stood still and our whole lives flashed before us. Most of the band, in desperate acts of self-preservation, had taken cover wherever they could, more or less leaving Gladwin standing alone, wielding a mic stand dramatically round his head warding off the seething aggressors. The outlook was grim.

Completely outnumbered, we didn't stand a chance and all we could do was pray. Just then, in a flash of blinding light our prayers were answered and a miracle happened. Like in the movies, the cavalry arrived just in the nick of time when the local constabulary came charging in to save us. Oh, thank you, Sweet Lord, God, Jesus, Mary, Joseph and every other bugger in the Bible. Thank you so very, very much for our deliverance and, just this once, for the boys in blue. The weirdest thing is, though; it was only by coincidence that the cops actually happened to arrive at that precise moment. By sheer fluke they had turned up to investigate reports of the weirdo CID detective from earlier who'd apparently been impersonating a police officer. Eventually things calmed down and it's safe to say we escaped fatal injury only by the very skin of our teeth. After a reprimand from the chief constable for inciting public disorder, we were given a police escort out of town and strongly advised not to return in any great hurry.

Newcastle Mayfair Mecca turned out to be another right roughhouse. It was actually quite a respectable-looking ballroom, typical of the period, with a large dance floor and balconies all round with a grand staircase leading to the bar upstairs. The Dimples were second band on stage and all seemed to be going well until suddenly, for whatever reason, the whole place erupted. Apart from ourselves, everyone else seemed to be involved in the biggest brawl I've ever witnessed.

The hall was packed and there must have been over a thousand punters battling it out, all screaming, kicking and punching. Within minutes the place was practically demolished. Chairs and tables were smashed into matchwood and bodies both male and female were being hurled down staircases like rag dolls. It was like a Wild West saloon, with people flying over the balcony with twisted and broken limbs, all piled up unconscious amongst the debris. Total madness. By now shattered glasses and broken bottles were strewn everywhere and the whole place was awash with gallons of Newkie Broon ale.

As we frantically tried to drag our booze-soaked equipment off the stage to safety, a couple of what I can only assume were corpses fell from above, impaling themselves on the remaining microphone stands. That was it. We just left the rest of the stuff and high-tailed it while we still had the chance. Hilariously we were later reliably informed that this is just a normal Saturday night for Newcastle.

All-night transport cafés always seemed to attract hassle for rock bands and we often ended up fighting off some bunch of morons in such places. Normally we'd have a team of roadies riding shotgun in the van but on this particular occasion it was just the five band members in a car. After a nosh at the Haven Café on the A1 north of Doncaster, we were about to top up with fuel at the adjoining filling station when a gang of thugs followed us out of the café and launched an all-out attack without warning right there on the garage forecourt. We made a run for it to make our escape, but Gladwin and Stixy, the drummer, didn't quite make it and started getting battered. We stopped and ran back, but by now Stixy was bleeding after putting his fist through a petrol pump and Gladwin was flat out with a broken leg. The gang took off, and by the time we got there, all that was left to do was pick up the pieces. Stixy was basically OK, but we had to rush Gladwin to Doncaster Hospital, where they fixed him up and stuck a pot on his leg. He subsequently recovered but for the next few weeks did gigs on crutches, though if truth be known I think he quite enjoyed all the sympathy and attention.

A couple of months later at the same café the gang struck again, but this time we had three roadies in the van that doubled as minders. They were Mick West, Crack and Big Mo, who were three of the hardest guys from town and local legends. The gang just assumed we were easy meat after the last time, but how mistaken they were. Just as we were leaving, one of the mob made the fatal mistake of having a pop at Big Mo and the roadies responded accordingly. The rest of the aggressors joined in but didn't stand an earthly with this trio in full flight. Watching seasoned street fighters at work is sublime. They are true master craftsmen in their own specialist subject: extreme violence. Poetry in motion. It was a massacre. Clinically and efficiently they did the business, and as a final touch, Mick pissed all over the gang leader's head as he lay there puking. Feeling elated, we triumphantly drove off, leaving the bastards scattered all over the car park. Justice had been served.

There was also a bit of a dust-up at the Watford Gap services on the M1 after four or five drunks started a bit of bother. The band plus two roadies, Mick West and Chris Adamson, had stopped off for a snack on the way back from a London gig. As usual we were sitting there minding our own business when this rabble began to upset the diners. We all looked suitably weird at the time, so eventually they started picking on us, though we tried to ignore it. But no, they wouldn't let it lie. The ringleader was mainly instigating the disturbance and the others were reluctantly getting dragged into the melee whether they liked it or not. Nevertheless, not really expecting any resistance they unwisely persisted.

The ruckus began in earnest when the ringleader had a go at Chris, who suddenly jumped up and, much to the bloke's surprise, chased him up and down the restaurant, leaping over tables to catch him. Mick was instantly up like a shot to deal with the most dangerous-looking one who was wearing a rugby shirt and we started on the others. By now, all the diners in the restaurant were cheering us on, aware that these arseholes had it coming and wanted to see them whooped. Chris quickly gave the protagonist a good hiding and then came over to help us out. We didn't have much to do as the stragglers immediately lost heart when their mate went down. The tough guy, however, fancied his chances, and he and Mick got stuck in.

With the others out of action, we all gathered round as spectators to watch the main event that had now worked its way through into the foyer. It was marvellous. Initially it was a battle of strength as they wrestled each other to the ground. They both struggled for what seemed like ages, getting in the odd thump until they were sweating and grunting with fatigue. Still puffing and panting away, the rugger scrumhalf suddenly seemed to run out of steam whist Mick retained his stamina and started coming out on top. At brawling and fighting, he was a real artist and so decided to put on a show.

Psyched up and sensing victory, he started to play to the audience, holding the crowd in the palm of his hand. The other guy had all but given up by now and you could see the fear in his eyes knowing he was completely at Mick's mercy. Totally in charge, Mick started toying with the sucker like a cat fooling with a mouse. He started cruelly teasing and taunting the bloke, who just stood there transfixed and so terrified that he was now crapping his pants. At that point Mick just nutted him as hard as he could and blood spouted everywhere. It was quite horrific. There was this almighty crunch and the guy went down like a sack of spuds and that was almost that, but not quite.

Mick had also managed split open his own forehead into the bargain which enraged him even more and he was heard muttering, "Now where's the cunt that started all this?" The crowd cheered and applauded in appreciation and anticipation of even more bloodshed. This included several Blue Boar security guards who were also clapping and happy to let us get on with it. In fact one of them came up to us later on, shook us by the hand and said, "Congratulations, lads, it's good to see the band win for a change." Mick, still hell-bent on retribution, had unfinished business, and off he went in search of the ringleader, who had been sneakily watching the proceedings whilst nursing the wounds inflicted by Chris.

He suddenly realised Mick was after him but was too scared to run. After making a pathetic attempt at blending in with the crowd so as not to be noticed, he ended up crawling towards the door on all fours like a frightened wounded animal. Mick was straight on his scent and strode towards him as he cowered by the entrance, no longer even daring to move. Mick just pointed and said, "Right, you're the silly cunt that started it," and literally kicked the bloke's teeth down his throat, thereby completing the mission. Without even breaking step, he casually strolled back into the restaurant and nonchalantly finished his fry-up. Magic!

20

Party Time

When not scrapping or gigging, we'd probably be back in town either resting up or rehearsing, but mainly partying at the band house that served as headquarters, hotel and harem.

Acquiring a reputation for twenty-four-hour fun and frolics, the place soon became a regular drop-in centre that attracted all the freaks from miles around. Drop-out centre more like. Day and night it was the throbbing hub of hippie happenings, music and merriment. A rock 'n' roll circus. It was also an occasional stopover for visiting bands to the town such as Jethro Tull, Robert Plant and John Bonham, etc. Come on, where do you think Led Zep picked up all their outrageous behaviour from?

Though boisterous and rowdy, most of the stuff we got up to was mainly just youthful exuberance. Pep pills were all the rage at the time and chemists were getting rolled nearly every night for fresh supplies. The Buccaneer coffee bar was the main centre for distribution as well as pick-up point for girls and gossip. Amphetamine, benzedrine, chlorodyne, dex, daps, ephs and in fact the full A–Z of uppers and downers were easily available for consumption in those early days.

Widely used during wartime to keep pilots and troops alert during long missions, they were in fact primarily slimming aids or mother's little helpers. These stimulants had recently been rediscovered by a new generation of mods and ravers wanting to stay awake at the Mojo Club, Castleford Crystal Bowl, Jazz Workshop and other similar all-nighters where we frequently performed. The two popular favourites were black bombers and blues, otherwise known as doobies, but best of all were glass phials of pure methedrine normally mixed with a bottle of Coca-Cola.

Of course, almost everyone dabbled and experimented to one degree or another and you could spot the symptoms of speed a mile off. The bulging wide-eyed euphoric intensity. The dry-mouthed, gum-chewing, jaw-achingly tedious, non-stop rabbit and relentless onslaught of verbal diarrhoea. Hyperactivity, sweating and copious consumption of cola, combined with an almost visible weight loss as the pounds dropped off before your very eyes.

Any thoughts of hunger would have completely disappeared. It was fantastic for dancing, but for a male, one of the strange and unfortunate side effects was the shrinkage of a certain vital bodily appendage to a fraction of its normal size. Not that it really mattered much, because having lost the urge you became kind of asexual and benign. Everybody in sight suddenly becomes your best friend and all's well with the world. Talking at twenty to the dozen, secrets and deeply personal confidences would eagerly be imparted and exchanged with total strangers in meaningful conversations that were bitterly regretted the following morning.

It was great while it lasted, but then surely as night follows day, there came the inevitable and dreaded 'comedown'. As the effects started to wear off you'd be physically exhausted but unable to sleep. You'd either stay up all night or go to bed to try and rest, but it was impossible. For hours you'd just sit there bolt upright with eyes wide open and your head spinning out of control. A multitude of brilliant revolutionary ideas and concepts that were going to change the world several hours before, now seemed completely ridiculous but continued to swim around your brain till they drove you almost crazy.

Another great buzz was the sleeping pill Mandrax, which made you feel extremely tipsy but also had amazing aphrodisiac qualities. More about 'Mandies' later.

Prior to discovering marijuana our first hallucinatory experiences came courtesy of Dimeryl cough mixture, which at that time could still be purchased legally from any chemist. It must have contained some form of opiate but tasted bittersweet and nauseating, which was horrible when you had to force down a whole bottle of the stuff to get the desired effect. It was weird gear that crept up on you about an hour after consumption. The sensation was one of being cosily cocooned in a dark womb-like abyss.

There was also a dramatic change in time and spatial concepts, although totally different to taking acid. It would seem to take forever to do the simplest task and virtually impossible to hold a conversation. By the third word of a sentence you'd have forgotten what it was that you'd started talking about. It just felt like very hard work trying to keep it together or do anything normal. Crossing a bridge would be like walking a tightrope, hanging on for grim death. Short strolls became epic marathons and watching TV or a film was a life sentence. I remember making the drastic mistake of going to see *2001: A Space Odyssey* at the cinema on 'Dim' and swear it literally lasted for light years.

Instead of expanding your mind like LSD, it sort of magnified in the opposite direction but wasn't a paranoia kind of thing. It would be possible to sit motionless for eight hours and just stare at something and watch its shape alter or blend into the shadows. When gazing into someone's face they'd turn into chimpanzees, Roman soldiers, reptilians or pirates and such like. Observing yourself in a mirror was the weirdest of all, like you could almost see into your own soul but not in a frightening way like acid, which could get totally out of control. At least with Dim you felt as if you were vaguely in charge. The room would slowly spin around with doors and windows randomly moving about, constantly changing position. Then imaginary figures would appear, sitting there on the sofa like the three wise monkeys as if it was somehow highly symbolic.

Unsurprisingly, I'm fairly sure it seriously destroys brain cells. Before taking Dim I had a brilliant memory but for ages after could hardly recall a damn thing. Unlike being on dope, sex was not particularly enhanced whilst under the influence and felt somewhat empty and unfulfilling. The after-effects too were prolonged and unpleasant, not unlike having the symptoms of mild flu for a couple of weeks.

Some idiots took the stuff every day for years and God knows how they must have ended up. I took it quite a few times and enjoyed it for the experience but no way could get hooked. It's the same with anything. There's always a small minority of people with addictive personalities who will be excessive and obsessive in whatever they do. Others who make up the vast majority are usually far more sensible and tend to experiment with most things in moderation but unfortunately get tarred with the same brush as addicts. The whole debate on drug policy is irrational, illogical and unfair. To be honest I don't really give a toss anymore, having given up all that crap long ago, though I must admit that it was pleasurable at the time.

21

Don Arden / Galaxy Entertainments

Apart from all the tomfoolery, The 'Dimps' (as we were now commonly known) were a reasonably accomplished musical unit and were out gigging several nights a week. By now our set consisted of all the usual popular soul, ska and Tamla standards. Increasingly we started covering material by The Impressions, Miracles, Esquires, Daryl Banks, Capitols, Marvelows, Solomon Burke, Major Lance, Monitors and Garnett Mimms. The more obscure the better. All the mods started picking up on what we were doing and began flocking to the gigs. Soon we were playing at packed all-nighters, colleges and clubs all over the country.

A booking agency called Galaxy Entertainments was advertising auditions in the Melody Maker and searching for new acts to add to their prestigious roster so we contacted them. They invited us along so we travelled down to Wickham Hall in Romford to share the stage with five other similar bands, all seeking fame and fortune. We must have 'done good' because they signed us on the spot. Big time, here we come. Amongst our new stable mates were the Small Faces at the height of their career, plus The Move, Amen Corner, Nashville Teens, Love Affair, Skip Bifferty, The Lonely Ones and a host of other greater and lesser names.

The company offices were on Carnaby Street right slap bang in the middle of the 'happening' '60s action. The big pop hit of the moment was Cat Stevens song 'Matthew and Son' which to me is so evocative of Soho during that brief era. For a giggle we used to wind John up by singing 'Gladwin and Son', that being the name of his father's insurance company.

During that 'groovy' period I guess we could best be described as freestyle mods where anything goes. At some point we all had centre partings and were wearing hipsters, spats and frilly shirts with long collars. Either that or Levi 501s, Ben Shermans, mobster suits and thigh-length pirate boots. Most of our crowd at the time were wide-eyed, pill-popping blue-beat freaks. You name it, we did it, wore it or swallowed it. The Dimples were lucky enough to be right at the heart of the scene in its absolute heyday and probably the best time ever. All our ultra-trendy gear was picked up from around there at Kleptomania, Carnaby Cavern in Ganton Street, Lord Kitchener's Valet, John Stephens, Anello and Davide, Lord Jon and the rest of them. We naturally thought we were the cat's cobblers, though my old dad always said we looked like something out of Fred Karno's Army.

Anyhow, we soon discovered that Galaxy was run by a right gang of hoods led by none other than Don 'Mr Big' Arden. Dangerous Don was noted for excessive violence to anyone who crossed him or owed him money. He had a couple of heavy-duty sidekicks and a massive minder who could lift two huge Selmer Goliath bass cabs at the same time, one under each arm. He'd often throw his own clients downstairs if they gave him too much lip. Once he famously hung rival agent Robert Stigwood upside down from his office window for trying to poach the Small Faces.

Also allegedly it's rumoured that he burnt down the Speakeasy Club in Margaret Street and had Jane Mansfield bumped off after some financial dispute. Although highly unlikely, nothing he did would surprise me. On the positive side he was very successful at promoting and breaking new bands. Having been in the game for a long time as a singer himself, he had learned the ropes the hard way. He started out impersonating Al Jolson and Enrico Caruso as well as film-star gangsters George Raft and Edward G Robinson, until discovering management was far more lucrative.

This is when he began bringing rock stars from America such as Chuck Berry, Bo Diddley and Gene Vincent. Eventually he really hit pay dirt with ELO and Black Sabbath, which is how Sharon and Ozzy got together. As it happens he was generally OK with The Dimps apart from running us ragged. For example, we had a gig supporting Lulu at some grotty holiday camp in Scotland and were summoned to attend a meeting in London for the following morning. So after driving down the A1 all night with no sleep, we arrived knackered to find no one at the office. The meeting had been cancelled and he hadn't even bothered to let us know. This was so bloody typical, but we soon wised up.

22

Decca Records

Regardless of these annoying traits, Dastardly Don was getting us some smart gigs and even set up a record deal with Decca, though his recent chart-fixing prosecution probably didn't help our prospects a great deal. The first song he offered us was 'Hi Ho Silver Lining', but we turned it down long before it was a hit for Jeff Beck. It was the type of rubbish we hated and refused to play. Even Jeff Beck couldn't stand it. Don wasn't too happy but gave it to another one of his bands The Attack, who had a resounding flop with it.

Next up was 'Love of a Lifetime' which was even worse, but we were reluctant to turn it down. You don't get too many second chances with guys like Don Arden. So really we were pressured into recording the damn thing because that's the way the industry worked in those days. Tin Pan Alley would convince everyone that some load of old crap was going to be a smash hit and that was that. Record it or you're out. His favourite saying was, "Stick with me, my boys, and I'll stud your arse with diamonds." The other one was, "Stick with me, my boys, and you'll be farting through silk knickers."

Upon release, the song got very little airtime and sunk without trace, which we were quite pleased about as it was such an embarrassment. The B-side was a John Gladwin composition called 'My Heart Is Tied to You' that was much better and more in the soul style of the band. It might have done well chart-wise if they'd have made it the A-side.

In 2007, a commemorative blue plaque dedicated to Don Arden and the Small Faces was unveiled outside the former Galaxy offices at 52–55 Carnaby Street by Faces drummer Kenney Jones. This was all organised by Val Weedon who'd been a secretary at Galaxy at the same time we were there. I managed to contact her and she kindly sent me some old Dimples publicity pics that were part of her collection of memorabilia. It turns out that Val has written several books about her life and times in the music business and is still involved with promoting noisy rock bands. It's quite funny, really, because in 1997 she received an MBE from the Queen for her contribution to the campaign for 'The Right to Peace and Quiet'.

The Dimples were definitely more of a live band and never got captured properly on vinyl. Regardless of that, the experience of recording at the Decca studios was something special with the help of our producer Tony Clarke. Also we managed to get a live promotional spot on Granada TV show *Scene at 6.30* up in Manchester. This was produced by Johnny Hamp, who later brought 'The Comedians' to our screens. *Scene at 6.30* was quite hip, having previously featured The Beatles, Hollies, Searchers and several other northern bands before they became famous.

The Dimples (Decca).

For the show we all wore red Sgt Pepper-style military gear from Lord Kitchener's Valet so heaven knows what we looked like. The broadcast playback wasn't actually all that bad or particularly cringe-worthy, though I doubt it was ever saved for posterity. They just wiped all the tapes back then to re-use and save money. Whilst hanging around before filming, I was chatted up by Irma Ogden from *Coronation Street*, who'd been rehearsing in the studio next door. She asked if I had any change for the phone and blagged three pence off me. I didn't fancy her, though. Ha ha.

So with stardom still eluding us we just carried on with the relentless grind of one-night stands. This was interspersed with the occasional recording session in search of a follow-up single. One such time was with songwriter Pete Dello from Honeybus, who'd had a massive hit with 'Don't Let Maggie Go', the Nimble bread advert on telly. He had a song for us called 'Roof Over Our Heads' about homelessness, which I think we made a demo of, together with another of his compositions. Neither came to anything and we were becoming disillusioned.

Greg and Gladwin were increasingly at each other's throats, which eventually led to a final bust-up. Greg quit and with him went Smithy, who decided it was time to settle down and marry Carol, his long-time sweetheart. Shortly after leaving the band he launched a successful chain of award-winning fashion shops called, would you believe it, 'Smiths'. Anyway, the remaining three Dimples decided to carry on and find suitable replacements. The obvious choice of drummer was a previously mentioned local lad called Steve 'Stixy' Cox, but finding a decent guitar player was more of a problem. No sweat, something'll turn up. It always does.

23

Mad Geoff

An advert in the *NME* seemed the best way to find our future ax-man. After several replies we whittled the choice down to a guy from Oxford called Geoff Eaton Tindle, or 'Mad' Geoff, as he soon became known. He'd paid his dues working with Jimmy Page, Screaming Lord Sutch, and Mal Ryder and the Primitives, who for a publicity stunt had their shoulder-length hair cropped off on the Eamonn Andrews TV show.

Mad Geoff came as a breath of fresh air, with his Pythonesque and Milligoon sense of humour. Though not as tall, he *was* Basil Fawlty before *Fawlty Towers* was a twinkle in John Cleese's eye. The way he spoke, his mannerisms and the way he acted was uncanny, even down to thrashing cars with a tree branch. He'd scream hysterically doing headstands in a bucket and do suicidal summersaults down the middle of the road if we got stuck in traffic.

He told such tall tales about his life in previous bands with Freddie Fingers Lee and Ian Hunter, that we mythically christened them 'The Exaggerators'. Later on we found most of the outrageous stories were actually true. On other occasions he'd dress up as a tramp and sweep the streets or raid litter bins and pick up used dog-ends from the gutter, just to get a reaction. The whole time he was constantly doing all this crazy shit and kept us permanently in stitches.

He'd been brought up in a pub by the Thames, but both his parents had died when he was young. A wicked step-aunt then became his guardian but more or less disowned him as quickly as she could. Also he had just split with his girlfriend so was obviously feeling lonely and sorry for himself. Realising all this, we tried to make him feel at home as he adjusted to our strange northern ways.

Meanwhile, he revelled in mock self-pity and milked the poor old tragic Geoff scenario for all it was worth as part of his comedy routine. One of his favourite pseudo-melodramatic cries for help was, "God I'm lonely." It was so convincing that you never quite knew if he actually meant it or was just messing about as usual. His imagination and acting ability was so incredible that he could make any situation funny. In fact the guy was wasted as a musician and should have been a comedy scriptwriter.

Having recently received a substantial inheritance, Geoff was forever buying lots of fancy new clothes, but even so he always looked slightly unkempt. Every day he smothered himself with 'Brut' aftershave and I mean really splashed it on. The whole house and van reeked of it. Never once did he ever bother cleaning his dirty clothes but instead just slung them out the bedroom window until they were piled high in the backyard.

As well as being called Mad Geoff he also acquired many other idiotic nicknames in the band. One of them was 'Hammy' because of the way he nibbled his food like a hamster. An annoyingly monotonous communal chant evolved for use in moments of boredom to mither Geoff that went 'Hammy the Hamster, Hammy the Hamster, Hammy the Hamster' for hours on end until everyone eventually got fed up. The band even clubbed together once and bought him a real hamster for a pet that lived in a box with an old deerstalker hat for a bed. Unfortunately it ate the hat and died.

Right from the start Hammy, aka Niff-Niff, and I hit it off. He was one of life's eccentrics and it was like having my own personal jester. The two of us formed our own little clique and started making home-brewed beer. At the time it only cost a couple of pence a pint and was twice as strong as pub ale so we made gallons of the stuff. We'd take a crate of hooch to every gig and get totally wasted. The taste was terrible but worst of all the bottles kept randomly exploding. It was like living with a ticking time bomb. Glass shrapnel would end up embedded in walls and thick brown sediment splattered the ceiling. With practice we finally got the hang of it and the bottles stopped blowing up but the evil flavour never improved.

The pair of us were always acting the goat and our behaviour became increasingly reckless and defiant. Sensing insurgency, Gladwin, who liked to think he was in charge, viewed our antics somewhat disapprovingly. And you guessed it, the more he disapproved, the naughtier we became. Yes, all very childish, I know, but so enjoyable. In many ways Niff-Niff was a bad influence but at other times he was really good. He made me look at the world through different eyes. View things from another angle and question everything.

At the same time I was getting into all the new alternative hippy shit and devouring the philosophical teachings of

Gurdjieff and Ouspensky, as well as lots of other similar mystical writers. On top of this, our musical horizons were rapidly expanding, taking on board gospel and jazz such as Art Blakey and Wes Montgomery. We also listened to stuff ranging from the Swingle Singers and Music for Zen Meditation to experimental classical compositions by Messiean, Boulez and Hindemith. Add to this any other pretentious avant-garde nonsense we could lay our hands on and you maybe get a hint of where we were coming from at this point. All these contrasting cultural influences were now incorporated into our own music and reshaping the sound of the band.

Inevitably by now we'd also discovered cannabis. The first time we ever messed with the mezz was after a Leicester gig with a band called 'Family' that was promoted by a boxer mate of theirs. We were ripped off and never actually got paid but were invited back to a 'Family' group party where their bass player Ric Grech (who later joined Blind Faith) started rolling a joint and offered us a toke. We were used to uppers and downers, but this stuff was new to us. Not wishing to appear uncool, we took our first puff of marijuana acting like old hands at the game and soon reefer madness took over.

Before long nearly everyone around had become regular heads and the whole scene began to change, as did the direction of the band. By now we had a brand-new van and plenty of dates pencilled in. Rehearsals with the new line-up continued apace as we added more and more new material to the set. Geoff picked up real quick and Stixy the drummer slotted straight in no probs.

Stixy was a natural but a bit of an enigma as it turns out. At the time he seemed such a simple soul (as do most drummers) and we admired his percussive expertise but merely assumed he was a big dumb blond. How wrong we turned out to be. With Gladwin and Wincott joined at the hip and myself and Hammy all cosied up, Stixy perhaps felt the odd man out but then again maybe not. Actually he was far too busy chatting up the birds to care less. We had our fair share but Stixy was just a glutton. He had a different girl at every gig we ever played and was a real rum lad, as we found out later.

24

Gospel Garden (1967-1968)

The group briefly carried on gigging as The Dimples, but it was decided a fresh new name change was in order. We'd recently been heavily influenced by a couple of albums, namely Jim Webb's 'Magic Garden' by 5th Dimension and 'Black Nativity' by gospel singers Madeline Bell and Alex Bradford. By mixing the two concepts we came up with 'Gospel Garden', which everyone agreed had a certain ring to it. Admittedly a risky image but we decided to take a chance. Whatever, we started incorporating some rousing gospel songs amongst our existing soul and ska repertoire, plus some jazzy guitar arrangements for Hammy to get his little hamster teeth into, and people loved it.

The concept seemed to work brilliantly and Gospel Garden went down a storm. We managed to wriggle out of our contract with dodgy Don Arden and found a new manager in York called Syd Hartas. He had an American DJ partner called Chicken Fat Charlie and was already getting work for another happening band called 'Roll Movement'.

Syd did us proud and got us loads of prestigious gigs all over the country and especially in London. One of the coolest and toughest was the Q Club in Paddington. Its clientele were almost exclusively Jamaican and I think we were one of the few white groups ever to play there. We'd been doing a lot of all-nighters with a black soul band who recommended us, but because we were called Gospel Garden the venue didn't realise we were all white boys until we got there. As we unloaded the van and started setting up the amps, the crowd was eyeing us with suspicion.

It was very dark and the audience were mean-looking and to be honest we were shitting ourselves. Just before going on stage we noticed that they had a price list of exotic Caribbean food available pinned up behind the bar. There were many unfamiliar dishes and we were getting increasingly fearful that if they didn't like us, we might end up as 'Beat Group Soup' on the following night's menu. Thankfully we went down better than expected and lived to play another day. Being accepted at the Q Club was quite an accomplishment for a band of bleach boys and we left there relieved and very happy.

Other notable London in-crowd gigs we played at were The Marquee, Scotch of St James, Speakeasy, Cromwellian, Flamingo, 100 Club, Sybillas, Blaises, Tiles, Revolution, Hatchett's, Ram Jam, Oscars and the Lotus Club.

Back oop north in the dressing room bog at York Assembly Rooms (1967) not long before we were due on stage, our drummer 'Stixy' shat the *biggest turd in the world ever*! Perfect and completely intact, this glorious lump was so huge that it blocked the U bend and stuck up above the toilet seat by a good six inches. So impressive was the stupendous stool that we decided to invite the whole of the audience to file backstage and view it. They were without exception awestruck with admiration and it received a rapturous standing ovation. We even seriously considered donating it to York Museum as an exhibit. Not unexpectedly, however, there was an acute lack of volunteers to remove and transport this prodigious item to a more appropriate place of worship. In fact, it wouldn't surprise me if it were still there lying dormant to this day. There is no way it would have flushed away in the normal manner, and no one in their right mind would actually touch it. As you can imagine it was a hard act to follow and the rest of the evening was something of an anticlimax after all the excitement. And yes, you've guessed it: the giant turd stole the show.

Another venue was Brandesburton Village Hall in East Yorkshire (1967), where, as a climax to the Gospel Garden show, Stixy did a prolonged drum solo whilst at the same time performing a rather tasteless strip tease for a gimmick. He got down as far as his underpants and was just in process of removing this last remaining vital item of clothing. At the critical moment, just in the nick of time, the local village bobby leapt up with his cape, draped it over Stixy and the offending parts, and promptly escorted him off the stage. As far as I remember the gig was abandoned and we never got paid. Barefaced cheek!

Yet another unsavoury Gospel Garden incident was in a dressing room with no toilet at Burton-on-Trent Rugby Club in 1968. After drinking about twenty-five pints between us backstage (remember this is a rugby club do), we didn't think it totally unreasonable under the circumstances to recycle the empty beer glasses into more pressing use as we relieved ourselves throughout the evening. Anyway, after the gig we packed up and went home, leaving the freshly refilled glasses there in the dressing room overnight.

The following morning the cleaners were horrified to find twenty-five pints of piss neatly lined up along the window ledge and stinking to high heaven. Unsurprisingly they threw a fit and refused to touch the stuff. Management was called in to do the dirty work and as a result we were never again re-booked at Burton, the centre of the British brewing industry. I don't know why. The beer tasted like piss anyway.

The only gigs we ever did outside the UK mainland were over in the Emerald Isle by which time we had recruited a new guitarist, Les Nicol. The first booking was on a Saturday night in Belfast at the Maritime Hotel, otherwise known as Club Rado or The Blues Club, which was the spiritual home of Van Morrison in the early days. Our support group was an outfit called 'Cheese' that very soon afterwards changed their name to 'Taste' when they teamed up with Rory Gallagher. They ought to have called themselves 'Cheese on Taste'. Boom boom. I think it was Rory in the audience that evening that came up to tell Les how much he enjoyed his playing.

Next night we were booked at the Embassy Ballroom in Derry (or Londonderry), which was a peculiar venue. Our dressing room was under the stage and there were official signs everywhere saying 'No Political Songs', 'Do Not Play "God Save the Queen"' and other such messages. For most of the evening, all the boys stood at one side of the hall and the girls stood at the other. It wasn't until much later on that they actually plucked up courage to meet in the middle and have a dance. Maybe that was because they hadn't consumed any alcohol, which wasn't allowed back then on a Sunday in Northern Ireland.

We were desperate for a bevvy before the show so nipped over the nearby border where it was legal. On the way back, right in the middle of nowhere, we happened to pass a racetrack that was swarming with ordinary family saloon cars, hurtling round the circuit at breakneck speed, packed with Mum, Dad, Granny and the kids all hanging on for dear life. It was an entirely unofficial 'free-for-all' with no one in charge or any safety precautions whatsoever. We could hardly believe our eyes but in a moment of madness thought we might as well join in for the craic. There were six of us in the van plus the gear, but even with so much weight on board we just dived headlong into the fray and careered round like maniacs with the best of them until we had to leave for the gig. Completely bonkers. Only in Ireland.

Gospel Garden
(L to R) Steve Cox, John Gladwin, Terry Wincott, Craig Austin, Geoff Tindle.

25

Pete Stringfellow / Camp Records

By now, even Pete Stringfellow from the Mojo Club in Sheffield had heard about us and fancied a piece of the action. After some wrangling Syd and Pete shook hands and became our joint managers. On Whit Monday, 3 June in 1968, the 'UK and American International King Mojo Festival No. 1' was organised by Stringfellow at the colossal Queens Hall in Leeds. As a result of the new management partnership, Gospel Garden was added to the bill alongside the Small Faces, Bill Haley and The Comets, Edwin Starr, The Herd with Peter Frampton, plus lots of other big names of the day.

Ridiculous as it sounds, we somehow managed to get bigger billing on the poster than all the other acts, including the almighty Bill Haley, for Christ's sake. Original King Mojo posters are now collector's items and changing hands for hundreds of pounds. Another rare collectable was a record given to us at the Mojo Club by Stringfellow called 'If This Is Love I'd Rather Be Lonely' by The Precisions. Gospel Garden was almost certainly the first UK band to include this great future northern soul classic in our regular live set.

One of the poshest venues we ever did was The York Theatre Royal. It was a proper stage show supporting Dave Dee, Dozy, Beaky, Mick and Titch, who were always in the pop charts throughout the '60s. Remember 'Bend It!', 'Hold Tight!', 'Xanadu' and 'Zabadak!'. Definitely not my cuppa tea but an extremely successful group nevertheless. Dave Dee was an ex-copper from Wiltshire, who was the first person at the scene of Eddie Cochran's fatal car crash in Chippenham. Later he became a justice of the peace. A little bit of trivia there. Anyway, he was watching our set from the wings and must have liked what he saw. There and then he more or less offered us a record deal and wanted to produce a single as soon as possible.

He was talent scouting for a London company called Double R Productions. Not Ronnie and Reggie but a couple of playboy jet-setters called Steve Rowland and Ronnie Oppenheimer. Steve Rowland was an ex-Hollywood movie actor turned record producer who also had his own band, Family Dogg. They were managing The Herd, who were the hottest band around at the time, with Peter Frampton dubbed 'the face of '68'. A meeting was arranged at their swish offices in Saville Row and they instantly offered us a deal. Again, as usual we were seduced by promises of stardom and shamelessly blew out poor old Syd with hardly a backward glance. He was mightily pissed off and I don't blame him. Still, this was the big time, so all's fair, I guess.

Anyway, we went right ahead and signed on the dotted line and immediately things started to happen. Straight away they offered us a TV advert for the launch of the new Humber Sceptre car via Robert Stigwood who was managing Clapton and the Heebie Jeebies. We were dead chuffed as we were massive fans of Humber cars and were already travelling to gigs in our own flash two-tone Super Snipe estate.

The advertising concept was that we were 'rock stars' being driven around the West End in a chauffeur-driven limo 'vis à vis' the new Humber Sceptre. Problem was that when we saw it, the Sceptre wasn't really a luxury limo at all but just a dull, normal family-sized car and by far the worst design Humber ever made. From the start the project was doomed.

The driver was an actor, whose chauffeur's cap was several sizes too small, so he had to cut a slit down the back to get it to perch on his head. Then all five of us couldn't fit in the car, so they got rid of Wincott with the excuse that his black beard made him look too sinister. Then filming took all day fannying about and left us bored shitless. For weeks we waited for it to come on telly and finally it did. I only ever saw it the once and it was pathetic. Sad to say, the crappy Humber Sceptre died a death and the car company went bust shortly after.

Next up we were offered a single to record called 'Finders Keepers'. We really detested the song, but it was more or less forced upon us yet again, surprise surprise. The B-side was a Gladwin composition called 'Just a Tear', which was much better and ought to have been the A-side. It was released on the ever-so-camp 'Camp' label, though I can't remember exactly if the producer was Dave Dee or Steve Roland. The place where it was recorded is also a bit of a blur but was probably De Lane Lea, Trident, IBC, Lansdowne or Wessex. Thinking about it, I do seem to have spent an inordinate amount of time and energy in professional recording studios over the years without very much to show for it. Hey ho.

Predictably 'Finders Keepers' failed to sell, so again we just carried on touring the length and breadth of the country.

One of the highlights was playing at the first televised Hippy-Fest in Newcastle dressed in our kaftans and beads, throwing flowers at the audience. Being Geordie-land, though, I reckon we were lucky to get out unscathed. The other band on with us was called the Mandrakes, with singer Alan Palmer, who later changed his name to Robert Palmer and subsequently became a huge superstar. It would be very interesting to see film footage of that if still in the archives.

Gig-wise we took the rough with the smooth just to keep up the momentum, but it didn't always pay the bills. Often half-starved we were reduced to raiding fridges and food cupboards at any gig that might shove us in the kitchen instead of a proper dressing room. Niff-Niff would stuff his suitcase full of ketchup as he was totally addicted to tomato sauce and drowned every meal with it, whatever it was.

In the middle of the night we'd stop off and raid fields for carrots, cauliflowers or anything that was free and available off the land. On balance I don't know how cost-effective it was to do this. As often as not we'd get caked in mud for a couple of bobs' worth of fruit and veg. One time poor old Geoff ruined his suit after falling in a slurry pit, losing an heirloom pocket watch into the bargain.

Another night we spotted three large sacks of onions in a garage forecourt, so we stuck them in the van. Back home at the band house they were stacked in the pantry ready for making huge pots of pilchard curry, which is what we more or less survived on. A few weeks later we were about halfway through the top sack when a strange smell started to permeate the house.

We didn't realise what it was for while and then suddenly there were flies everywhere. The smell got worse and worse till we twigged it was the bottom two sacks that had gone completely rotten. Well, when we tried shifting them the stink became unbearable. The sacks had all turned to mush and were impossible to lift without getting covered in stinking gunk. There were gallons of festering onion juice crawling with maggots, just sloshing about the kitchen floor. We eventually cleaned up, but it took forever to get rid of the lingering stench.

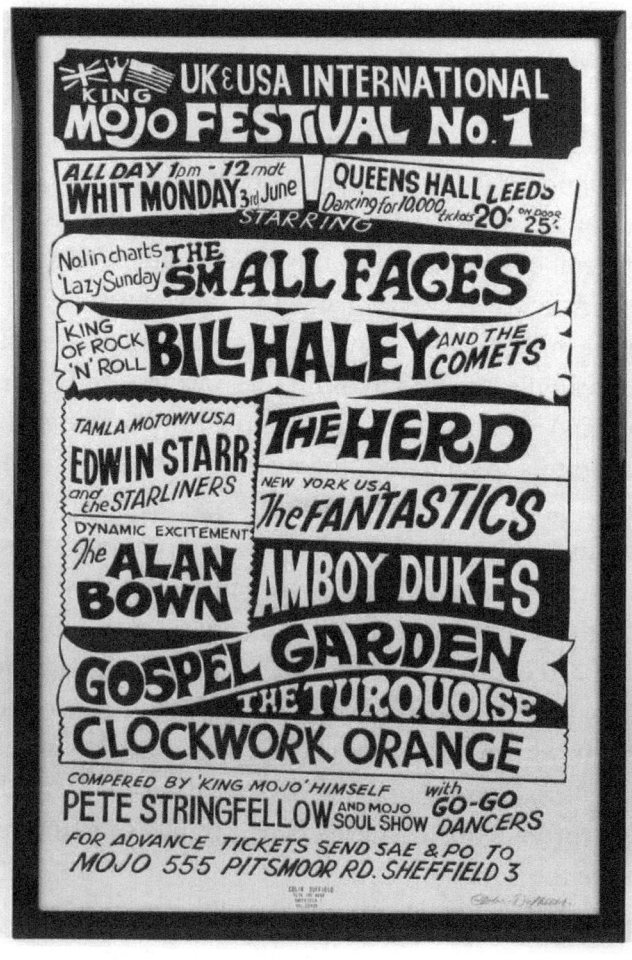

King Mojo Festival Poster.

26

Groupies

Winter arrived and we'd carry on regardless as usual. It was never a problem getting to venues, whatever the weather. Together with Tax, our roadie, there'd always be at least six of us on board and we'd carry spades and wooden planks as a survival kit. That's all we ever needed to get over the snow-covered Pennine hills on a cold winter's night. If necessary we'd all jump out and literally push the van for miles across the frozen moors. It was a big six-wheeler, but if it got really stuck we'd just shovel our way out. I don't think we ever missed a gig because of bad weather conditions.

Once on a trip to the 76 Club at Burton on Trent we had to travel via Derby. Because of deep snow, the Derby ring road was gridlocked in every direction, but we weren't about to give in that easily. Without missing a beat Tax just said, "Fuck it," and drove the van straight up onto the pavement and we circled Derby by footpath for the next ten miles. It felt so exhilarating sailing past all the stranded traffic, much like you might imagine the thrill of a joyriding buzz. Back then we didn't give a shit and always took these sorts of chances when nobody else had the bottle to do the same. Now, with nasty Big Brother and CCTV to track our every move, I somehow don't think we'd get away with such mad manoeuvres today.

Bit by bit they've taken all the spice out of life. Drip by drip they're banning everything, and not only drugs and tobacco. Pubs are closing wholesale because of breathalysers and no-smoking rules. Health supplements, organic food and natural herbs are restricted whilst multinationals patent GM crops with their despicable and immoral terminator seeds. Our water's being poisoned with fluoride and the sky is contaminated with chemtrails full of barium and aluminium oxide. Depleted uranium weapons and fallout from knackered reactors are polluting the planet whilst forests are burnt and chopped down wholesale. Earthquakes and tsunamis are triggered by HAARP geo-engineering and weather modification.

This abused Nikola Tesla-type technology causes droughts and floods to destroy crops that create shortages in the world's food supply. Lethal for the masses but great for the corrupt elites and their control of commodities and the lucrative war machine. Much of this organised chaos is instigated by government alphabet agencies using false-flag operations.

Since the Reichstag fire, other suspected false flags have been Pearl Harbour, Operation Northwoods, Gulf of Tonkin, 9/11, 7/7 and the Oklahoma City bombings to name but a few. Artificial intelligence and 'The Internet of Things' will be the final nail in the coffin. On the other hand, maybe only a coordinated 'one-world government' strategy can ultimately save an overpopulated planet – who knows? *Rant over.*

Anyway back in the '60s when life was much simpler, we'd play 'knuckles' to pass the time away en route to gigs.

Big mistake. It was never a fair contest. Stixy was a big lad who had hands like a cave man's. His fists were like huge mallets so you didn't stand a bleedin' earthly if challenged. The game always started off amicably enough, but having received several savage blows the mood changed. After being clobbered a few more times the loser, now with a fixed rictus grimace, would be on the verge of tears with pain and humiliation. It really, really did fecking hurt. By now we'd be cursing each other and falling out big-style, with the backs of our hands bruised black and blue. They'd be so damaged and swollen by the time we got to the gig, it was a minor miracle how we ever managed to play any of our instruments at all. Knobheads.

At a Scarborough gig, a very friendly young groupie came backstage and kindly offered herself to the band. There was a gang-bang for starters and then for main course she came back with us to the band house. It was an almighty orgy and she was up for anything, though I'd best not go into the sordid details. Predictably, a few days later, most of us came down with the same distressing symptoms.

We called in the quack, who resentfully came to the house and immediately lined us up in a row with our willies hanging out. We felt so stupid and childish as he gave us the once-over, and of course diagnosed a multiple outbreak of the clap. With that he made us turn over and he jabbed us up the jacksy with a huge oversized syringe to teach us a damn good lesson for being 'time-wasting little shits'. To be honest I don't think we actually learnt very much 'cos it just seemed to happen time and time again. Hey, you're only young once.

I always had plenty of tasty totty passing through what was known as the windy room. Why windy room? Because everyone said that I'd enter my boudoir with some willing wench, looking immaculate, and then re-emerge an hour later, flushed and dishevelled with wild hair and the appearance of someone who just survived a force ten tornado.

Two utterly stunning Swedish chicks had just come over on the ferry and turned up at a gig somewhere near the port of Hull. They both had the biggest knockers we had ever encountered. Apparently one of the girl's fathers was a cosmetic surgeon and had performed both their boob jobs personally. Maybe our Viking cousins are just more broadminded and liberated than us Brits, but come on, kinky or wot? Stixy steamed in as usual and got off with one of the girls and someone else pulled the other.

After the gig we lured them both back to the band house for some high-jinks, when Stixy's girl secretly handed me a Mandrax and then slipped Stixy a 'Mickey Finn'. Her devious plan was to knock him unconscious and have her evil way with me. Fair enough, I wasn't complaining and the plan seemed to be working. Stixy appeared to be out cold and the lusty, busty Scandinavian strumpet ended up in my bed. I was warming to the encounter when suddenly, Stixy's huge great fist smashed through the bedroom door. He'd obviously come to, sussed what was going on and was after my blood. Like a shot I was up and outta there escaping down the back staircase, half naked and running for my life. By the time I'd summoned enough courage to dare venture back, the sexy Swede had managed to calm Stixy down and persuaded him not to kill me.

Anyway they must have made up, 'cos next thing we knew they were getting married. Stixy took off for Sweden with his bride-to-be and we never saw him again. Later we heard they'd split up and he went to study at some college, which was not at all like the Stixy we had known. The last thing we heard was he'd got a whole bunch of qualifications and had become a top professor at some Swedish university.

Unbelievable. Apparently he did come back to the UK once to visit his mother but had forgotten how to speak English and could now only speak Swedish. How weird is that?

At around the same time mad Geoff also decided to quit the group and marry Norma, a girl he'd met at one of our Liverpool gigs. All of a sudden we almost didn't have a band, so we auditioned a load of drummers with a guy called Mick Bradley proving to be the best choice. He was from Rugby and previously in a Midlands band called The Sorrows, who'd had a big hit with 'First You Take a Heart'. Mick was a superb drummer with a huge, impressive kit and twin bass drums. To be honest I don't remember that much about him, other than he'd been a draughtsman at Rolls-Royce and seemed quite serious and intelligent.

That is apart from the time we shared a bottle of full-strength Black Swan Australian Sherry at a very prestigious Mayors Ball. He wasn't a big drinker and this legendary Aussie liquor was deadly. About halfway into the set he violently threw up all over his drums but continued to play like a demon, splashing vomit every which way over audience and band alike. The mayor and his fellow civic dignitaries were not at all impressed and we were subsequently banned from yet another venue.

As for our replacement guitarist, whiz-kid Les Nicol from 'ABC' was the only man for the job. He was Mick 'Ronno' Ronson's archrival in Hull (Kingston upon Hull to be precise) and could give anyone a run for their money. We were still signed with Double R, who had big plans for us but didn't think Gospel Garden was a commercial-enough name. We agreed and started racking our brains for a new one. Before we had time to come up with anything ourselves, they had already made the decision for us. So, what would it be?

27

Methuselah (1968-1969)

Methuselah. As they say, shame about the name. It was the kiss of death and we despised it, but wheels were already in motion. They'd brought in makeover stylists, photographers, graphic design teams, record pluggers, the press and the whole caboodle. It was fait accompli. At least it proved they were keen to get moving, which was fair enough, I suppose.

Elektra, the most prestigious record company in the world, wanted us on their label, so Double R Management set up a meet with big Elektra boss Jac Holzman. He was over from the States to discuss and arrange everything, so we all met up at his luxury penthouse just off King's Road, together with our dogs. We had a Great Dane called Jacob and he had an Afghan hound called Fido, or whatever. The dogs bonded, which I think really clinched the deal. So that was it. A three-album contract signed and sealed. Sorted. By strange coincidence and unbeknownst to us at the time, our old pal Iain Matthews from The Imps and Fairport Convention was also about to sign with Jac Holzman at Elektra. So, all in all quite an achievement for a bunch of wild young Lincolnshire Yellerbillys.

Over the previous year, the band had been introducing more and more Gladwin compositions into the set until it was now almost exclusively his original material. We had performed it all live so were more or less ready to record without further ado. Kenny Young, who had written 'Under the Boardwalk' for the Drifters, was brought in as co-producer, so he and Steve Roland could work together. Once the recording was complete, publicity shots were taken and album sleeves designed. To showcase the new band they threw a huge glitzy launch party at The Revolution, the newest, trendiest, hippest joint in town. This was where The Beatles, Stones and the in-crowd all hung out. After a sound check we were sitting around chatting up Marsha Hunt from *Hair* when along comes *Ready Steady Go!* presenter Cathy McGowan demanding we turn down the volume. Whaaat? Who on earth does she think she is? Out of spite we just turned up the sound even louder, egged on by a devilish Marsha Hunt.

So here we are, all bopped up and hot to rock, and I'm trying out a brand-new image for the occasion in the form of cool toothbrush moustache. Of course when our two managers see it they almost have a nervous breakdown. The place will soon be crowded with specially invited Jewish agents, managers, top TV and film execs, so like it or not the taboo tash has got to go. Just before we hit the stage I slink into the dressing room to begrudgingly remove the Schicklgruber stubble but run into a spot of bother.

My shaver's on the blink and the battery on its last gasp, when midstream it grinds to a halt. Well, it's just dangling there, resolutely glued to the unwanted whiskers and going nowhere. The razor won't prise loose and we're due on any second. It's now stuck hard and fast and I'm panicking. I obviously can't go on stage like this, so all I can do is try and make good with a pair of very sharp, pointy nail scissors that I find in my wash bag. The result is a mangled mess of shaggy tufts with cuts and blood dripping everywhere. Not quite the image we were trying to project on our big debut night, but as they say, the show must go on.

Now we were spending more and more time in London, our hotel of choice was the 'Madison' on Sussex Gardens in Paddington, which catered exclusively for rock bands. It was located just off Hyde Park, which is central and very handy. Everyone who was in town stayed there. Regulars were Ten Years After, Family, Dave Dee and Co, The Walker Brothers, plus a few all-girl groups. It was dirt cheap and the rooms were like dormitories with six or eight beds in each one. Although we never actually trashed hotels back then or threw TVs from windows, bands would frequently raid each other's rooms or use them for entertaining groupies and other such capers.

Round the corner from the hotel was a proper Italian ristorante where instead of the Heinz tinned stuff, we discovered what real authentic spaghetti Bolognese tasted like. Spag Bol is what we survived on whenever in London. We had a meeting in there once with prospective manager Long John Baldry, who offered to 'handle' us, but we knew exactly what he meant by that. He was about seven feet tall and had an impossibly loud and booming voice that rattled the walls. Cutlery and plates would vibrate and be dancing round the table every time he spoke. He was quite intimidating considering he was a friend of Dorothy's and indeed Elton John. In the end we had to decline his kindly offer because of the deal happening with Double R. Great singer, though.

Methuselah (1968-1969)

METUSELAH (From L to R) Les Nicol, Terry Wincott, Mick Bradley, Craig Austin, John Gladwin

28

Romantic Interlude

Guitarist Les Nicol was a real blues purist and a gifted player, but I was always puzzled why he'd joined an eclectic outfit like ours. Maybe he wanted to broaden his scope or just saw it as a stepping-stone to a more successful career.

He turned up one day with a couple of snooty little cuties in tow that I'd never seen before. As soon as I clapped eyes on one of the girls, the old ticker skipped a beat and I was instantly smitten. Up until then I'd always had loads of sweethearts, girlfriends, flings and crushes, but this was different. Like the thunderbolt scene in the film *Godfather II* it was lust at first sight. She probably didn't notice me or even know I existed, but from then on I was in a terrible state and couldn't function or think about anything else. Admittedly I was always an irresistibly handsome devil but figured I might be punching above my weight with this one.

Then to my astonishment at a party one night, it turned out she also felt the same about me. After weeks of agonising, playing it cool and trying to keep the magnetic attraction under control, we couldn't hide it any longer. In a flash we were drawn together and from that moment on were inseparable. She was a real-deal Sloane Ranger dolly bird who'd cruise around in a Mini Cooper, wearing micro skirts and kinky boots, looking like a supermodel. As it happens she later went to the Lucy Clayton modelling agency and charm school to learn the important things in life such as balancing books on her head and how to get out of a car without flashing her knickers. With a cut-glass (or should I say glarse) accent and private school education, she was a genuine socialite deb. Throughout the 1960s, hanging out with musicians and working-class oiks was de rigueur for the upper crust and happily I slotted nicely into both categories. True to form, she would eventually revert to type and rejoin the gentry, but for the moment I was where it was at.

When the band wasn't gigging, she would either come over to see me or I'd visit her home in a rather select part of the county. It all was very civilised, stylish and comfortable, as one would expect for such a well-bred girl. By now our little love affair was consuming so much time and energy that I was going soft in the head. So much so I was starting to lose any interest in the future of the band and dreaming instead of cosy cottages with roses round the door and white picket fences.

We'd sit around getting stoned listening to 'Hey Jude', 'White Room' and 'Fire' by Arthur Brown. Or sometimes we'd take long romantic walks on empty beaches with her dogs, though it drove me crazy the way she fussed over these pedigree pooches and talked to them in a silly high-pitched voice like a proper upper-class twit. Before we finally went own separate ways she taught me how to say yah, trite, grise and hice (translated to yes, trout, grouse and house respectively). Also to say napkin not serviette and loo or lavatory instead of toilet. At mealtimes I was introduced to avocado vinaigrette, shown how to eat peas properly with a fork and told not to fart at the dining table. Only joking. Oh, well.

Back in Palookaville I'd had enough of the band house and fancied a change of scene, so found a nice new knocking shop and moved in with a couple of cohorts to share the rent. When not on the job either bandwise or birdwise, I continued the beer-brewing tradition and decided to start producing wine as well. Vital ingredients were desperately needed so a night-time raid on next door's rhubarb crop swung into action. My flatmate Laurie volunteered to be big chief tealeaf and I was recruited as lookout. Come nightfall I kept watch as he crept out down the garden and over the fence with a big box to carry back the booty. He was busy chopping and loading carefully selected sticks of barb when a police squad car with headlights blazing pulled into a car park overlooking the crime scene. Oh, shit.

Laurie laid flat and kept his head down wondering what best to do. Had they spotted him? Maybe someone had dialled 999 and they were there to catch us red-handed. Should we leg it or hold tight? Well, the patrol car parked up and switched off its lights as we held our breath expecting the worst. Strangely, nothing happened and after twenty minutes, off they went. How the hell could they have not seen us? Maybe they'd just stopped for a quick fag or flask of coffee or even a swift bunk-up, who knows? Shortly after, 'Rhubarb Lol' returned covered in crap but with the produce intact and we breathed a sigh of relief.

Still slightly paranoid in case we'd been spotted, the haul was hastily stashed out of sight and crammed in the bottom of the cooker until the coast was clear. Sometime later the final result was an impudent little vintage with the aroma of toasted crumpet, essence of skunk and hint of London bus tyres. To be honest it was all such a faff we just stuck to beer after that. Well, cheers, m'dears.

29

Elektra Records

During that summer, we got well into gardening whilst living at the new drum. Mainly lettuce, carrots, beans and all the easy veggie stuff. There was an old concrete air-raid shelter at the bottom of the garden so we decided to get a bit more adventurous and grow mushrooms in it. What we needed was tons and tons of horse manure. So, with a promise of a share of the bounty, we persuaded a friend to take us to a local beauty spot favoured by the riding fraternity called Burton Hills, in his classic '60s bank-robber-type Jaguar. Rather a stylish method of transporting nag turds, don't you think? With a pile of sacks and a spade apiece, off we went in search of the magic ingredient.

After spending best part of a day ruining clothes, shovelling shit and filling sacks to capacity, the car boot was loaded up ready and we headed back with the windows wide open. We laid the stinking equine effluent a foot thick on the bomb-shelter floor and spread it evenly ready for planting. Then off we popped down to Woolies for a packet of fungal spores and followed the instructions to the letter. A week later, nothing. A month later, nothing. A year later, still nothing. Not even a toadstool. What a complete waste of human endeavour. We had more bloody mushrooms growing on the bathroom wall. My mate obviously never did get a share of the failed crop and must have been royally cursing us as he fumigated his beloved Jag. Anyway, I came to the conclusion that I just don't have green fingers, though very much admire those who do possess the gift.

In London if we ever needed pills or gear of any kind we would score from a couple of junkies that shared a seedy bare room just off Piccadilly Circus. The place had no furniture whatsoever apart from two single beds without sheets or blankets, just a pair of filthy stained mattresses. A single naked light bulb swung 'Callan' style from middle of the ceiling and the walls were streaked with blood squirted from dirty syringes. The stuff was stashed behind an electric meter, which was the only other thing in the room, and the whole place reminded me of a deeply depressing scene from some squalid film noire.

We'd make a swift purchase, usually blues or bombers, and then get out as quickly as possible. On one occasion we were also offered some small gold spherical pills that looked like cake decorations, which is what we suspected they most probably were. After assuring us they were powerful aphrodisiacs, we were persuaded to try a few. They were cheap enough, so just to get away without being hustled further, we risked a modest handful that were then duly shared out amongst any interested parties. Still sceptical about these so-called 'Spanish Fly' pills, I hid mine away for a rainy day and almost forgot I even had them. Eventually that particular rainy day arrived and I tried a couple out to see what might happen. They kicked in about an hour later and soon dispelled any previous nagging doubts about their effectiveness. By the time we went back for seconds, the junkie boys had disappeared. Dammit.

Inexplicably, the debut Elektra album imaginatively titled *Methuselah* was only released in America but not here in the UK. It didn't sell many copies, though a follow-up double album was due to be recorded as soon as possible. Most of the tracks on the first album in my opinion were rather poor, but the material for the second was truly dire. It's a shame, really, because John had previously written a few decent songs.

We still continued gigging when not recording but the spark had gone. In between our regular boring band spots, Les, Mick Bradley and I would indulge in spontaneous Cream and Hendrix-style free-form jamming sessions as a trio. It was a blast playing the sort of stuff we really enjoyed. Likewise Gladwin and Wincott would do their own separate mellow acoustic spot, so it was almost like two bands painfully sharing the same stage. Chalk and Cheese would have been a more relevant name than Methuselah and by now the rot had well and truly set in.

Proverbial musical differences were now so obvious that we had no option but to call it a day. It was a tough decision to be giving up everything we'd spent years working for, and most people thought we were mad. To us, though, the integrity of the music was still the most important thing, and if we weren't enjoying it what was the point? As a result of the split-up, Elektra never released the double album, so thank heaven for small mercies.

Gladwin and Wincott went on to form ye olde Englishe folk group 'Amazing Blondel' that signed with Island Records and made umpteen albums. Interestingly, a young Dave Stewart from Eurythmics was a huge Blondel fan who once secretly stowed away in the back of their van, so guess they must have been a big influence on him. Mick Bradley joined Steamhammer but sadly died of leukaemia shortly afterwards. That just left myself and Les free to go anywhere and do anything we liked. Yippee. Excited and without a moment's hesitation we both decided move down to London permanently and put a post-psychedelic trio together. All that's needed now is a drummer.

30

Distant Jim (1969)

So, full of the joys of spring, Les and I took off for the capital in search of the third member of our little trio. Just in case the adventure went pear-shaped, I decided to hang on to the northern flat for now as an emergency precaution. An old mate of Les's offered to put us up at his place, deep in no-man's land somewhere south of the Thames near Catford. He seemed a decent bloke whose claim to fame was that he used to babysit for John Mayall's kid, Gaz Mayall of Gaz's Rockin' Blues.

Other than that I can't remember much about the place, except it was a dump miles from anywhere and once a year was invaded by huge swarms of flying stag beetles the size of cricket balls. In a demented frenzy, these hideous kamikaze critters with huge pincers attacked anything that moved and scared the bejesus out of you if they got tangled in your hair.

Most of the time we spent listening to Django Reinhardt LPs and smoking strange lumps of dope that had obviously been smuggled into the country disguised as potatoes. We called it Spud-U-Like. It kept us laughing hysterically all day long and was possibly the best 'happy hash' I've ever had. There was a trap door up onto the roof where we'd lay zonked out for hours in the sunshine, watching the planes flying out of Heathrow to far-flung exotic destinations. Well, you can but dream.

We were now so flat broke that a trip to Catford dole office was our last resort and what a palaver that turned out to be. I had occasionally signed on back home without too much aggro. In fact we called it the 'Department of Enjoyment and Inactivity' but the Catford SS office was truly Kafkaesque. Catford even sounds like Kafka and was probably named after him. Talk about being given the bureaucratic run-around. You'd have thought it was the supervisor's own personal life savings we were trying to blag. To them, musicians were the lowest of the low and we never got a red cent, but at least it finally spurred us on to the true task at hand. However miserable our existence seemed to be at that brief moment, neither of us had the slightest doubt things were going to work out fine and the future looked bright ahead.

What happened next was uncanny. I think I've always been a little bit psychic, especially during my teenage years when I'd often see blue florescent orbs floating about the room. They would follow me about and I'd get premonitions. Nothing mega, just little intuitive insights that would guide me along the righteous path. Whether it was a ghost, aliens or a guardian angel, I really don't know. Or maybe it was just an optical illusion, though it does sometimes feel like I'm being watched over.

Anyway, Les kept banging on about this guy called Steve Chapman that he'd seen with a band called 'Juniors Eyes'. According to Les he would be the ideal drummer for our new trio, although I didn't have a clue who he was or what he looked like. Half joking, we decided to head up west and search for this elusive Steve Chapman bloke, even though we didn't have the faintest idea if he lived in London, Paris or Timbuktu. In fact we didn't know anything about him whatsoever.

No sooner had we hit Leicester Square, which was teeming with tourists, than I pointed over at this guy who shone out from the hordes like a beacon. "There's Steve over there," I said very calmly to Les, whose eyes nearly popped out of his head with astonishment. And lo and behold who should it be but the man himself. Un-bloody-believable. Must be odds of zillions to one. The gods had intervened. Well and truly shaken, we went over and introduced ourselves to Steve, who didn't know who the hell we were but was equally amazed when we told him what just happened.

It was such a fateful and bizarre chance meeting for all concerned that we decided it was a mystical sign. Destiny had brought us together and 'Distant Jim' was born. Even the fact that Steve had just left Junior's Eyes and was looking to join another band was serendipitous. He seemed to really like what we were doing, so everything was falling perfectly into place, just as we knew it would.

Not only that, as an added bonus we were offered a new place to stay by some acid-freak friends of Steve's up in North London at Friern Barnet, near to where he lived in Finchley. It was a lovely big old house, with a beautiful garden and a conservatory that was to be our temporary home for the summer. We shared bathroom and kitchen and survived almost exclusively on dry cream crackers and cold baked beans. Still, it was a vast improvement on crappy Catford (no, not cat food).

Other than being penniless, we were having a great time and things were coming together nicely with the band. The new songs were all our own original material, freshly written by myself and Les. We figured if Gladwin could do it, then so could we. We needed somewhere more permanent to cobble our brand-new set together so persuaded Steve to venture from his suburban comfort zone and head north to my old flat in order to rehearse with no distractions.

After his initial culture shock it started sounding pretty good, but we still needed more equipment and a PA system, not to mention a van. So, left with no other option we decided to subsidise our otherwise meagre resources with a few odd jobs. Within a few weeks we'd made enough dough to buy everything we needed, so quit the monkey business and got on with the task in hand. Night and day we rehearsed solid, and even recruited a roadie called Nigsy... Distant Jim are Go.

Distant Jim on Parliament Hill.
(L to R) Les Nicol, Craig 'Tex' Austin, Steve Chapman.

31

Cosmarama / LSD

After finally getting the act together we handed in the keys to the flat, headed back to London and moved straight into our new abode. Steve had a large circle of friends down there and one of his mates offered us a room at his hippy commune in the quiet Mock Tudor suburb of East Finchley. It didn't stay quiet for long. His mate's name was 'Tall' Paul, who was a great bloke and very generous but a real wide boy.

Now we had a tad more 'brass in pocket' we lived like kings on trusty pilchard curry every night, served up gourmet-style for the whole entourage. It was a bit like the scene back up north but in a more upmarket neighbourhood, and we still had the knack of driving the neighbour's potty at party time. Tall Paul was always holding folding and had accumulated all the quintessential accoutrements of trendy hippydom. A huge record collection, very long hair, Jesus beard, an obligatory VW campervan, plus the biggest stash of illegal substances you can imagine.

He loved having lots of friends around and hanging out with musos, so everyone was happy. At one shindig for a laugh I tied my hair with a ribbon, put on a dress and slapped on some lipstick. It went down well and I looked so damned attractive I almost fancied myself. With such shapely legs as these, I thought it would be spiffingly hilarious to go out and see if I could thumb a lift by hitching up my skirt. The stunt quickly backfired when a truckload of wolf-whistling workmen pulled up and started giving me the come-on. Mortified, I bottled it and tottered back to safety as fast as my sexy sling-backs could carry me.

Steve, or the Reverend Chapman, as we started to call him, was very well spoken and had charming manners. He was an all-round shrewd dude, cool and very stylish but at the same time reminded us of a rockin' vicar. Since leaving school he'd worked in publishing, record plugging and numerous other aspects of the music biz. So as well as drumming in various bands, he was also clued up as to how the recording industry functioned behind the scenes.

Then a chance encounter with Geoff Gill, one of the old York crowd, proved fruitful. He'd had a big psycho-pop hit 'My Friend Jack Eats Sugar Lumps' with his band Smoke, and was now a session musician and producer at Morgan Studios in Willesden. He had some spare studio time and invited us to record a few original songs, which we did and he'd get publishing rights. Although we all had differing musical tastes, the common denominator was striving for originality. After being turned on by the Grateful Dead, United States of America and HP Lovecraft we concluded that post-psychedelia was the best route for us to take.

We put down an album's worth of home-grown tracks, plus an old blues cover called 'Just a Little Bit' by Rosco Gordon that was released as a single on the Dutch Negram label. Our particular version was inspired by a Mad Magazine flexidisc entitled 'It's a Gas' by Alfred E Neuman, and was enhanced with lots of gassy burps and belching. Although no trumping was involved, this misguided marketing gimmick resulted in the record getting banned in the UK for gross vulgarity, hence no airplay and no sales. Third single and same old story. Loozers.

The B-side of the single was one of mine called 'Cosmarama' and was about the best of the bunch that we recorded at Morgan. However, being well into the rock 'n' roll lifestyle by now we were permanently out of our heads, which is a recipe for disaster in any studio situation. Judgement becomes impaired, resulting in a rubbish performance. Because of this, the rest of the tracks proved disappointing and were never finished properly so probably ended up in a dusty vault somewhere. Remarkably 'Cosmarama' was re-released in 2010 as title track on the Psychic Circle record label. This was a compilation album of obscure '60s bands put together by Nick Saloman, highly respected front man of 'Bevis Frond' and it received rave reviews. Still waiting for my royalties, by the way!

Though frequently spaced out during this period, neither Les nor I had actually ever taken any LSD, but that was soon to change. It seemed that the Finchley crew had already taken acid plenty of times before and were due for another trip. Did we want to tag along? Well, why not?

32

Tripping

So, came the big day and after sucking on our sugar lumps we set off on a cosmic rollercoaster ride. Everyone was in the back garden buggering about and sniffing flowers as the freakiness took hold and the fun began. Actually it started out as anything but fun when I was suddenly maliciously targeted by a giant bumblebee in relentless pursuit. I was screaming and running for my life until I was distracted by another trauma when I noticed a tiny blister on my thumb from plucking bass guitar. In an instant it seemed to blow up, big as a football and was ready to pop. Terrified, I rushed indoors to escape the increasing horror but inadvertently stood in front of a mirror.

As I caught my reflection I could clearly see my insides and internal organs pulsating in graphic detail. Veins, blood vessels, sinews and muscles were all exposed and writhing wildly about. I could see cell structure down to atomic level and my skin disappeared as I watched my whole body turning inside out. At some stage later I was offered a piece of cooked chicken and it immediately struck me how horrifying it was that we killed and ate other creatures. For about a year after that I went on a macrobiotic diet and ate nothing but vegetarian food.

Meanwhile, the rest of the gang were creating such a racket that the neighbours called the cops, who proceeded to raid the premises. I had some amphetamines hidden away but thought it best to down the lot rather than risk getting busted. So now I was not only tripping but also blocked out of my skull as well. The cops inexplicably didn't find anything but gave us a stern warning about noise and disturbance. To be honest, I don't think they could be arsed to deal with the escalating pandemonium and just buggered off, shaking their heads in disbelief.

One of the girls from the Finchley crowd was Kate, and before long we became soulmates. She had amazing pre-Raphaelite hair and was very beautiful, both physically and spiritually. Not only that, she was super-smart, bright and streetwise with a prodigious inventory of other desirable qualities. Not a bad CV then? We got together and decided to make a go of it, though our timing wasn't brilliant as she had already planned a big trip around America. Upon hearing this I was obviously downcast, but we agreed to reunite again upon her return and see if we still felt the same. Then take it from there.

Not long after Kate's departure, Les and I fancied taking some more acid so we met up with a couple of old girlfriends who were living in a Fulham Road flat, and the four of us dropped a tab apiece. This was only our second trip and it turned out completely different to the first time. Because we couldn't really go wandering the streets of central London completely off our heads, we were more or less confined indoors. Without a nice big park to frolic about in it was starting to feel rather oppressive and claustrophobic.

I realised it was taking effect when one of the girls suddenly dumped the entire contents of her handbag on the floor and started flinging all her belongings around the room. Talcum powder, make-up and God knows what was flying everywhere, creating huge dust clouds that covered the four of us and everything else in sight. By now the two mad cows had totally flipped and were busy scrawling graffiti and lipstick up the walls. Meanwhile, Les was in the corner pounding out a tuneless cacophony on an old piano, searching for the lost chord, and the whole scene was turning into something resembling a war zone. I was hopelessly trying to stop them demolishing the entire flat, but they were flying high and convinced this was perfectly rational behaviour. All at once I felt very isolated and retreated into a dark cocoon for the rest of the trip. Involuntarily I found myself time-travelling and just sat there for several earth hours circling the universe until it wore off. After all that we were just glad to get the hell out of there and into the fresh air. Strange gear, this LSD.

Some excellent Distant Jim publicity photo shots were taken by a photographer friend of Steve's on Parliament Hill, ready for the big promotional push. Unexpectedly it turned out that we actually only ever did one gig and that was at Klooks Kleek in West Hampstead. It was OK but didn't exactly set the world on fire, and after the Morgan Studio calamity it was all beginning to look like another disastrous waste of time. In the final analysis, even after all the hard work and initial promise, the band never really quite seemed to gel properly.

The acid trips were literally mind-blowing and started having a profound effect on my whole worldview. Any ambition of wanting to be a rock star suddenly seemed shallow and fatuous. Things were no longer black and white. Possessions and materialism felt immoral. The system was exposed as hypocritical and corrupt. Nothing meant anything anymore. Essentially everything was all falling apart and for the first time I was having doubts about the future.

With this and the fact that acid was still messing with my head, everything was getting me down and, ridiculous as it now sounds, I had to get away and find myself. With that I quit the band and Distant Jim was no more. It was all a bit sudden and impulsive so I obviously felt very bad about letting the guys down. Not surprisingly Les and Steve were dismayed after all we'd been through together but realised I'd lost any desire to carry on. Anyway, that's acid for yer.

After the initial shock Les and Steve went on to to form another band called Coast Road Drive and after that joined Leo Sayer, who was a big name at the time. They eventually moved to America, touring with different outfits, and became very successful. Especially Steve, who joined Sutherland Brother and Quiver, Al Stewart, and finally Poco. I'm really glad it worked out well for them both, but for me all that was left to do was tidy up a few loose ends and move on.

33

Freak Out

Having quit the band and burnt my bridges, I bid farewell to Finchley and retreated back to my parents' house, which proves I can't have been right in the head. It was only meant as a temporary arrangement and I planned to be out of there as soon as possible. In the meantime, I started hanging out again with Barry 'Baz' Roberts, an old childhood friend. We'd more or less been brought up together since we were youngsters, and his mother Doreen and my mum were best friends. Doreen was a capacious, forceful woman and my mum was very slight and unassuming, so they were a bit like a female version of 'Little and Large'.

They first met when Doreen caught me pulling up her newly planted hedge and chucking shrubs at their kitchen window. When she went to complain, my poor old mum broke down in tears and told her how she couldn't cope with me anymore. I was always running away or up to some terrible trouble and this latest stunt was the last straw. Anyway, Doreen, or 'Aunty' Doreen, as she became known, ended up comforting my mother and they became inseparable companions. She was a loud American, originally from Ohio, but was brought up on Merseyside so had lost her accent. Oddly enough she didn't have a Scouse accent either. She was from quite a wealthy background and her mother had several large properties by the river and a fancy place in Hamilton Square, Birkenhead, where we'd stay on holiday as kids.

Whilst there I vividly recall the amazing Liverpool overhead railway that ran right along the waterfront past the docks from Dingle (where Billy Fury was born) to Seaforth and Litherland. It was the world's first elevated electric system, very similar to the later iconic ones in New York and Chicago, but due to structural defects was demolished in 1957, more's the pity. I also remember lots of beautiful old Sentinel steam lorries chugging round Stanley Park, some of which remained in service until as late as 1961. Sounds silly, but something else that intrigued me were all the little round manhole covers along the pavements, where coal was delivered to the terrace houses and tipped straight down into the basement coal bunkers. Oh yes, and one final recollection from Liverpool was my first-ever Chinese restaurant meal, although I must admit I've never tried the famous local delicacy which is, of course, scouse (or lobscouse stew). But I digress again.

Bazzer was now married with a child and living in a flat down Frodingham Road, Scunthorpe's version of Jack the Ripper's Whitechapel. An exciting immigrant ghetto and Latin Quarter full of sleazy pubs and dodgy mob-owned coffee bars with names like Angelo's and Dino's. Local novelist Ted Lewis must have taken his inspiration for *Get Carter* from this shady part of town. The book's original title was actually *Jack's Return Home* and was located in Scunthorpe and not Newcastle, as portrayed in the 1971 film version starring Michael Caine. Not many people know that. Sorry, couldn't help myself.

Barry was a talented painter and studying at Doncaster Art College that was part of the ubiquitous drug scene and rife with illegal substances. From here he scored some acid and against my better judgement I was persuaded to again partake. After my last dodgy experience I was expecting the worst, but it turned out really well. I was visualising Buddhist mandalas and Hindu yantras clear as day. Whether I was creating them in my mind's eye or directly connecting with ancient archetypes I don't know, but searching for an answer to life's eternal, imponderable questions seemed to be all that really mattered.

Later on into the trip we were just lolling around when Baz and I started communicating by ESP. We were sitting more or less back to back at the time holding a nonverbal conversation and reading each other's minds. When we turned around we realised we'd both been interacting mentally by scanning our cupped hands at each other like satellite dishes. Esoteric or wot? It always amazes me that some people can casually smoke dope or drop acid and then go out raving or down the pub for a normal night out. I could never do anything like that. For me it was a deeply spiritual experience to be savoured in quiet contemplation, even if it didn't always work out like that. To say that LSD is unpredictable is a massive understatement, as I was soon to find out the hard way.

Acid can definitely make you paranoid and reading *One Flew Over the Cuckoo's Nest* didn't help. Like many people, one of my greatest fears is being mistakenly locked away in a mental hospital with no way of convincing anyone that I'm not really nuts. This phobia worsened after I heard about a friend who had completely flipped on lysergic acid and jumped through the windows of a whole row of bungalows. This obviously created quite a commotion and climaxed with him attacking a resident with a shovel. Before long the cops arrived on the scene and chained him to some railings until the 'green van' came to cart him off to the loony bin.

Over the following weeks we were becoming more and more concerned for his welfare but were actively discouraged by the authorities to get involved or even visit him in hospital. In defiance, we began to hatch a plot to help him escape. After making few enquires to find out which ward he was on we drove to Bracebridge, a booby hatch for the barking just outside Lincoln. They obviously wouldn't let us in see him so we crept round to a side window and knocked to attract the attention of one of the inmates whilst taking care not to alert any of the staff. Obligingly the inmate went off and fetched our friend back to the window.

We were all set to spring him when it dawned on us what a truly shocking state he was actually in. He was barely recognisable and he certainly didn't recognise us. The guy was no more than a drooling zombie. No way could we help him now or take responsibility for him in this condition. We had previously assumed that once the acid had worn off he'd be fine and they were just keeping him in as a form of sadistic punishment. OK, he'd done some heavy crap whilst under the influence and arguably should get a slap on the wrist, even though he was actually a really decent, intelligent bloke. It wasn't premeditated and could easily have happened to anyone.

As I said, LSD is just so fickle that anyone who takes it risks losing their mind at any time. Disastrously for him the effects never really wore off, which left him permanently doolally. It was ages before he was let out and I don't think he ever properly recovered. Last we heard he was working as a park gardener even though he held a fistful of university degrees. What happened seemed inconceivable and it's hard to imagine what he must have been through. As fate would have it I was soon to find out for myself first-hand. Like any self-fulfilling prophecy I'm convinced one's own worst fears eventually come true. Now isn't that a cheery thought?

One perfect summer's afternoon, Barry turned up with some more acid. Having enjoyed the previous dose I decided to risk it again and we dropped a couple of tabs. It was such a beautiful day, the sun was shining and birds were singing, what could possible go wrong? At first it was great. We wandered through the park and down to the woods, getting off on the glorious complexity of birdsong. We just looked each other in amazement and in that moment realised where Jeff Beck pinched his licks from. Then after going through various stages of euphoria, swirling patterns and sparkling colours, I felt the sudden compulsion to return to the gates of Hades and face my demons.

This was possibly the worst decision of my life. To cut a long story short, I dived headfirst through a top-storey window, as you do, and managed to break an arm and a leg in the process. Whoops-a-daisy. After a short period of 'recuperation', the scars were healing and even though hampered by two plaster casts I was getting around famously on crutches. So, having had my full-blown, mystical experience, I decided not to drop any more acid and also lay off the esoteric literature for the time being. Strangely, I was seeing everything with such clarity and it seemed anything was possible. Suddenly the world was my winkle. This was like a whole new beginning and I figured maybe I should do something useful or practical with my life for a change.

34

Bell-bottom Blues

The '60s were all but over and it felt like the end of an era and the end of a dream. In all the time I'd spent in bands I never made any decent dosh and was heartily sick of being skint. I was to all intents and purposes a bum and seriously needed to get my act together. Luckily my noggin was always overflowing with mad inventive brainwaves, and now my voodoo whiskers were twitching again, sensing something in the air.

There was a notion in the back of my mind that I wanted to design clothes. I'd always been into fashion and worn flamboyant outfits on stage and off. Much of my gear was custom-made by whoever I could persuade to sew stuff for me, especially my dear old gran. Since I was a teenager she'd tapered all my Teddy-boy drainpipes and knitted some really groovy tops, though not those dreadful Aran sweaters I hasten to add.

For ages I'd been fruitlessly looking around London's fashion hot spots, searching for some seriously flared jeans but couldn't find anything close. The nearest thing they had were flap-front sailor pants that weren't even proper bell-bottoms. Suddenly I realised there was a huge gap in the market, and on cue, the old familiar blue fluorescent spheres started flashing overtime. It was obvious I was getting a psychic message directly from the almighty himself, to go forth and make silly trousers for the benefit of all humanity. But where does one start?

After bribing my dear sister Jane to help out, she kindly knocked up the first prototype in plush green velvet. Then, as luck would have it, an investor pal of my dad's heard about the design idea and kindly offered to stake me £200 to get things up and running. Brillsville. With me being the ideas man, I needed a partner to handle all the boring stuff, like administration and finance. My brother-in-law Stuart 'Zonk' Knox, who was at the time (and still is come to think of it) an irritating smart-arse, fitted the bill perfectly, so we teamed up.

The plan was to buy an industrial sewing machine and overlocker plus some fabric and get stuck in as soon as possible. We found a dealer from the Yellow Pages and for £80 secured a job lot of bewildering contraptions that we didn't have a clue how to operate. Slowly, by trial and error, we made some progress and decided to employ a couple of machinists.

One of them happened to be the girlfriend of my mate Pete Macklin who was currently dossing at my newly rented gaff. Pete was a waif I'd rescued from the streets 'cos he looked so cool. He had waist-length hair and was sporting a gold braided pink frock coat and cowboy boots, which was quite far-out daywear clobber even for back then. He was down from Middlesbrough, probably on the run, so I put him and his girlfriend up in the flat till he sorted himself out.

His girlfriend Eileen was handy with a needle and thread, so we set her and another seamstress to work making prototypes on the new machines. To say the least we had a few teething troubles but managed to make several dresses to sell at a local boutique, plus a 'coat of many colours'. This complex patchwork jacket was made of hundreds of random bits of material and took weeks of hard graft to complete. Even Joseph himself would have been proud of it, as would Roy Chubby Brown, but the disproportionate cost, time and effort almost bankrupted us.

We moved the machines into a spare room at our former band house, but with all the problems and breakdowns the pressure was intense. By now the girls were literally living and sleeping underneath their machines, which made me feel like Sir Jasper, the wicked Victorian mill owner with the waxed moustache. If she wasn't working hard enough I'd yell loudly at her and shout, "Come on, Eileen." No, I didn't really. Health and safety would have had a field day (whatever a field day is), so it's a good job they never found out about the orphan children I had sweeping chimneys and collecting night soil for a bowl of gruel a week.

Because the girls proved so inexperienced and all the jobs were so time-consuming, they worked all hours to achieve next to nothing. Money was fast running out and the situation was getting ridiculous, quite frankly. It became obvious that the current approach was unrealistic and we were getting side-tracked instead of making ultra-wide flared jeans, which was of course the primary objective.

Drastic steps had to be taken, so we shut up shop and considered our next move. I felt terrible but sacked the girls and sold back the machines at a fraction of the cost to partially retrieve some of our investment money. With what we had left in the kitty we found a much better way of utilising the dwindling funds.

Jenny Squires, a student friend of ours from the fashion department at Doncaster Art College, suggested we speak to her tutor who might be able to assist us. This turned out to be a brilliant solution and better than we could ever have hoped for. The tutor was a lovely lady and within a couple of hours had run off a set of master patterns, sizes 26 to 34, purely as a favour. I shall be eternally grateful for this kindness, though I'm abashed for not being able to recall her name. She was a gem.

This help was free and achieved more in one afternoon than we did in all the previous months put together. I think it's what they call a learning curve. It taught us a valuable lesson not to personally get involved in the production process but instead hire qualified seasoned professionals. From now on subcontracting became the name of the game and don't get your own hands dirty.

35

Loon Pants / Isle of White Festival 1970

A few weeks after finishing her fashion course, our friend Jenny moved to London and invited us down to her housewarming. By chance there was a clothing factory directly over the road so we popped over to see if they'd make some samples of our new designs. The factory guy said yes and we sent him the patterns. The samples turned out really well, leading us to place an order for a trial run to sell at the forthcoming Isle of White music festival.

He needed fabric so we delivered several rolls of assorted coloured cotton drill and then we waited. And we waited and waited and waited. After weeks of delay and constant begging and pleading with the guy to pull his finger out, we finally snapped. By festival opening day there was still no sign of any stock, so in a rage we drove down in Stuart's clapped-out minivan and physically laid siege to his factory.

I've still no idea what the hold-up was all about, but after a few angry threats, 250 pairs of preposterous 27" bell bottom trousers finally rolled off the production line to a victory fanfare. Though not yet officially christened Loon Pants, these little beauties were nevertheless the very first batch ever made. It would be some months before the Loon name was finally coined after briefly being known as Elephant Flares.

It was heady, deadline stuff for a couple of space cadets with zero rag trade mileage. Just a mad adventure. A make-or-break gamble as to whether we could ever sell these killer kecks or even make it to the festival. Rip, shit or bust the deed was done as we parted company with our last few shekels for the schmutter, all the gelt in the world. Not quite sure why I suddenly came over all Yiddish, but we finally pulled away from the factory gates with the little van creaking and groaning, packed to the gunnels. Would the old girl make it?

Squeezed in amongst the Loon Pant stock were our camping supplies, consisting of macrobiotic brown rice, giant marrow, primus stove, moth-eaten tent, emergency bog roll and a crate of good old home brew. Perched on top like a couple of fried eggs, sat myself and bemused business partner Zonk, wondering what we'd let ourselves in for. At long last Craig Stuart Fashions finally hit the road, so it was goodbye Harlesden Blouse Company (which wasn't actually in Harlesden but on Maygrove Road in West Hampstead) and hello Isle of White.

Well, not quite! First, the poor old minivan, struggling under such harsh punishment, constantly overheated and we were forced to take on water every few miles. Then, after eventually fitting a new thermostat we were then stopped by police roadblocks for drugs and vehicle search. Especially for the event, the constabulary had commandeered all school premises en route to the festival and were apprehending virtually anything that moved. Lines of suspect vehicles were being processed in every schoolyard on the way down to the coast and of course the van had to be completely unloaded and then repacked each time, which was a real balls-ache... and they still never found the stash!

We were lucky. My old mate Rhubarb Lol got busted twice on the way down then got bitten by a snake. After much heat, hassle, wailing and gnashing of teeth we mercifully found ourselves aboard the ferry, savouring the delicious ozone and cool sea breezes blowing in from the English Channel. The weather, just for once, was perfect, nigh on tropical. Touch wood, it was looking good and with no immanent prospect of mudbath or bloodbath, we arrived intact. Were the gods finally with us?

DAY ONE – Find place to park, pitch the tent and break open the... erm... bubbly? Ah, home sweet home brew. Chill out. Sleep like babies... zzzzzz.

DAY TWO – Once the hideous and unspeakable morning ablution scenario is dispensed with, we set up stall next to the coach park and confronted a tidal wave of incoming festival-goers. Bad mistake. After two hours, total sales reach zippo, not a skerrick. Mild panic. However, it doesn't take long to twig that the arriving hordes are only interested at this juncture in setting up camp, not in shopping. Desperate measures are needed, so time to implement Plan B. At very high risk of a severe going-over by the 'Fiery Creations' security torpedoes, we manage to sneak the van onto the official marketing and merchandising compound, saving ourselves a pretty penny in site fees. Boldly raising our banner, we set up shop and try again. Then just like that, bingo, we're overrun with punters. Hot cakes or wot! Three quid a shot. Half the stock gone in a flash. *Elderado!* Looks like we've finally hit the jackpot.

DAY THREE – A sell-out. Van empty. Pockets full. We're wearing green! Rags to riches and this is just the start. Yippee. Perform a silly idiot dance.

DAY FOUR – Because brown rice takes about two hours to cook we'd run out of camping gas within the first couple of days so by now we were queuing with the best of them for fish and chips, kebabs, and poisonous rat burgers. Never mind, let's go watch some bands. Hendrix, The Who, ELP, Chicago, Free, The Doors, Miles Davis, ad infinitum. The climax, of course, was the wonderful spectacle of Piss Pissedofferson being mercilessly booed offstage by half a million people all hurling Coke cans at him. Deep joy.

DAY FIVE – Head for home, a serious bath, some proper food and sleep for a week.

36

Kensington Market / Loondon Showroom

After selling the initial batch of Loons, the search was on for a more reliable supplier. This turned out to be a firm called Booth and Fielding (overall manufacturers) in Scunthorpe. Then as sales increased we started using their Sheffield branch as our headquarters, where my business partner Stuart was now based.

Immediately, I started punting Loons around Kensington Market, which was now taking over from Carnaby Street and King's Road as the world's top fashion Mecca. Our first customers were Lionel Avery at Pam Todd's stall and wholesaler Ian Grieg at Flarewear/Whispering Kite. As orders started flooding in, we decided to treat ourselves to a whopping great Jaguar Mk X so we could deliver direct to the door in style, rather than using the old clapped-out minivan. This was just prior to the installation of parking meters on Young Street, so it was still possible to park right outside the market entrance for free. It was easy to get a thousand pairs of Loons in the huge boot, so we'd be zipping up and down the motorway at breakneck speeds every few days to satisfy demand.

The insane thing was that the brakes on the Jag were virtually nonexistent and it took two miles to stop, rather like an oil tanker. This was still in the days when people used to thumb rides, so on the way back up north I'd pick up a few hitch-hikers and drive flat out, scaring them and myself half to death. When not doing deliveries I'd be schlepping all over the country, searching for new customers and picking up orders at places like City Stylish and Marcus Price in Newcastle, Boodle-Am in Leeds, Jons City and Western plus dozens more in Manchester, Sheffield, York, Bristol and in fact most everywhere.

It wasn't long before we acquired an office and showroom at Kensington Market on the top floor in Young Street, right next to Ken Todd's den. Miraculously we even had a key to our own private bog, the only one in whole of the building. However, being somewhat young and irresponsible at the time, we were soon in trouble with the market security bouncers for taking pot shots from our window at traffic wardens patrolling the newly installed parking meters directly outside. Also for pouring water onto the customer's heads immediately below us for a laugh. Understandably some of them didn't find it quite as funny as we did and so complained to management, leaving us on our final warning.

By now the company had taken on an office manager and a van driver, so there were usually three of our vehicles parked more or less permanently on Young Street during working hours. Almost daily we would receive up to half a dozen tickets, which soon started piling up, gathering dust in the office. True to form we just ignored them until months later, a very scary official-looking meter maid in full regalia, goose-stepped through the door, demanding payment for literally hundreds of outstanding fines.

After the initial panic it gradually became apparent that she was actually quite amenable, so we sat her down and promptly proceeded to ply her with alcohol from our amply stocked 'hospitality' cabinet. After a right skinful, a mutually acceptable deal was agreed by offering an initial 'incentive' followed by regular minimum 'token' payment to cover all future tickets, which saved us an absolute fortune.

All this was slap bang in the middle of the oil crisis, petrol shortages and the three-day week that caused endless power cuts and lengthy blackouts. As cosy as it was living by candlelight, there was rubbish and even corpses piling up in the streets, not to mention IRA bombs exploding all over London. On the upside we had smarmy unemployed merchant bankers queuing at our door begging for a job. Even whilst all this was going on we would think nothing of walking around the market with a couple of grand stuffed down our boots.

By this time I was off my crutches, though I still had an arm in plaster for the next twelve months or so. Every few weeks I was backwards and forwards to the hospital for a check-up, but it never did heal properly. Also, I was supposed to report to the trick-cyclist a couple of times a year about how I was recovering from the acid trip. When the shrink asked me what I'd been doing for the past six months, I told him about our little business venture and how we'd just made forty grand since my last visit (equivalent to £600,000 in 2022). He nearly fell off his chair and said not to bother seeing him again.

To put it in perspective, the average British wage then was about £28 per week. After only six months' trading we were paying ourselves a fortune by comparison, as well as claiming expenses and receiving a substantial bonus. We were quite comfortable, thank you very much, though I'm not bragging, just telling it like it was. In truth I've never been much of a bread-head or particularly materialistic. This rag trade adventure was just a sideline that basically started as a hobby making stage clothes. Luckily a very lucrative one because like I said, I've never made a bean playing in rock groups.

Stuart and Craig (AKA Zonk and Tex).

37

Hebden Bridge

By 1972 we needed even more production, so one day our factory manager and mentor Ken Carmichael took us across to Hebden Bridge, where the main holding company had its headquarters at Foster Mill. They were called Redman Brothers, affiliated with Sutcliffe Melbourne, English Fustian and Hebden Bridge Estate Company. With factories the full length of the Calder Valley stretching almost from Halifax to Burnley, they ran the place like their own personal fiefdom.

This was a revelation, as we had no idea it was such a massive organisation. Scattered around Todmorden, Sowerby Bridge and Mytholmroyd, they had jacket factories, trouser factories and coat factories. Not only that, they had flat cap factories, whippet factories, racing pigeon factories and ecky-thump black pudding factories for all I know. There was also a cotton-weaving mill that made drill, denim, moleskin and gambroon in Hebden, plus a large plant producing corduroy, velvet and God knows what else towards Heptonstall.

This was long before Hebden Bridge became a picturesque beauty spot and tourist gateway to the Pennines and Yorkshire Dales. The whole place was dark, cobwebby and almost Dickensian with toothless hags, ragamuffins and prostitutes jostling for trade in the foggy gas lamp-lit streets. You could buy a house for a few hundred pounds and someone started advertising them in the back of *Time Out* magazine in London. Before you knew it, all the ageing hippies were snapping them up and moving en-masse to Yorkshire.

The huge Foster Mill factory was so ancient it still had the original water wheel that was used to provide power pre-industrial revolution. To get there you had to run the gauntlet of bed sheets and old ladies' bloomers hanging out to dry in a maze of tenfoots, ginnels and back alleys. It was like stepping back in time but had so much character it was fantastic. You could almost imagine the women in their shawls, clacking around in clogs along the steep cobbled streets.

In fact there was an old clog factory and a museum of fighting clogs with pointy metal toecaps that they'd kick each other to death with. It was always a treat to go somewhere this special while still unspoilt. Within a few years most of the industry would have vanished and the factories flattened. Fortunately, a few of the historic 'dark Satanic mills' did survive and were converted into luxury apartments, though many have been replaced by dreary Wimpey and Barrett-type homes.

By now, we were doing so much business and giving so much credit that we'd developed serious cash-flow problems. Redman Bros offered to help bail us out for a stake in the company and we agreed, thinking it would relieve us of the massive financial burden. They had expert accountants and almost unlimited credit, so it would be much less for us to worry about. Also as part of the deal they would start churning out stuff for us in their Calder Valley and Rotherham factories, thus increasing production substantially. This meant sacrificing half our shares but gaining many other positive benefits. Besides, we couldn't really afford to carry on without this assistance, so we signed on the dotted line at the old Martins Bank Chambers and the deed was done. It worked perfectly for a while and we expanded to the point where we had about a dozen factories making various items. Happy with this new arrangement, we headed home looking forward to enlarging our empire even further.

So, as well as increasing our clothing range we decided to branch out and set up a graphic design studio with my old mate Baz Roberts and his sister Caz in Doncaster. We also financed another pal called Mike Von Joel (whom I always thought looked like a composite of all the Rolling Stones), to produce a trendy new magazine called *New Style*. He had previously been a student at Winchester Art College and was making a packet selling our Loons to all the other students, including members of Roxy Music. *New Style* was quite successful and led to his career as editor of various other art and photography magazines, including *State Media* and *State f22*. Talking of the Rolling Stones, curiously enough he later married Mick Jagger's ex-girlfriend Chrissie Shrimpton, whom I met once and she was absolutely lovely. Mike was a very amusing fella and I often wonder what became of the old scrote.

Alas, as it turned out, the graphic design studio idea fizzled out and all we ever got out of *New Style* was a measly credit in the first issue. There were a couple of other similarly doomed projects, so wisely we decided in future just to stick to the fashion game. Having said that, what we really wanted to do was buy property in central London whilst it was dirt cheap. Problem was, no matter how hard we tried, it was impossible to persuade our new parent company to invest in this sure-fire winner. To this day it pains me to even think about it.

38

Luckie Mucklebackit's Experimental Clothing Laboratory

By 1973 every bloke and his pet gerbil had copied our design and were knocking out Loon Pants with a vengeance. They were now being advertised in the back of *NME* and *Melody Maker*, and cheap imports were flooding in from Hong Kong, India and Pakistan. Astonishingly, this only seemed to increase demand and we started selling even more pairs in cotton drill, moleskin, velvet, tartan, split knees, PVC leatherette, gambroon, you name it. We couldn't make them fast enough. The burning question was, how much longer could this phenomenon continue before the bubble finally burst? Especially considering that most fashion trends were lucky to last a single season.

At its peak, Craig Stuart had a dozen factories churning out ten thousand pairs a week plus all the other stuff and we were basically coining it in, to put it mildly. By now we had already added shirts, jackets, dungarees, Oxford bags and even hot pants to the range, but figured it might be a good time to start dabbling with something even more adventurous for the future.

Vague delusions of grandeur were slowly creeping in as I began to imagine myself as a legendary fashion guru and creative genius of the century. Our styles became more and more outrageous, and because the main business was doing so well, it was naturally assumed any new ideas would be equally successful.

Glam rock was all the rage and I felt this was the direction that fashion would continue to move. For instance, I honestly believed that platform boots would just keep getting higher and higher until we'd all be staggering about on stilts. This meant houses would soon have to be re-designed with towering ceilings and doors nine feet high. I was already mentally planning an architectural consultancy and building firm, ready to cope with all the coming changes. It was just a matter of time before the great unwashed caught up with my exalted utopian vision.

To me it seemed inevitable that everyone would soon be skating around on motorised rollerblades, dressed in self-contained, germ-free and air-conditioned space suits for travelling in complete privacy on public transport. They'd be available in multi-colours and come with a phone, computer, in-built entertainment centre, drinks dispenser and even an integral Portaloo. It simply never occurred to me that there might be a backlash, and that flat shoes would come back into style or short hair ever be popular again. This genuinely all came as a shock to my system when the climate finally changed. And that, folks, was my wildly distorted version of reality during those halcyon days. Maybe the acid hadn't quite worn off yet after all.

Meanwhile, back on Planet Earth, a prestigious sales and marketing trip to the massive international exhibition hall at Cologne in August of 1973 was on the agenda to promote the new range. With this in mind, the company went ahead and employed our designer and pattern-cutter friend Jenny, to help create a radical new collection that in our wisdom we christened 'Luckie Mucklebackit's Experimental Clothing Laboratory'. This consisted of glam rock-style winged jackets, pedal pushers, baby doll tops, hooded pixie duffle-coats and all sorts of other daft outfits.

Luckie Mucklebackits Catalogue (Back Page)

So, with a deadline set to complete all the samples, we rented a dedicated design studio at a Mews in Paddington from a guy with a glass eye, who used to play guitar with Billy J Kramer and the Dakotas. Apparently, a string snapped and took his eye out. Anyway, we got stuck in and everything was going swimmingly with all the samples finished on schedule and everything ready to go. Then of course disaster struck. Jenny arrived next morning to discover there'd been break-in through the skylight and the bulk of the pieces had simply disappeared. Whether it was just a random theft or industrial sabotage is still a mystery, as no one was caught and no items were ever recovered.

Because the exhibition was already paid for, with all the flights and accommodation pre-booked, we really had no other option but to go and make the best of a bad job.

Craig Stuart Fashions Catalogue (Front Page)

39

Cologne Exhibition / Wuppertal Monorail

To get to Cologne we took the ferry and then drove by car to Germany. As soon as we crossed the border, we immediately got pulled by the jackboot brigade for nothing worse than driving with side lights, which is verboten over there for some idiotic reason. We escaped with a warning, but it left a sour(kraut) taste in the mouth. Welcome to Das Vaterland.

Predictably, the exhibition was a catastrophe with only a few sad remaining remnants of the collection left to display, together with some Loon Pants that were rather old hat now at such a prestigious gathering. The final straw was when we sold the last odds and sods to some Dutch bastard who subsequently ripped us off. Whilst there, I happened to notice that Cockell and Johnson from Ken Market were also on the same British Export Council-sponsored trip, so hope they had more success than we did.

To me, Cologne was a cold, soulless dump, apart from the amazing cathedral that miraculously remained intact

Cologne Exhibition / Wuppertal Monorail

after the Allies bombed the crap out of the place in 1942. By complete contrast, at nearby Wuppertal, we discovered the most incredible and charming hundred-year-old suspension monorail called the 'Schwebebahn' that snakes its way around the city. I strongly recommend you visit, or at least check it out on YouTube. It's an incredibly efficient form of transport that could easily solve the world's traffic congestion problems if only town planners had two brain cells to rub together.

On our day off, we decided to take a healthy constitutional in one of the many beautiful Wuppertal parks to get a general feel of the place. As we walked briskly along the gravel pathway, the crunching noise began to sound strangely reminiscent of SS storm troopers marching into Poland. Yes, you've guessed it. Stuart couldn't help himself and spontaneously started doing outrageous impersonations of the Fuhrer, sticking a comb under his nose and wildly goose-stepping in classic John Cleese style. His eyes glazed over as he pointed skywards in a mock Nasty salute, screaming and babbling indecipherable Bavarian profanities, which is all highly illegal in Germany.

I was desperately struggling and grabbing at his arm trying stop him, but this simply made him more and more determined. We were falling about helplessly laughing, but at the same time I was seriously cacking myself, as quite a few people were looking round to see what was going on. Luckily no one actually reported us and 'I think we got away with it'.

Apart from that, I can't really remember much else about the place, although I must say the beds and especially those V-shaped German pillows are the most comfortable I've ever slept on. However, their toilet bowls (jerrys – had to get it in somewhere) are gross in the extreme, with pervy viewing platforms that allow you to poke about and proddle your poo with a stick. Or is that just me?

Luckie Mucklebackit designs.

Whilst there we also managed to spend a few tedious hours in Düsseldorf. Stuart's big sister Elaine had married a Fritz and we'd been asked to pay her mother-in-law a courtesy call to make sure she was coping on her own and such like. We couldn't speak German and she couldn't speak English, so as you can imagine it was a rivetingly interesting afternoon, though we did get a nice slice of Battenburg cake.

Stuart's sister Elaine was an ex-'Bluebell Girl' and international professional dancer, who has a few exotic tales of her own to tell of her exploits whilst touring the world. Amazingly she can speak six languages fluently but can't say no in any of them. Boom boom. Only kidding, Elaine. Anyway, she was old mates with Rory Storm, Alvin Stardust and many other showbiz names and celebs. She even taught Paul McCartney to waterski, so not a bad claim to fame. Talking of which, my old buddy Pete Macklin from Demon Records has two claims to fame. One is that he knows the guy who invented Twiglets. The other is that he knows the guy that invented Loon Pants. Yes, little old me. What an accolade. I'm very humbled and choked with pride. Just for the record it was in fact Pete who christened me the 'Loon Pant King'. Hence the title of this book.

Craig Stuart Fashions Stand at Cologne Exhibition.

40

Into Europe

After years on the road I was getting slightly fed up schlepping round flogging stuff, so in a moment of deluded optimism we decided to try using European sales agents for a change. We were offered a brokerage by a girl in Holland, so thought we'd check it out. Any excuse for a freebie trip abroad. So, looking like a couple of Soho rent boys dressed in our poncy winged jackets, peddle pushers and platform soles, we set sail across the North Sea towards the land of gin and windmills. These days it's hard to imagine Stuart ever wearing clobber like that, but wear it he did, and somewhere there are incriminating photos to prove it.

After loading the car onboard the ferry, we started climbing the long, steep stairway from the parking deck, right the way up to the passenger deck. On the stairs there were just the two of us, plus a girl in a skimpy mini skirt a few steps up in front. Stuart, the bastard, did an almighty wolf-whistle and ducked behind a bulkhead, leaving me on my ownsome, stood there like a lemon as the angry girl turned around to give me the filthiest look I've ever seen. Talk about dying of embarrassment. Quite funny, though, I'll give him that.

As there were no cabins available, we headed straight for the bar, obviously. After a few bevvies we got chatting to a Catholic priest who was on his way to a big symposium in Amsterdam. He told us he was there to discuss the merits of skullcaps and other religious headgear worn by the various clerical hierarchies within the orthodox Roman Church. Well, you can imagine our bitter disappointment at not being able to attend his lecture the following day, but somehow we quickly managed to get over it. Then things took a strange turn. It gradually became apparent that our new friend was actually a somewhat unlikely man of the cloth as he set about drinking us under the table. Not only that, but he started offering us a selection of Mandrax and various assorted pep pills that he'd got hidden somewhere onboard. We declined his kindly offer, bearing in mind the prospect of a body cavity search courtesy of Dutch customs officials if we got caught.

Then as the evening wore on, a couple of drunken Irish navvies took a strong dislike to our girly attire and were determined to throw at least one of us overboard. I'm not sure if they were after Stuart's blood to the same degree, but they ended up chasing me round the ship a few times as I legged it for my life. I managed to escape best I could in my six-inch stack-heeled boots and went into hiding until they hopefully calmed down.

For survival's sake it was now imperative that we blagged a cabin and do whatever it took to get one. We started asking around if anyone wanted to sell their cabin at a premium and eventually struck lucky with a couple of willing girls. They seemed happy enough to take our cash, though I think they figured we'd invite them along as part of the deal. That way they'd get their money back plus a free bunk-up. By now we were pretty plastered but still didn't fancy either of them enough to share a bed. Besides we had to be up bright and early as there was work to be done.

Now that was all sorted out it was agreed that a final brandy was in order, so we sneaked back up to the bar. Earlier we had promised the pill-head priest a lift into town the following morning so thought we ought to make arrangements before retiring. When we got there he was nowhere to be seen, but someone informed us he'd fallen down the full length of the ship's staircase and was found in an unconscious heap at the bottom. Holy Mary, Mother of God. Miraculously he'd survived and was sleeping it off so figured we'd see him at breakfast. Next morning we were all slightly worse for wear but after a good fry-up felt right as ninepence. Having dropped off Father Ted at the station looking like butter wouldn't melt after the previous night's shenanigans, we had another little job to do before meeting the agent girl later on that evening.

A potential Dutch customer had recently contacted us for samples, so whilst there we thought we might as well pay them a visit. It was in some little town we had never heard of way out in the sticks, so we drove far out into the wilds to find this godforsaken place. It turned out not to be a shop or even an office but someone's house, which was rather odd. However, we were very warmly welcomed by a young couple who must have run the business from home. After the usual pleasantries we showed them a few samples and chatted about the products for a while, but something didn't feel quite right. The guy seemed to be sounding us out for something other than buying a few pairs of jeans. He almost seemed to be offering his very attractive wife to us on a plate.

You hear about these kinds of things. Did he want to watch a threesome or take kinky pictures or wot? The whole situation was starting to feel distinctly uncomfortable.

In fact it got so weird we made our excuses, grabbed our samples and got the hell out as soon as possible. For all we knew they were probably a couple of serial killers and no one else in the world knew we were there in the back of beyond with Fred West and Myra Hindley. We could have been raped and tortured or held captive in a secret dungeon, ending our days in some horrific snuff movie. Or had we just simply imagined it? In fact I'm still scratching my head. That's how weird it was. Still, they do say foreign travel broadens the mind.

Recovering from our unnerving experience, we drove to Amsterdam and found a very nice centrally located Art Deco hotel. It was The Schiller on Rembrandtplein and after freshening up we toddled off to meet the agent girl at a fancy restaurant called 'September'. A few bottles of wine later and it all went blank. I vaguely remember making some inappropriate, clumsy, oafish pass at her and getting a good slap for my trouble. Strangely enough we never heard from her again after that. It's just unbelievable what appalling manners some of these foreigners have, ha ha.

All that aside, probably the main reason we were in Amsterdam was to track down the twat who'd bought our unwanted stock at the Cologne exhibition and still owed us the money. We tried to get legal advice and discovered the law is very different in the stupid Nether Regions. Apparently, he had declared himself bankrupt and set up under a new name the very next day with all the same stock and there was nothing we could do about it. Wonderful bloody legal system they've got in effin' Tulip Land.

Finally, we tracked the thieving bastard down and he obviously thought he was in for a beating, even though he had a nasty Alsatian devil-dog alongside for protection. Yes, it would have been so satisfying to have kicked the crap out of him, but in all honesty can you really imagine either of us two unisex-clad clowns seriously getting mistaken for hatchet men? When the arsehole twigged we weren't really going to whack him, he started getting cocky. Feeling even bolder, he threatened that his gang would find us and we'd never get out of Holland alive.

In broad daylight, there was really nothing we could do except leave him to it and keep a low profile till we could get out of town on the next ferry. Which is what we did and we never saw him or our dosh ever again. Mind you, we've still got his name (plus a few others) on our fantasy hit list come the day of judgement. Yes, they're all there in Stuart's little black book of no rubbing out, ready for retribution when they least expect it. Anyway, after all this assorted aggro, we decided it just wasn't worth the effort and with some relief, ditched our 'Into Europe' export campaign and returned to the safety and relative sanity of Merry England.

41

Typical Day at Kensington Market

A typical day for me and the 'Craig Stuart' crew at Kensington Market would start when I eventually rolled in after a short walk from my Cornwall Gardens flat. It was a lovely apartment that overlooked a private square and was very civilised indeed. The little old landlady told me the place was formerly occupied by Robert Beatty from *Dial 999*, a cop series on TV, which I thought was pretty cool. However, the poor dear was obviously a bit confused because it turned out that the former tenant was in fact American matinee idol Warren Beatty, which was even cooler. I was told this later by the mincing thespian downstairs who often had Warren's sister Shirley MacLaine staying there as his regular guest. Now Warren (You're So Vain) Beatty has quite a reputation as a ladies' man, if you get my drift, but I promise you I gave him a damn good run for his money whilst living there.

Throughout the 1970s I permanently had the horn and the old bedsprings were kept working overtime. Amongst the usual 'wham bams' were plenty of truly stellar performances as well as a couple of cringingly embarrassing flops that still haunt me to this day, but like they say, you can't win 'em all. This certainly wasn't generally the case and I often had several women on the go at the same time. I'd be sneaking one up into the flat as I smuggled another one out, whilst concealing a third in a cupboard or up a stairwell, not unlike a Brian Rix farce. Ah, those were the days.

Not long after, in case you were wondering, Kate returned from her American travels and we ended up living very happily together for many years, which 'more or less' put an end to my philandering. Anyway, as I was saying, a typical day at the market started when we arrived about ten o'clock-ish, or at least Pete Burkinshaw the office manager did. I'd probably stagger in with a hangover about eleven and head straight down to the Belly Buster café in the basement for a steak sandwich breakfast to set me up for the day. Strictly speaking I suppose it was 'brunch', which was a cross between breakfast and lunch. Or 'lust', as we called it, which is a cross between lunch and breakfast.

At some point, Stuart would show his face and we'd proceed to entertain our customers and friends who breezed in from all corners of the globe. Many prestigious designers like Paul Smith at Birdcage and Jeff Banks were regular customers. We even had students calling in from universities and colleges who were acting as our agents, selling Loon Pants to their classmates and making more money than their tutors. One of these ambitious young high-flyers was Nigel Cabourn at Newcastle College of Art and Design. Nigel was a mate of mine who later started up several hugely successful worldwide clothing brands including 'Cricket' and the 'Army Gym' based in Covent Garden.

Our showroom was much like a social club or drop-in centre. Many regular visitors that crossed the threshold were friends and fellow musos from my '60s Beat Group days. By sheer coincidence, as if by magic, all our skint mates would happen to turn up just before lunchtime, knowing full well we'd invite them to tag along for a meal, cheeky sods. We didn't mind really as it was always good fun and we could afford it, so what the hell. Occasionally it was the Greyhound pub or Angus Steak House, but more often we'd go to the Cherry Pie on Church Street.

Although cheap 'n' cheerful, the food at Cherry Pie was sensational. Unfortunately it was also a bit of a health hazard. What we at first thought was flock wallpaper was in fact hundreds of flies congregating to form pretty patterns on the backdrop. If disturbed they'd swarm and dive-bomb the diners before heading back to sneakily disguise themselves as part of the decor again. This is probably where the world's first 'Waiter, there's flock wallpaper in my soup' joke was invented.

For posh nosh, Maggie's just off Church Street was usually the restaurant of choice. It was reputedly Princess Margaret's favourite dining establishment, hence the name presumably. To get in you had to clamber over a huge dog that was always lying on the floor blocking the entrance. Having negotiated the canine obstacle, a gang of us would usually go down into the basement section where they'd automatically bring a huge vat of wine to the table with a measuring stick that worked out the amount of alcohol consumed. The flaw in their system was that we'd drink ourselves senseless and then top the level up with jugs of free water. They never twigged and must have thought we were all teetotal.

After lunch we'd have a wander round the crowded market, which always reeked of incense, to mingle with an eclectic mix of punters and showbiz types in search of the latest 'thing'. The place was a labyrinth of stalls on three floors selling brica-brac, belts, leathers, antiques, ethnic gear and a myriad of other assorted apparel, including Loon Pants, of course.

Many musicians regularly frequented the market, either buying stage outfits or actually working on the stalls. Most famously, of course, was Freddie Mercury, who was in charge of selling Alan Mair's legendary platform boots, just before Queen made the big-time. Alain Mair was also quite famous himself, having played bass in top Scottish '60s band The Beat Stalkers and later with The Only Ones.

After casually but unavoidably checking out all the stunning bra-less babes in their impossibly skimpy hot pants, we'd maybe buy a few clothes or yet another pair of stack-heel boots. Each new pair would get higher and more outrageous than the last. It was myself and Ken Todd that pretty much started the trend for platform soles, ages before Elton John and Slade started wearing them. Which reminds me of the corny old chestnut about Noddy Holder who was at a stall in Kenny Market when the salesperson asked him if he'd like a kipper tie? Ooh yes, that would be very nice, he replied, milk and two sugars, please.

Moving swiftly on. We were all very slim back then and I was a 28" waist before starting to pig out so much. Every evening we'd head off to somewhere like The Hungry Years burger joint on Earls Court Road that was full of celebs and dishy waitresses, if you'll pardon the pun. Or for the best curry in town it would be either the Standard Indian or Khan's on Westbourne Grove. Khan's was quite trendy and more like a traditional fast-food Indian canteen with a high roof, ceiling fans and potted palms. Needless to say, after several years of over-indulgence I was struggling to squeeze into my Loon Pants, having shot up to a 32" waist. Alas, they never looked quite as good with a beer belly. Still, never mind. Eat, drink and be merry, for tomorrow we diet.

Kensington market stalls

Some of the Kensington Market stalls that I can remember include Cockell and Johnson, Ruskin, Deans, Knees, Ken Todd, Pam Todd, Noddy's Nipples, McQ, The Clothing Clinic, Tranquil, Rowley and Oram (Mokies), Stirling Cooper, Make Believe Dreams, Palace Museum, Rag Toy, Bruno Sampson, Bill Buck Boots, The Wooly Pully Man, Sheep in Wolfs Clothing, Alan Mair, Freddie Mercury and Rodger Taylor, Bullet Jeans, Flying Down to Rio, Forbidden Fruit, Nitin Shar (Pepe Jeans), Murphy Brothers Records, Che Guevara, and of course our own stall Luckie Mucklebackits Experimental Clothing Laboratory.

42

Release / The Beast

Kensington Market was a lot of fun. We worked hard and played hard, but it wasn't always plain sailing. Many people smoked hash at the time so the place was rife with the all-pervasive pong of pot and patchouli. However, undercover plod were everywhere and one day Charlie, our van driver, got busted for allegedly dealing drugs, which he definitely wasn't.

Now, Charlie was a really decent guy whose passion was racing motorcycles at the Isle of Man TT. It finally dawned on me why they always called him 'Ton-Up Charlie' after the raving lunatic gave me a nightmare lift to work on the back of his bike at 100mph along the length of Gloucester Road. Jeez, never again.

Anyway, his unfortunate predicament all kicked off after he nagged us to get him a new van after claiming the old one was knackered. We finally conceded and bought him a flash six-wheel Ford Transit in vivid pink which instantly became known as the 'Pink Elephant'. The actual incident happened after it was reported to the police that someone was dealing drugs from a van next to the market. There is no way Charlie boy was involved, but the Pink Elephant was so conspicuous, and such an easy target that the feds decided to fit him up by planting dope behind the van's sun visor.

He was immediately detained, but luckily we knew about a legal organisation called 'Release' run by Caroline Coon and Rufus Harris that handled police corruption and drug-related cases. Thankfully they got poor old Charlie off the hook, though it still rankles that the drug squad got off scot-free after illegally planting evidence.

Another escapade that ended on a sour note but was fun while it lasted, was the acquisition of a monster Hot Rod Buick we called 'The Beast'. After making a few quid, Stuart and I decided to treat ourselves to something frivolous, when we spotted an advert in *Time Out* for a 1938 Buick McLaughlin, Straight 8 drop-head coupe with 'Albemarle' coachwork. Following a quick phone call we set off with cash in hand to the village of Denham in Buckinghamshire to meet the guy selling the car. It turned out the vehicle actually belonged to the Robert Stigwood Management Organisation and was previously driven by both Eric Clapton and the Bee Gees.

Although not in original condition, having been customised with a Jaguar 3.8 engine and wide racing wheels, we didn't really care. It looked the part and drove fantastic. The guy just wanted rid, so we clinched it for the bargain price of £400. OK it needed a bit of work but was roadworthy and all set to go. The thing was huge at about twenty feet long and a pig to park but proved an absolute hoot to pose around town with. The seating position was really high up and the whole thing kind of lurched about in a very scary fashion, making girl passengers scream with fear and delight. And a few blokes too.

The acceleration was simply awesome and it could burn off anything else at the traffic lights Grand Prix. It was such a gas that I even took the crazy clunker around the country on a mega nationwide sales trip. These were the good old days when you could just pull up and park right outside the boutiques you were visiting, so the 'Beast' turned out to be a tremendous attraction and promotional gimmick.

After the initial novelty began to wear off slightly we decided to give the old gal a complete makeover with full re-spray and new hood. It took a while, but we eventually put the revamped Beastie back on the road looking very striking in her fancy new cherry-red livery and white folding hood. So smart, in fact, that we were asked to exhibit her at a classic and vintage car festival. It was gorgeous weather on the big day and we parked alongside Bentleys, MGs, Morgans, steam trucks, ancient buses plus old crocks of all shapes and sizes. Then all the jalopies set off in procession around the showground to admiring glances as proud owners waved regally at the cheering crowds.

After a couple of laps, they decided that the Mighty McLaughlin had won a prize in its category and we drove over to pick up the rosette or whatever it was. The carnival queen was perched on a podium handing out prizes and as the car slowly approached, we thought it would be a good laugh to give her a scare. I can't remember who was actually driving, but as the car drew alongside, one of us honked the deafeningly loud air-horn which made the poor girl jump out of her skin. She tippled over, hit the deck and collapsed into a crumpled heap, losing all composure and dignity in the process. Immediately we felt really bad and very guilty for what we'd done. After making sure she was OK, we skulked off to a lot of well-deserved boos from the crowd, but then again it was quite funny. Anyway, it was probably all that Stuart's fault, so I blame him, ha ha.

It's hard to express what an enormous thrill it was to drive the Beast and never quite knowing what might happen next. Although she'd had a face lift, the car was already thirty-five years old, highly strung and altogether very temperamental. There was always a risk she could blow up or break down at any given moment. At speed the bonnet would flap about wildly, always on the verge of flying up and smashing through the windscreen. The wipers were so primitive it's a wonder they functioned at all and we lived in dread of rain. Steering was all over the place, finding gears was guesswork and basically it was like flying by the seat of your pants. But wow, what a great buzz. And she never did actually let us down as far as I can remember but there was always that nagging fear in the back of your mind. Still, as long as you were always respectful to the old girl she might be generous and decide not to bite you.

My daily runabout in London at the time was a souped-up, custom 'Sprinzel' Mini 1275 GT. It was a trendy chocolate-brown colour with tinted windows, wide wheels and sunroof, plus all the trimmings. One evening, my roadie mate Pete Burke had a trucking gig with Steely Dan at the Rainbow Theatre in May 1974 and he invited me along. I went down there in the Mini and after the concert drove Pete back to the Curzon Hotel in Mayfair, together with Skunk Baxter the guitarist with Steely Dan who had blagged a lift.

Now Skunk Baxter was not only high as a kite after the gig but was also 'Crazy Man Crazy'. We stuffed him in the back of the car and set off back to the hotel when he started rambling on about how much he loved the Mini. Full of enthusiasm, he suddenly became totally fixated on the idea of renting a workshop first thing in the morning, hiring some tools and replacing the existing 1275cc Mini engine with a huge American V8. I was listening to all this gibberish with amusement and eventually dropped the two of them off at Park Lane. Next morning arrived and of course nothing actually ever happened regarding installation of the new V8 engine. Poor old Skunk had obviously forgotten everything about the previous night's garbled conversation, so all I can say is thank Christ for that. Just thought I'd mention it whilst on the subject of motorcars.

Time for a quick rant
Other than the Buick I've never been a big fan of convertibles and wouldn't thank you for one. Also I'm very much in two minds about all-electric cars, although hybrids make more sense, as do hydrogen engines. Even some 'as yet' undiscovered technology or mini nukes sound potentially better than electric, but what do I know. Call me a Luddite, but those autonomous, self-driving vehicles are much too clever by half and blatantly begging for trouble. Amongst many other problems is the permanent risk of being hacked and control taken over by a third party. Also the loss of human driving skills needed in case of emergency, as well as endless moral and ethical dilemmas in the event of a fatal accident, and so on.

The worst thing of all, though, by far are those so-called 'smart motorways' with no hard shoulder. What a joke. Could they possibly be a pile-up waiting to happen? Too late, mate. They're happening all the time with dozens if not hundreds of fatalities already. And that's just in the short time they've been operational, so there are certainly many more deaths still to come. Whichever stupid criminals that dreamt up such a ridiculous concept (or the new Highway Code) should be forced to go out on patrol with the emergency services for a couple of weeks. Then see if they still think it's such a bright idea after spending a fortnight clearing wreckage and scraping corpses off the road. A very worthy *rant*, don't you think?

1938 Buick McLaughlin Drophead.

43

Shit or Bust

The Beast moved to several new homes with us after that, but we decided to mothball her for a while in Sheffield. One of Stuart's peculiar friends (and he had a good few) was an American who expressed an interest in buying the Buick, though we had no real plans to sell. He was the type of cheeky twat who never knocked before walking into your house and without so much as a by-your-leave would just help himself to the contents of the fridge. Or pocket anything else that was lying around as we were to soon find out. Reluctantly we agreed to a test drive and that's the last we ever saw of him or the car again, at least for a while. We were simply astounded at the brazen audacity of this so-called 'friend'. Later we heard he'd moved back to the States and was now Chief of Police in Chicago, would you believe? Yeah, I do believe.

After some nifty detective work scouring specialist car magazines, I spotted her for sale at a showroom in Wembley.

So she'd somehow found her way back to London. We contacted the police and reported it stolen, but the useless bastards said there was nothing they could do, even though we had all the paperwork and documentation as proof. It should have been an open-and-shut case of theft but they shrugged it off as a civil matter. Unbelievable.

There was no option but to get ourselves down to the Temple Bar and find a good lawyer. That was a trip and a half in itself but amazingly we got a barrister through legal aid, which was going to save us a fortune in fees. An injunction was issued and we ended up at court in a tense battle as to who actually owned the car. The motor dealer claimed he'd bought it in good faith, even though there was no logbook, which was obviously dodgy to start with. It was touch and go, but justice prevailed and we won the case. All that was left to do now was to arrange a time to pick her up.

Next day I made my way to Wembley with the intention of driving the car away, but upon arrival was horrified at what I saw. The poor old thing was lying there in a shocking state, hood ripped and paint stripper poured all over the back end. To make matters worse it wouldn't start. The dealer turned out to be a right villain and had sabotaged the Buick out of spite, making sure it wouldn't even run. Clearly I was livid and threatened to go straight back to court and claim compensation for all the damage and aggro.

At this point he turned really nasty and his two gorillas grabbed me, pinned me against the wall and started roughing me up big-style. I was thinking my time had finally come when he suddenly produced a camera and started taking snapshots of me for future reference. Angrily I said, "What the hell do you think you're doing, moron, that's my bad side," which didn't go down too well and I got another slap. He proceeded to explain slowly and very precisely, as if I was a complete imbecile (how ridiculous), that once I'd taken the car away, if he ever saw or heard from me again I was a dead man and I sort of believed him.

Accepting the situation stoically, all I could really do now was organise a recovery truck to come and tow her away. Zonk knew a mate with a trailer so I arranged to meet him in London a day or two later. He was a big, rough-looking lad so I was hoping for no further bother from the Wembley mob as we winched her aboard. It was a struggle, but by early evening we finally made it and headed north to find a suitable resting place for the injured wreck.

What a nightmare journey that turned out to be. The recovery driver was a maniac. His vehicle was a souped-up, short wheelbase V8 Landrover and the Buick on the trailer behind us towered ominously above our heads just inches away. If you glanced around or happened to catch a glimpse in the wingmirror it was like being pounced on by an evil red fiery dragon. This is the kind of terrifying imagery that was spinning round my head as the lunatic hurtled along the motorway at 90mph. I was grateful for his assistance and didn't want to upset the guy but felt the need to ask him if we could possibly slow down a tad. Being a man of very few words, all he said was, "Nah, shit or bust." In fact that's all he said on several more occasions as I pleaded with him to slow the fuck down. But that wasn't the worst of it.

My nerves were already in tatters by the time we pulled in for a break at Watford Gap services, but what I saw next totally freaked me out. As I jumped down from the passenger side, I spotted something out the corner of my eye that almost gave me a heart attack. The trailer tyre had a deep gash in the side and the inner tube was bulging out like a balloon.

"Jesus fucking Christ," I screamed at the driver. "Have you seen this?"

He looked a bit sheepish and said, "Yes, but I didn't like to mention it."

I said, "What do you mean, you already knew about it?"

He just shrugged his shoulders, and guess what he said? Yep: "Shit or bust, mate," and he went for a cup of tea.

By now it was pitch black and the madman had no intention whatsoever of fixing the wheel, so we just carried on the nightmare journey in much the same way as before. If the tyre had suddenly blown it would have meant an almighty pile-up and certain death. Until then I was pretty much a non-smoker but now desperately needed a fag as never before. There were twenty Marlboroughs sitting in the glove compartment so I asked him if I could blag one. He said, "Sure, mate, help yourself." By the time we got home I'd pretty much polished off the rest of the packet. As a result, I chain-smoked for the next thirty years. The loony tow trucker should have called his bloody company 'Nervous Breakdown'.

Astonishingly we arrived back safely and an old buddy of mine, Steve Bird had kindly agreed to let me leave the car in his yard until I could fix it up. He already had his own classic Mark 2 Jag and an American Airstream caravan parked up so it would be in very good company. Time slipped by and two years later the broken beast was still there gathering dust. By now we'd lost interest and the once-beautiful Buick proved to be something of a curse with a whiff of the 'Monkey's Paw' about it.

Time to get rid. She was definitely worse for wear and rather a mess after standing out in the elements so long. We figured she wasn't worth much in this state so just stuck an ad in the local rag. I think were only asking about a grand or so for a quick sale. No doubt we could have got a lot more nationally but in the end, we were quite glad to see the back of the blessed thing. Having said that, I often think back fondly and wonder whatever became of 'The Beast'.

44

Hong Kong Pong

With the incredible success of Loons, Craig Stuart Fashions wanted to follow up with a new range of brushed denim jeans and decided to call them 'Angry Pants'. They were named after the Angry Brigade that had just bombed Biba, although I hasten to add we had no affiliation with the organisation but just liked the name. All our own factories were flat-out, so to relieve the situation, myself and business partner Stuart decided to fly to Hong Kong and find some cheap production over there.

It was a Chinese social club charter flight on some inscrutable airline that nobody had ever heard of and took more than twenty hours to get there. The plane was packed with families and hordes of noisy little brats running wild, so we weren't exactly travelling first-class. Within a few hours the toilet had overflowed and was swilling up and down the aisles, which was an extra added bonus. Luckily I had downed some very strong travel-sickness pills that knocked me out and sent me to sleep for most of the journey, which was an absolute flightmare.

We stopped off in India on the way to refuel but it was too hot to even get out off the plane. To make up for it, though, arriving at Kai Tak, the old Hong Kong airport, was utterly amazing. The landing manoeuvre was almost impossible as we banked steeply over the harbour and flew in so low that most of the city's buildings were towering way above us. It was surreal and terrifying, but what an experience.

Upon arrival we booked in at the very swish Excelsior Hotel, though I shall always regret not staying at the 'Peninsula' with its spectacular views and rows of courtesy Rolls-Royces lined up outside. It was supposedly the best hotel in the world and featured in the James Bond film *Live and Let Die*. It's not that we couldn't afford it, so I don't know why we didn't stay there, unless they had a strict 'No Riff-Raff' policy, ha ha.

For days I had terrible jet lag and could hardly keep my eyes open with the after-effects of the travel-sickness pills. Stuart seemed to cope quite well though, and whilst I was tucked up in bed he was out at some sleazy nightclub owned by a geezer we'd met on the plane. Don't worry, Stuart, Mum's the word!

During the day we were visiting factory after factory until our heads were spinning. There were so many it was impossible to make a choice, but every one we went to had 'South Sea Bubble' jeans in boxes stacked to the ceiling ready for shipping to the UK. Millions of them. All day long we were courted and chaperoned everywhere in luxury limos. We were taken to exclusive floating restaurants in Aberdeen harbour or for afternoon tea on the verandas of the private clubs overlooking Repulse Bay.

On a rare day off, we managed to visit the old Forbidden City and the endless maze of shops and stalls that put even Kensington Market to shame. Then we hired a car and did all the touristy stuff, like exploring the New Territories and seeing the Chinese border, where we stuck our toes over the boundary line to see if we'd get shot. Don't forget Hong Kong was still a British colony until 1997. This, by the way, is the location where a traditional Chinese couple sit all day saying, "*Cheese*," for hoards of idiot foreigners like ourselves who each paid them one dollar to take their photograph. With no shortage of customers they were seriously coining it in and must have been about the richest pair of hustlers in China.

Most days we travelled across on the Kowloon (pants) ferry and marvelled at the bustling harbour full of exotic colourful junks and the half-sunken wreck of the *Queen Mary,* which also featured in *Live and Let Die*. So much to appreciate and so little time. The whole place was atmospheric with pungent smells and the distinctive Hong Kong pong that permeated everywhere. The contrast between the luxury skyscrapers in the affluent areas and the shantytowns stretching up the hillsides was almost unbelievable. These slums probably don't exist anymore and Hong Kong property prices are now almost unaffordable.

An old crony of my father's happened to be the HK Chief of Police and we were given a letter of introduction to meet him. He seemed genuinely pleased to give us a guided tour of his domain, especially around the most dangerous gangland areas where Triads and Tong mobsters would normally inflict 'death by a thousand cuts' on the likes of us '*gweilows*'. Roughly translated that means 'white devils', the derisive term for westerners. After this chilling insight to the seedy underbelly of the city, we finally concluded our business with a British-based agent who would now liaise with the Hong Kong factory on our behalf.

At the end of our stay, we arrived at the airport like a couple of right twonkers, only to find we'd turned up a day early for our flight. Duh. This meant we had to find another hotel as the Excelsior was now fully booked. Purely at random we picked one which seemed perfectly acceptable at first sight but to our stupefaction turned out to be the most notorious gay and transsexual hotel in the whole of the Orient, which is saying something. Still, whatever turns you on. Live and let die and all that.

Anyway, we were now resigned to being stuck there for the night so figured we might as well make the best of it. When in Rome etc, or in this case Hong Kong. So in the end we just thought, *Oh, sod it,* and lubed each other up, got hammered at the disco fetish party, popped some amyl nitrate and then got ravished at a mass orgy down the local opium den. No, not really.

Just before we left I bought some traditional Cantonese folk music albums and a few other knick-knacks to take back as presents. However, the sexy satin 'Suzie Wong' dress with slits up the side that I took home for my girlfriend unsurprisingly went down like a lead balloon.

Just for a lark we also purchased a laughing machine in a cloth bag. Like they say, you can't buy class. Later, in an overhead locker on the airplane I'd stashed this ridiculous laughing machine which, triggered by the constant turbulence kept accidentally going off, cackling hysterically all the way back to London. It was hilariously funny at first but after twenty hours the novelty had pretty much worn off. By Heathrow we were definitely the least popular passengers on board and so ended our little Asian adventure.

Six months later the Angry Pants finally arrived on a

slow boat from China after endless problems and frustrating delays. By now the whole project had lost all momentum and as a result this was the only batch we ever ordered. Enjoyable as the trip had been, it proved to be a somewhat futile exercise and all we could do was sit back and watch South Sea Bubble corner the brushed denim market. Lucky for us, Loon Pants and our other products continued selling for another year or so until we finally got bored, divvied up the proceeds and moved on to pastures new.

Tex in Hong Kong.

45

Hampton Court Daze

Craig Stuart Fashions basically ceased trading around 1975 and my girlfriend Kate and I moved from Cornwall Gardens to Royal Crescent in Holland Park, where incidentally the front door of our flat was used to make the Colgate 'ring of confidence' toothpaste TV advert.

Talking of front doors, just up the road lived Frank Windsor who played DS John Watts in TV cop series *Z Cars* and *Softly, Softly*. One night on the way back from our local pub the Prince of Wales, we had to stagger past Frank's house which was at the end of a terrace. We thought it would be a jolly jape to ring the bell at his back gate and run off and hide round the corner. However, by the time we reached the front of the house he was standing at the door with a vicious-looking guard dog and caught us red-handed. It's a fair cop, guv. Another day, another collar, as they'd say down at the Newtown nick.

Now effectively retired, I fancied a change of scene so we decided to move out to Hampton Court for a while. A couple of muso friends John Cox and Ronnie Hunt lived out at nearby Sunbury and they invited us over to check out the area first. The scenery was really nice with boats on the river and a pleasant holiday atmosphere, so we felt it was an ideal spot.

John had played guitar with the Soul Foundation in Belfast and also worked with Van Morrison. He'd been sharing a pad with top Irish bluesman Sam Mahood from Just Five but eventually moved back to London. Ronnie was a 'Flash Harry' who seemed to know all the faces on the manor, one of them being Andy Galton, whose father Ray wrote *Hancock's Half Hour* and *Steptoe and Son* with Alan Simpson. Andy was keen collector and had a huge stack of old comics, magazines and records, etc. He was also fellow car freak with a Ford V8 Pilot and kindly let me park the Buick in his garage when it was off the road for a while. Another local face was the fat actor bloke that played the wicked Landburgher Gessler in TV's *Adventures of William Tell*, who now ran the local sweetie shop. We found this quite amusing and was the final deciding factor for us renting a lovely four bedroom house just over the river from Hampton Court Palace.

The sun at Hampton Court did nothing but shine, so no wonder good old Henry VIII thought it was a great place to live. It was brilliant weather for the next couple of years and was the first time I'd ever managed a decent tan. There was also plenty of fun and games with lots of live music happening after we set up a drum kit and a few amplifiers permanently in the main room so we could rehearse at any old time we fancied.

It all went a bit crazy after Ronnie moved in with John Cox and his brother Mick, who had also worked with Van Morrison in Belfast. Loads of other musician friends were living in the area so we started regular jamming sessions at the house. Some of these guys were quite famous at the time and included Steve Holley from Wings, Herman the German from The Scorpions, Steve and Charlie from Poco, and Pete Arneson from The Rubettes. Lots of different musicians and girlfriends were in and out all day, including Ron's bit on the side, sexy Sylvia, the husky blonde Maplins yellowcoat from television holiday camp comedy *Hi-de-Hi*.

Part of the scene we had going in Hampton Court was at Andy Galton's house, which was actually more like a mansion that I assume was formerly part of the palace grounds. Andy shared the place with his sisters Sarah and little Lisa, who was a member of our gang and a good friend of Kates. It was all pretty free and easy, and the Galton get-togethers were legendary. There were also plenty of rave-ups at our own gaff if not quite on such a lavish scale. We had lots of different activities going on, such as the time I challenged Ronnie to a drinking competition, which was really rather stupid.

Ron was a regular heavy boozer, twice my size and had the constitution of an ox. He was into full-strength cider and I'd just started making home brew again after a long lay-off, so was now only a moderate drinker since the gin-soaked years of my yobby youth. Anyway, egged on by the usual suspects we downed five pints each in quick succession, no problem. I just opened my gullet and the whole lot almost slid down in solid lumps, just like the old days. Easy peasy. Ron seemed OK and was ready for another. I still felt in with a chance and was about to sup a sixth when without warning the room started to rotate. A nasty woozy sensation that I'd not felt since throwing up at midnight mass in 1962 left me desperately in need of a good lie down.

Feeling quite poorly, I'd no sooner put my head to the pillow when the bastards burst through the door, whooping and yelling like a bunch of retards and began bouncing up and down on the waterbed. By now I was feverishly sweating buckets as the nausea began to peak and my poor head spun wildly on its axis. Next came that deceptively calm few seconds just before the dramatic re-enactment of the projectile vomiting scene from the film *Witches of Eastwick*.

Then without fanfare or further ado, copious quantities of technicolour chunder cascaded forth at lightning speed, exquisitely redecorating the room and jazzing up the bedroom carpet. Diced vegetable soup on an industrial scale erupted from the bowels of Beelzebub, creating a masterpiece that would put even the most flamboyant of post-modernists to shame. By now I really didn't care anymore. I'm ready to die. Sweet Angel of the Lord, please take me now. I need a priest and I'm not even Catholic. At long last, merciful sleep descended, putting me out of my misery until next day's impending and inevitable hangover. Not sure if Ron suffered any ill effects but I suspect he fared much better than me. Anyway, cheers, Ron, old mate. A worthy winner.

46

Taggs Island

By that point Kate decided enough was enough and I can hardly blame her for wanting to get away from this madhouse. It wasn't that we were splitting up permanently or anything. but she decided to stay for a while on her friend's houseboat nearby on the 'Thames Riviera', as it was known. And it wasn't just any old boring, run-of-the-mill houseboat but a converted ex-naval MTB (motor torpedo boat), which was a pretty cool craft. Like having your own mini battleship.

It was moored up on Taggs Island next to the fabulously named Cigarette Island and neighbouring Ash Island. Maybe it should have been called Faggs Island? At one time the island belonged to a wealthy lawyer who evicted all the squatting tenants. One of these was a spiteful pikey called Tagg who put a gypsy curse on the island stating no business would ever prosper. Several tried but failed, including a luxury hotel and casino built by Fred Karno, the famous impresario who discovered Charlie Chaplin. The semi-derelict 'Karsino', as it was known, featured in the film *A Clockwork Orange* but burnt down shortly after. By this time it was just a picturesque wooded atoll, surrounded by assorted flotilla and accessed by a little rickety bridge over the water.

Kate's friend was an ex-hippy-type traveller who had a very rare VW twin-cab pickup truck, plus a collection of classic vintage showman's wagons and tinkers caravans. These were all parked up next to the boat, making the place look like an upmarket Romany encampment. If my own drum ever got too hectic, I'd spend a few days with Kate on the MTB just to get some peace and quiet.

Back at the house, a healthy alternative pastime between bouts of boozing and bonking during those crazy, lazy, Hampton Court mazy, daze was the sport of badminton. The back garden was large enough for a makeshift badminton court, so we strung the net across the lawn tied to a couple of trees. Sounds primitive, but it worked a treat, and we had a tournament every day for the whole summer. I'd never really played much before, but in a very short time got pretty damn good and ultra-fit in the process. It was fantastic fun with the whole gang taking turns and it soon got very competitive, especially between myself and Mick Cox, who hated losing.

As previously mentioned, Mick had played guitar with Van Morrison in Belfast and worked on the original Astral Weeks demos plus several of his albums. The guy was a seasoned pro who had also toured America with 'Eire Apparent' and was managed and recorded by Jimi Hendrix. Eire Apparent were Jimi's protégés and he and Mick hung out together and spent many hours in the recording studio. On top of all that Mick was Gary Moore's favourite guitarist whilst in another band called the Alley Kats in Belfast, so he came with one hell of a pedigree. Which made it all the more enjoyable to thrash him at badminton. Ha ha.

We did eventually do a gig at a pub in Shepperton billed as 'Nervo and the Fleet', but I got so drunk that I forgot all the lyrics and then tried to start a fight with a leather-clad 'Road Rat' in the audience. Luckily Andy knew the biker and persuaded him not to kill me. Needless to say we never actually did another gig with that particular illustrious line-up.

A visiting acquaintance to Hampton happened to mention that she did all the merchandising for rock promoter Harvey Goldsmith. She desperately needed loads of T-shirts and asked me if I might be interested in helping out. I was happy to assist and the first ones I managed to locate were some two-tone designs for Alex Harvey Band and Rick Wakeman. In particular she wanted T-shirts for the forthcoming Elton John 'Louder than Concorde' tour and also 'The Rolling Stones Tour of Europe 1976'.

This was no problem, and I started sourcing and supplying all sorts of tour merchandise, including exclusive paper 'crew jackets' for Elton and the Stones from an agent chap in Kenny Market, whose name I now forget. It was quite funny when he told me they were made by a firm in Utoxeter, which he couldn't pronounce properly and always called it Uto-Oxeeter. I only wish I'd kept a few prime examples of these garments, which are now rare collector's items.

The only regret I had whilst living there was not realising that a huge rockabilly resurgence was going on around Hampton Court. It was hosted by DJs Geoff Barker and Stuart Colman, who were holding regular vintage rock 'n' roll revival sessions in a local club. If only I'd have known, I would have been down there like a shot.

47

Dingwall's

Whilst living on Taggs Island, Kate and her houseboat buddy had found themselves waitressing jobs at the legendary Dingwall's Dancehall in Camden Town. So after leaving Hampton Court it seemed like a sensible idea if we moved to Camden.

Although Dingwall's was called a dancehall, it had more of a nightclub atmosphere and was definitely *the* place to be seen in the '70s. For a live music venue it was the perfect size and shape, not too big, not too small, with stage and dance floor at one end and restaurant at the other. Not forgetting the bar, of course, that ran nearly the full length of the room. It was in a great location at Camden Lock next to the canal amongst craft workshops and the antiques flea market. Close by were other major venues such as the Roundhouse, Electric Ballroom and the Music Machine, later to become Camden Palace. In addition were all the famous music pubs like the Dublin Castle, Monarch, Carnarvon Castle, Devonshire Arms and The Falcon.

It was a real happening scene, so after Hampton Court, Camden felt like the obvious choice of place to move to. Apart from anything, it would be handy for Kate and her new job, which I think she really enjoyed. We found a ground-floor flat to rent in nearby Delancey Street with patio doors out into the back garden, which was very handy for lounging about and letting the cat out. Not so great was having faulty under-floor heating permanently full on, which was like living in a sauna. Also the noisy French couple in the flat directly above that never seemed to stop bonking.

We soon settled in and spent most free evenings enjoying the Camden nightlife before finally ending up at Dingwall's, simply because it was the best place to go. It was celebrity central and everybody who was anybody propped up the bar at Dingwall's. All the current bands either played there or just hung out, and it was the spiritual home of Hawkwind and the Pink Fairies. Also Mick Farren's Deviants used it as their headquarters and Dingwall's was always regarded as the anti-establishment establishment.

There was always a nice mix of musical styles, from Doctor Feelgood or The Pirates, to country acts like Pete Rowan or Tex Mex accordionist Flaco Jimenez. Amongst my own favourites at the time were Paul Carracks band Ace, who'd just recorded 'How Long', plus a great little Cajun outfit called the Electric Bluebirds. Much later on Blur, U2 and all the other 'Johnny Come Latelys' gigged there, but this was the early days I'm talking about when the place was properly hip.

Kate was well in with the owner Tony Mackintosh and usually blagged all the best shifts. She was also mates with Boss Goodman the DJ and the rest of the staff, even though I was regarded by them as something of a liability and merely tolerated. Though not in the same league as O'Toole, Harris or Reed, I had by now turned into something of a drunken hell-raiser and all-round loose cannon, hence never quite flavour of the month at Dingwall's. They put up with my antics 'cos I spent so much bloody money. Also for Kate's sake, the bouncers must have turned a blind eye whenever I was squirting beer at customers or tipping drinks over some poor sod's head.

Even though all these high-jinks and riotous behaviour was massively inspired by *Tiswas*, basically I was just being an obnoxious jerk. In retrospect I was probably acting like this from some form of mild depression. Although I'd never felt particularly manic before, and my life was one long rambunctious hoot, in truth I was increasingly like a ship without a rudder. With no business to run and a failed musical career behind me, I'd lost my way, with nothing much to look forward to. Since the '60s my view was that the world was living on borrowed time anyway, so what's the bleedin' point? Getting 'out of it' seemed to be the answer. Also I was feeling guilty about taking Kate for granted and not always giving her the respect she deserved. On a more mundane level I was on the Fatkins diet and piling on the pounds. Well, I'd had a lot on my plate. Boom boom.

Approaching thirty and already past it. Most of the time I was generally feeling bored shitless from any lack of ambition, so maybe this was a midlife crisis that I'd so far refused to accept. Whoa! Definitely time to get a grip, pull my socks up, smell the coffee and, er... can't think of any more relevant clichés.

At Dingbats I got my final warning from the bouncers after a couple more incidents. Mind you, bearing in mind they were a notorious bunch of Belgian ex-mercenaries I'd managed to get away with murder for long enough. This was just further confirmation that I had to get my act together, but how? It would be tough, but for starters I cut back on the hard stuff, dug out a pair of trainers and began a strict new jogging regime in earnest. Every day I'd run several miles around Regent's Park and Primrose Hill, getting fit and taking in the scenery. There were some very smart architectural buildings to admire round the periphery and it was a great way of exploring parts of London that you never get to see by car.

Even so, all this exercise didn't stop me popping back to Dingwall's from time to time just to keep my hand in. Most of the waitresses were very attractive and one girl I got on well with was Deirdre, who worked in the cloakroom or on the door. Some of the others, though, were heavy-duty drug users and a couple of them would stand on their heads in the toilets and inject stuff direct into their eyeballs for a quick fix. Quite a few of them ended up either as junkies or lesbians for some reason. Admittedly I was something of a heel when under the affluence of incahol, which understandably hacked Kate off. Then again, she was always getting chatted up, which I wasn't too happy about, but as usual whatever happened, we always ended up back together. Camden was OK, but after a while we got sick of living in temperatures hotter than the surface of the sun and decided yet again it was time to move on.

48

Musical Chairs

Mark Jacobs, an old friend of Kate's, had a hippy shop in Portobello Road called 'Hindu Kush' selling joss sticks, skins, ethnic furniture and such like. He was going away for a couple of months on one of his 'buying' trips and said we could stay at his house whilst he was away if we looked after his dog. He was supposedly out there in Nepal and Afghanistan purchasing items for the shop, though I can hazard a guess that's not all he was bringing back.

Anyway, he had a very swish drum in East Sheen near Barnes, which was rent-free, so we jumped at the chance. Like I say, all we had to do was feed and walk the mutt. When we arrived, a friend of Marks called Nils Stevenson was also staying there with his girlfriend, which was slightly unexpected but not really a problem. That was apart from her leaving mucky knickers in the shower tray and playing Bob Marley non-stop twenty-four seven. Still, we soon got used to it and carried out our dog-walking duties in earnest at nearby Richmond Park.

It wasn't long before we started getting chummy with these other two occupants of the house, who weren't at all hippy types like Mark, in fact quite the opposite. Nils, we discovered, had been organising gigs for the Sex Pistols and was now managing Siouxsie and the Banshees. I was quite interested in the whole new punk phenomenon so he took me down to The Roebuck pub on the King's Road, which was one of the main punk haunts. He knew everybody and we met all these crazy cats with spiky haircuts and wild clothes, which I thought were great. Mind you, I wasn't so keen on the safety pins or the actual music. At the time I was more into Ry Cooder, Donny Hathaway and proper bands like Little Feat who'd eat the Clash-Pistols for breakfast. There is nothing worse than being forced to endure inept wannabes struggling through their musical growing pains, or in any other sphere of life, come to that.

Frustratingly most of these UK punk bands could barely play yet imagined they were creating something new and revolutionary. Re-inventing the wheel is always a tedious process to endure for a grouchy old bastard like me. Can't say I've ever enthused much about any punk bands who (IMHO) were nearly all over-hyped and overrated. The only exception possibly was 999, who were quite good live, but maybe I'm missing the point. OK, I must admit that something vaguely exciting was obviously happening with all these young upstarts blowing out prog-rock and injecting fresh blood and energy into the whole jaded scene. Problem was, they weren't actually replacing it with anything better, only providing a mega marketing scam for Malcolm McLaren and some of his other creepy cohorts.

After a while, Mark arrived back from the Himalayas looking suspiciously spaced out so we said our goodbyes and shook paws with the pooch for the last time. Our next port of call was with my old mucker Les Nicol in a posh part of Willesden and yes, there actually is one! How he could afford such a fancy mansion I don't know but thought it best not to ask. Les was living with a strange girl called Ez, short for Esmeralda, who was into astrology, I Ching and all that Enochian magic stuff. Ez reminded me of gypsy fortune teller or a witch. She even had a 'familiar' in the form of a black cat that mysteriously disappeared, leaving four kittens behind. As we weren't paying rent, I felt obliged to look after the kittens and had to feed them by hand for the next couple of months with a pipette.

Sharing digs wasn't an ideal situation so we started putting feelers out for somewhere more permanent. The Royal Borough was always our favourite stomping ground, and as luck would have it, a friend's flat became vacant in World's End. It was offered to us by Pete Bardens at a peppercorn rent and was too good to pass up on. Pete played keyboard with a band called Camel and had just been offered a plum job with Mick Fleetwood so was now moving upmarket. It was a real muso house and although a bit of a dump, had potential and was well salvageable.

My old drummer Steve Chapman and his Icelandic chick Gullah had just acquired the ground-floor flat from guitarist Tim Renwick, who worked with Sutherland Brothers and the Alan Parsons Project. It was like a revolving door of different musicians and when bass player Charlie Harrison and his lady left for the States, session guitarist Chris Spedding moved into the basement flat with his girlfriend Penny. Chris played rock and jazz working with such people as Robert Gordon, Sharks and Roxy Music, not to mention the Wombles. I said not to mention the Wombles. He was a great musician, if somewhat reclusive, although his girlfriend Penny was a friendly, outgoing American ex-model.

Someone said her rich daddy was boss of some mega bank in New York, so it was probably him that sponsored her new fashion design venture based in Lots Road just around the corner. She was making stage outfits for Chrissie Hynde of The Pretenders (whom I later discovered was Andy Galton's girlfriend when she first moved to England), though I never heard much about Penny's career after that. Then after Penny and Chris left, Debbi from Buggles, who sang 'Video Killed the Radio Star', moved in, thus continuing the house's musical tradition.

Anyway, we collared the top flat and spruced the place up best we could. It was always a bit down-home funky but had 'character'. There was only one bedroom, but the front room had a genuine Victorian open fireplace and original features. So after bumming around for months it was very nice indeed to have our own place again, so we just got on and enjoyed it for a while. By the time we'd finished it was very cosy and felt like home apart from the sad state of the carpet that we never quite got round to replacing.

Pete the previous tenant and his missus had a stupid little pug dog that just shat and peed everywhere, so it hummed a bit at first. The pong eventually dissipated but the shiny carpet became increasingly threadbare and worn smooth like glass. We never could get rid of the embedded muck and dog hairs so instead we just got a lovely little moggy called Tom to add to the grunge.

One day I was having a ham sandwich and left it half eaten on a plate on the floor. Whilst my back was turned, Tom sneaked a piece of meat which must have had a blob of hot English mustard on it. A split second later he expelled a huge turd and took off round the room like the wall of death. I never realised cats could defy the laws of gravity and levitate with such dexterity. Poor old Tom never touched the floor and remained airborne for several laps until the Colman's finally wore off. I'm happy to say he quickly recovered, though it maybe made him think twice about nicking my lunch in future.

49

Upcerne Downcerne

The flat itself was situated down by Chelsea Creek where all the film stars now live. Back then it was rather run down but on the verge of gentrification and I wish I'd bought the place cheap when I had the chance. Anyway, we all lived together in this incestuous lunatic asylum, riddled with gossip and intrigue. Our street was called Upcerne Road, which we re-christened 'Upcerne Downcerne' in tribute to the popular TV period drama series *Upstairs Downstairs* with all the obvious similarities. It was very much like a real-life soap opera, where there was always some game afoot with gangster friends of Gullahs feuding over dope deals or hiding out from some rival mob. Very relaxing when you're half expecting the Richardsons to kick the door down and nail your head to the floor.

Gullah also had some posher pals in the countryside so we all piled down to Wiltshire on one of our binges. Nobody seemed to know the directions so we travelled in convoy and just followed the leader. The place we were looking for was called Surrendell Farm, which we found hours later in a confusing maze of country lanes. It turned out this rural retreat was actually a Jacobean mansion, albeit slightly ramshackle that was set in a large sprawling estate and not at all the humble smallholding we had imagined.

Not only that, it turned out to be the hippy commune where Princess Margaret and toy-boy lover Roddy Llewellyn were being relentlessly hounded by the press. They weren't around on the day we turned up, which is probably just as well. Everyone, including her closest friends, had to call Margaret 'Ma'am', but there's no way you'd ever catch me doing that. I'd have defiantly refused and probably been beheaded for treason or something.

The girl that owned the house was Sarah Ponsonby, who was somewhat eccentric to put it mildly. In the middle of her living room was a weird throne-type affair, which if I remember correctly was an actual working lavatory. She was always in the thick of the action and mistress of ceremonies. Allegedly, on one occasion her anarchic entourage wearing gimp masks hijacked a primetime TV news bulletin and were arrested after handcuffing themselves to various pieces of studio equipment as part of some gay rights protest.

At Surrendell gatherings, everyone wore costumes where the girls would dress up as French maids or nuns and get rat-arsed at the village pub, much to the annoyance of the yokels who hated all these toffee-nosed pranksters. The bumpkins eventually wreaked their revenge when they shopped Sarah to the feds for growing pot. She got busted and fined, which more or less put an end to such visits down on the farm.

Another hangout was Vicky Moore's place out by a forest somewhere near Reading. We'd all shoot down there and get out of our skulls for a couple of days whilst watching all the semi-naked girls prancing round the woods dressed as fairies. Vicky was tall and rather glamorous, and she later opened the best ever designer shop in London called 'Miracles' selling weird and wacky artefacts unlike anything I'd ever seen before. The shop was brilliant, although very few people seem to remember it now, so I don't think it was around for long. Now resident in Majorca, she sells lotions and potions online under the name of Victoria Moore Skincare. A little plug for you there, Vix. She still regularly hosts parties on the island with select members of the King's Road mafia and keeps inviting me over to stay for one of their illustrious doghangings. Sounds tempting, but I'm not sure I could handle the excitement these days.

We were big fans and friends of cowboy country music singer Hank Wangford, who in real life is celebrity gynaecologist and rock 'n' roll doctor Sam Hutt. One weekend our posse moseyed on down to his Heathfield ranch for a six-gun shoot-out and the grand final of the UK cowpat-flingin' competition. No doubt we had a real root 'n' tootin' time but the only thing I remember is the bleedin' khazi didn't work and meant we had to make like the pope and shit in the woods. And just so you know, wiping your backside with a dock leaf isn't as easy as you might think. Hee haw.

One famous Upcerne visitor was Hendrix drummer Mitch Mitchell who incidentally played Wendover in *Whacko* as a kid actor. Who could forget headmaster Jimmy Edwards's immortal words, 'Bend over Wendover', just before a giving poor Mitch a good thrashing? Another guest was record producer and Roxy Music bass player John Porter, who was originally from Leeds. I only met him the once, but we had a 'reet good yarn' about our mutual influences and northern rock 'n' roll roots.

Directly behind us on Uverdale Road lived Marianne Faithfull during her druggy anorexic period. One of our regular chores was lobbing empty bottles at her annoying junkie mates from our balcony at the rear of the building if they started getting out of order. In a nutshell there was always something going on at Upcerne Downcerne that kept life interesting.

50

Asterix

Kate soon found herself a waitress job round the corner at Asterix on King's Road and was earning good money and great tips. Asterix was a really popular creperie (pancake house, to you and me) named after a French cartoon character. I'm not sure but they may have changed the spelling later to Astrix so as not to get sued by the Frogs. Or was it Belgians? Anyway, one evening we popped over to the Roebuck pub with a few staff members and the restaurant manager to relax after Kate's shift. I must have had one too many 'cos I dropped myself in it after volunteering to do the washing-up at Asterix and cover for the regular guy who was due a night off. No problemo, baby, bring it on. Hic!

Not imagining for one minute they were serious, I'd forgotten all about it when a few days later there was a phone call asking me to come in that evening. Thinking it was some kind of wind-up I just laughed and said what the fizzing heck are you talking about? It was the manager on the line, but unfortunately he wasn't jesting. The guy was totally relying on me so I couldn't let him down, plus it would reflect badly on Kate if I didn't show. With no real option I went down there and was handed an apron and shown to my spot behind the service counter at the sink.

Piled high on the draining board stood a mountain of sticky and slimy plates ready to wash. Was I seriously expected to deal with this lot by myself? It must be some kind of joke they play on new recruits like being sent for a long stand or a big weight. But no, it was all for me and I had no choice but to get stuck in before it got any worse. After the initial shock I started making modest headway and was feeling quite pleased with myself. Then it suddenly got so busy we were rushed off our feet with dishes stacking up thick and fast again.

The pace was relentless and by now the floor was swilling about in soapy water and oil spilt from the grill so was like a skating rink. The whole sweaty experience was awful, like being on an endless conveyer belt. Since that day, kitchen and catering staff have my full sympathy. Thankfully as the evening wore on, things slackened off and slowly I worked my way through it all until home time. Thank Christ that was over. To paraphrase Derek and Clive, it was 'the worst job I ever had'. To my surprise I was thanked by everyone for saving the day and treated almost like a hero. I would have actually done it as a favour, but they paid me anyway and in the end I felt quite proud. Never again, though, no way, Gonzalez.

After that little drama we decided we both deserved a break and took a short vacation that was in complete contrast to our life in London. It was a visit to my mad 'Aunt' Cissie's haunted house in Argyll on the west coast of Scotland where I'd spent most of my childhood holidays. Actually she was more eccentric than mad and also very frugal. For example, she hoarded tiny bits of string, perished rubber bands, plastic bags and mountains of other useless old junk all stuffed away in cupboards, which we thought was hilarious. She was so tight that even well into old age she'd thumb a lift back and forwards to Glasgow rather than pay a train fare. I remember her telling me once that she got a ride with Jimmy Shand and his band in the back of their van like a geriatric groupie.

And although I'm not sure if the spooky old house was genuinely haunted it certainly felt that way. It was very ghostly with dusty cobwebs and ancient Victorian decor that was at least a hundred years old. There was no telling-bone or any of that modern elec-trickery and the only lighting was candles or paraffin lamps. We cooked fish freshly caught from the loch on the trusty old Rayburn and drank milk that was straight from the cow. Back to nature with no mod cons. Sounds crap, but it was brilliant.

The views were breathtaking with spectacular walks over the mountains to Ardentinny and beyond. To get there in the early days we'd take the ever-so-romantic steam-hauled 'West Highland Line' train up to Arrochar and then catch a little MacBrayne's post bus to our remote destination. It was single track all the way with very few passing places along the twenty-mile switchback route, which could be quite hairy at times. Once there we'd go out collecting mussels and giant clappy-doos from the shoreline to use as bait, then spent much of our time fishing. Cissie had a lovely wooden clinker-built dingy that we'd take out to the middle of the Loch and hook so many fish it was unbelievable.

Sometimes the boat would get caught between a submarine travelling one way and a paddle steamer going the other, which created an almighty wash that was rather unnerving, considering none of us could swim. Every trip we'd be catching two or three fish with each cast, usually cod and haddock or sometimes skate or mackerel. We never caught any live kippers though, funnily enough. After an hour, the boat would be almost sinking under the weight. There'd be so much fish on board that we'd struggle to even give it away. This all changed one day when a Russian factory ship sneaked up the loch and trawled it clean, right under the noses of the useless Admiralty boats that were supposed to constantly patrol the area. It was never the same again as far as the fishing was concerned but still remained a beautiful part of the world to visit.

For supper it was always Milander crusty bread from Milngavie (pronounced Mulguy) with their clever advertising slogan 'Demanda Milander'. We had local cheese, tomatoes that actually tasted of tomatoes and real scotch pies followed by macaroon bars, snowballs and Tunnocks tasty teacakes for afters. All washed down with a wee dram to end the day. Heaven. Sorry about that, folks. Just a brief, tearful bout of sentimental and self-indulgent nostalgia. Also to honour the memory of my parents, whose ashes were scattered in the loch.

After the highlands we went to visit a friend of Kate's at Innerleithen, about thirty miles from Edinburgh. The girl was married to a luthier (guitar maker to you and me) and they lived in one of a row of farm cottages on Colin Tennant's estate by the River Tweed. All the other cottages were occupied by various members of The Incredible String Band who had been very popular back in the '60s and were mentored by the Laird Glenconner himself.

They had massive cult status with sold-out concerts at the Albert Hall and the Fillmore West in San Francisco during their heyday. Although still very popular, they had lost their commercial edge and weren't selling so many records but were heavily into Scientology. As it happened I was destined to meet up with one of the band's strongest Scientology advocates a few years later.

51

Greece / Poros

There were plenty of other jolly jaunts and excursions where Kate and I had a great time together, but sometimes we took off on our own. She regularly went off exploring India and Sri Lanka, or more often America, so this was the lifestyle we were used to. And while Kate's away, Craig will play and all that. I'd usually find some new love interest whilst she was on the road and she would no doubt do the same.

On one of these occasions our former office manager Pete and his wife Heather had booked a flight to Athens and invited me along plus a friend. At short notice I picked up a lovely little waitress whose name I now forget and whisked her off to Greece for a couple of filthy weeks of extracurricular activity in the sun. It was too hot and stuffy in Athens, so we caught the next ferry to Poros and rented a villa in the hills overlooking the main fishing village and harbour. By this stage I was looking forward to some hanky-panky but to my horror discovered she wasn't on the pill. As neither of us had brought any protection it was left up to me get hold of some form of contraception before I was allowed to play hide the sausage.

Easier said than done. I immediately shot down to the island's one and only chemist shop and discretely asked for a packet of condoms. The pharmacist just looked back at me with a blank stare and shrugged his shoulders. Now, did his shrug mean sorry pal, we don't have any condoms or I don't know what the fucking hell you're talking about? It soon became apparent he couldn't speak a word of English which at least meant that I was still in with a chance.

Then in a flash of inspiration it occurred to me that the word 'prophylactic' would do the trick. I mean, what word have you ever heard in all your born days that sounds more Greek than prophylactic? They probably invented the damn things three thousand years ago, for God's sake. Or Eros's sake, in this case. The chemist guy would surely latch on and was bound to be impressed, especially if I communicated in his own native tongue. So with a flourish and theatrical wave of the hand I bestowed upon him the Greek prophylactic word with more than a hint of Hellenic inflexion for extra effect. But no, not a flicker. Total incomprehension.

With hopes now dashed on that front I abandoned the intellectual approach and just started shouting things like Durex, sheath, French letter and rubber Johnny very loudly in the time-honoured traditional English way of getting across to foreigners. But still no joy. What a complete tosser. Apart from *ouzo, retsina*, Metaxa and *dhio birres parakalo* I could barely speak a word of Greek but optimistically hoped it might still be possible to explain what I wanted in sign language.

By now a small crowd had formed to see what was going on as I stood there dementedly pointing at my crotch, waving an imaginary dick around and pretending to pull on a phantom Johnny bag. Even this didn't work so I was seriously beginning to wonder what was wrong with this drugstore dipstick. Everything thus far had failed, so whatever next? I was now reduced to the final act of desperation and was left with no other option but resort to the art of mime. As you can imagine I was already feeling pretty silly, but this was my final chance to make the moron understand my essential needs, so basically whatever it took.

So in a last-ditch effort I started acting all sexy and began wildly humping the shop counter, moaning and grunting in mock ecstasy. The customers lapped it up as I climaxed with an almighty fake orgasm and with that the penny finally dropped. Hallelujah. From the back of the store Stavros or whatever his stupid name was emerged with a choice of cock socks and I grabbed four boxes of a dozen just in case. There's no way I was going through that humiliation again.

In retrospect I'm pretty sure the whole thing was a clever wind-up or a Greek joke played on every gullible tourist who goes in to buy a bulletproof vest. Anyway, as I left the shop bloody Stavros gave me a sly wink as if to say 'gotcha'. Either that or he fancied me, which is, of course, something else they invented in Greece three thousand years ago.

You may wonder, was this little pantomime and all the accompanying rigmarole worth the effort? Well, let me just tell you that the willing waitress in question turned out to be a double-jointed contortionist and that's all you need to know. Anyway, a couple of depraved weeks later it was back to Blighty.

52

Punk Scene

Kate was still away so I started hanging out with a rascal called Neville. He played guitar with a punk band called Mean Street and invited a gang of us down to one of their gigs at The Roxy Club in Covent Garden. Intrigued, we all piled down there to watch them perform at the first actual punk gig some of us had ever been to. They had a loony cook called Kenny who played the drums in his chef's hat and chequered pants, plus a charismatic young singer called Gary Numan, as yet undiscovered. Everyone was out their heads, pushing, shoving, pogoing and gobbing the night away, filthy bastards. It was all pretty disgusting even though everyone seemed to be having a jolly good time of it. Let me just say that I enjoyed it so much I never went back again. Don't get me wrong, I still loved the haircuts, clothes and amazing fashion ideas, but not really their music or notion of hygiene.

Around the same time I met Lisa, an American girl who was a friend of Ez and Neville's, and we hit it off immediately.

She was attractive, intelligent, rich and culturally unbiased so took everything on board such as fine art, films, theatre and, yes, even punk. It turned out she was big mates with The Clash and her sister's boyfriend Mickey Foote was working for them at the time. Funnily enough, years later I spotted this same boyfriend on a television documentary about Donald Dump's controversial golf course development near Aberdeen. Trump had dug up all the ancient sand dunes and the locals were up in arms. Mickey now lived up there and was one of the main protesters, so more power to your elbow, mate. Not really relevant, just a little aside. Feckin' golf, eh?

The Clash all lived together in a big mansion overlooking Regent's Park that was owned by Terence Conran, who initially made his pile with the Shabby Tat shops. His son Sebastian also lived there and was working with the band helping design record sleeves, posters and also their stage outfits. Lisa took me round there one day to meet the guys and somehow managed to purloin a pair of Joe Strummer's designer canvas trousers which she gave to me as a present. They were an absolute perfect fit, though disturbingly I was starting to get mental images of poor old Joe, wandering about in just his underpants three months later, still searching for his missing strides, ha ha.

She also wangled some tickets to a film premiere at the ICA about the British punk explosion centred around the Roxy club where we'd previously seen Mean Street. Imaginatively entitled *The Punk Rock Movie*, it was all filmed on Super 8 and directed by former Roxy DJ Don Letts. This anarchic DIY hotchpotch is now regarded by many as an all-time classic, featuring seminal punk bands of the era including the Sex Pistols, Clash, Siouxsie, Alternative TV, Generation X, Slits and Subway Sect. A darker side to the film shows junkies shooting up in the bogs and a guy slashing his chest and stomach with a razor, so it definitely ain't for the squeamish. To give him credit, Don Letts was a man of many talents and something of a visionary to have had the foresight to capture such rare movie moments for posterity.

It was now the late '70s and, having been so inspired, I fancied having a crack at making some post-punky-style jackets myself but needed assistance with cutting patterns. Before Lisa went to back to live in the States, she had suggested I should visit a designer friend of hers who could maybe help me out. Her name was Alice Pollock, though I had no idea who she was at the time. She didn't have the phone number but gave me an address on Fulham Road, so I wandered down there on the off chance, not quite knowing what I'd find.

53

Alice Pollock / Circus

So, off I went in search of this mysterious Alice Pollock at the address I'd been given on the corner of Fulham Road and Ifield Road. Upon arrival there was a sign above the door saying 'CIRCUS', which intrigued me as it had actually caught my eye several times previously when passing. There didn't seem to be a doorbell so I just walked straight in and up the winding stairway. The top of the stairs opened out into

Photo credit: Tony McGee / Harpers and Queen magazine.

a large airy room with a beautiful polished wooden floor and it looked fantastic. All very minimal and converted tastefully into a wonderful spacious work area. The atmosphere was so harmonious and inviting that I knew immediately I was in a very special place.

In the room were three people busily at work. One girl was cutting patterns, another was knitting and the third was a guy on a sewing machine whom I recognised instantly. It was none other than Jasper Conran, brother of Sebastian, who made gear for the Clash. I wasn't expecting that. He was Britain's latest top 'wunderkind' designer and in demand all over the world. Not surprisingly I was feeling slightly awkward with these three looking quizzically at me as if to say, who the hell are you?

After regaining a modicum of composure I asked to speak to Alice. The girl cutting patterns smiled sweetly and said, "I'm Alice, how can I help you?" It was such a soothing and dreamy voice that I was immediately enchanted. After explaining who I was and why I was there we relaxed, got chatting and had the most amazing conversation. It was instant chemistry and by now the pair of us were so engrossed that we'd almost forgotten about Jasper Conran and the other girl. Eventually we were introduced but they both seemed rather put-out by the amount of attention I had been receiving.

Alice obviously ruled the roost round here, but who the hell was she to hold so much sway? We had obviously clicked and a further meeting was arranged to discuss ideas over dinner. After combining business with pleasure, one thing led to another and suddenly we were an item. On the surface, Alice appeared quite casual and unassuming, but there was obviously something about her that made everyone pay her such respect. Gradually I learnt that during the '60s she was probably one of the most influential fashion designers in world, up there with Mary Quant and Jean Muir.

She had initially started with a small shop at 52 Radnor Walk just off King's Road called Quorum with her legendary partner Ossie Clark. Between them they literally kick-started the whole swinging sixties thing, making custom clothes for The Beatles, the Stones and every other superstar of the era. Even before that she was PA to Orson Wells and dressed people like Glenda Jackson, Liza Minnelli and Charlotte Rampling.

Trading as Alice Pollock, she generally kept a relatively low profile and was not conspicuously a big household name like Zandra Rhodes or Biba. However, it was Alice pulling the strings in the background who was the real impetus, even with Ossie Clark, who was a genius and generally acknowledged as number one. Those in the know realise this. Even into the '70s after selling out to Radley Fashions, she told me how she went on to design the classic parachute jacket and other significant punk stuff for Malcolm McLaren's shop 'Seditionaries'.

Like I say, Alice just beavered away quietly behind the scenes in her own unique, inimitable way. Zen-like, she fastidiously kept her workroom spotless, routinely spring-cleaning every morning before starting daily operations. But when she did get grafting, boy, you should have seen her go. After a final briefing on my new designs she instantly set to and made samples until we got the jackets exactly right. At the same time she was also busy doing her own thing with her current brand label 'A Nice Pear' as well as mentoring the other girl in the workroom. This was Catherine, an American girl who was hand-knitting the most incredible multi-coloured woollen creations. Jasper drifted in and out when he felt like it but eventually disappeared off the radar.

By now she knew about my own rag trade background and how successful Loon Pants had been during my time at Kensington Market. Even so, I still felt very much in awe of her amazing abilities and achievements. Also by her impressive number of personal contacts. Throughout the '60s, Alice had also been involved in the music scene, which went hand in hand with fashion, and was good friends with the likes of Lulu and Cleo Lane. After hearing some of the songs I'd been writing, she said I ought to record them and rang a friend of hers who had a studio. The guy who owned it was her former van driver at Quorum who happened to be none other than Dave Gilmour from Pink Floyd.

54

Dave Gilmour / Alice Pollock Fashion Show

Hey presto, after speaking with Dave Gilmour, the next thing I knew was we were booked in at his Britannia Row recording studio in Islington with head producer Nick Griffiths at the helm.

This was fantastic, so I roped in my bass player mate Johnny Bentley from Squeeze and drummer Gordon Coxon from Blood Donor, whose keyboard player Keith Hale had just written 'It's a Mystery' for Toyah Wilcox. They were a very good group of musicians but like the rest of us were wrestling with the all-pervasive backdrop of punk. So if you can't beat 'em, join 'em and I wrote a bunch of hooligan songs for the session with our little trio 'Racket of Three'.

Nick engineered the backing track for the first song, which I can't remember the name of, and we made a start on the second one called 'Aggravation'. Halfway through, Dave Gilmour shows up, likes what he hears and takes over the desk from Nick. We finished off with another daft song called

'Jesus Elvis Hitler' that Dave thought was great and he told us to come back later and add the vocals. I often kick myself for not doing so but at the time I was feeling quite blasé about the whole thing. Everything was going so well with Alice and it felt like I had all the time in the world to finish off at the studio but for whatever circumstances it never happened. Motto: seize the day.

Perhaps the reason was because we were right in the middle of planning a fashion show and it was all systems go to get the exhibits ready on time. My jackets were almost completed and looking fabulous in heavy black canvas, punk-ish but still tasteful. The knitwear was stunning and totally original, quite unlike anything seen before. Alice included several choice items of her own together with a few zany accessories and we were all set to go.

The models were various waifs and strays that Alice had taken under her wing. One was a beautiful six-foot jet-black African girl called Princess Agnes of Toro and another was an aspiring singer called Tilly. There was also a gay guy called Piggy who was quite famous at the time plus a couple of others I don't remember.

It wasn't a massive event but just a few select guests and press by special invitation. The location was a low-key but supremely elegant restaurant called '11 Park Walk', now owned by Gordon Ramsay. During the afternoon we took over the basement where the models made their grand entrance down a spiral staircase to mingle with the guests. This allowed them to get close up and fully appreciate the quality of the items on display. Everything went without a hitch and was a phenomenal success.

Within the next few days we had rave reviews from the main *Times* fashion writer plus a whole load more favourable editorials. The crowning glory, though, was the front cover of

Vogue, which looked stunning. Or was it *Metropolitan*? Or was it *Cosmopolitan*? Whichever, it was one of the big three at the time. Hey, come on, this was five decades ago and I can't remember every flippin' detail, for heaven's sake, ha ha. Anyway, for years I'd been trying in vain to get this kind of publicity for my own designs, then Alice goes and clinches it with a couple of phone calls. The gal got clout.

Meanwhile, I was staying half at her place and half at mine in World's End whilst thinking of how to earn some extra cash until the 'Circus' thing really took off. Just around the corner there was always a buzz and lots going on in Lots Road, hence the name, most probably? It had a lively pub called 'The Ferret and Firkin in the Balloon Up the Creek' and the 606 jazz club plus a recording studio where I once got roped in to play triangle on a John Cale session. There were also several clothing companies, one of which was called Pinto Sportswear.

Out of curiosity I stuck my head in at Pinto's headquarters and got chatting, only to learn that one of the owners had previously been somehow connected with our old Kensington Market rivals 'South Sea Bubble'. As successful as South Sea Bubble appeared to have been in the mid-1970s, they suddenly disappeared overnight almost without trace. This seemed strange at the time, but I later heard they were part of some huge money-laundering operation that went badly wrong.

The Pinto guys had set up this big wholesale warehouse to hold stock for their retail shops on King's Road and elsewhere but were struggling to get the designs made in sufficient quantities here in the UK. Styles were changing so rapidly and it took far too long to bring stuff in from abroad. Because I still had all my old factory contacts I agreed to set up a few deals for them on a consultancy basis, which turned out to be a nice little earner for a while. Then I heard they were about to rent a retail outlet in Kensington High Street. To my surprise I discovered that the leaseholder was one of our former Loon Pant customers from Kensington Market who was called Bruno Sampson.

Bruno had certainly come up in the world since running a single stall in Kenny market. He now seemed to own half of King's Road and Kensington High Street including Pontings Kensington Super Store. They wanted to do a grand opening of this latest Pinto shop on a lavish scale but weren't exactly sure how best to go about it when they learned of my involvement with Alice. Obviously they must have heard about her awesome reputation and asked me if she might be interested in organising the launch. It's the sort of thing that was just up her street so after a meeting with Bruno and the boys she agreed to do it.

The big Pinto Sportswear launch came and went very successfully, and Bruno seemed well impressed. He said if Alice and I ever needed financial backing for a project of our own he'd definitely be interested. This was great news because we'd been thinking of setting up a fabric screen-printing operation and needed tables, steamers and other specialist equipment as well as suitable premises.

So to help draw up a master plan, Alice brought in a few PR friends including Prince Andrew's former lover and baronet's daughter Vicky Hodge and an ex-model called Nancy. There was even a white witch called Diana Warburton to put a good luck spell on the proceedings. There was also another nutty wild cat dude hanging round at the time called Cosmo, though I'm not sure if he was involved or not. All I remember is him jumping up and down, dancing like a complete bozo on top of the washing machines at the laundrette over the road, so probably not.

We set up operational headquarters at Nancy's house and began to fine-tune all the different ideas for what we now called 'The Project'. After some research and a several brainstorming sessions, things were shaping up nicely when suddenly Vicky Hodge's boyfriend turned up unexpectedly at the front door brandishing a blood-stained carving knife.

55

John Conteh / John Bindon / Ossie Clark

It turned out that Vicky Hodge's boyfriend was notorious Fulham gangster and hardcase John 'Biffo' Bindon, who arrived right in the middle of a business meeting clutching his trademark carving knife dripping with blood. He had obviously just stabbed some poor sod and needed a place to hide the weapon. Apparently this was a fairly regular occurrence and I heard one time he hacked someone's arm off.

He was seriously bad news. I remember him showing off outside the Water Rat pub when just for kicks he lobbed a beer glass through a taxicab window. The driver pulled up and jumped out ready to confront the perpetrator when he saw John Bindon sprinting at full tilt towards the cab. He realised instantly who it was and took off at the double before 'Biffo' could rip his head off. Such was his fearsome reputation round West London. Everyone knew who he was and would be very careful when he was lurking around.

When not maiming people, however, he could be quite sociable and held court at various drinking establishments in the manor. He was renowned for the size of his manhood and his party piece was to hang six beer mugs on his willy in front of all the pub clientele. Even if they found this trick offensive, no one would dare complain.

As well as being a hitman and running protection rackets he was a tough guy actor in films like *Get Carter*, *Quadrophenia*, *Poor Cow* and *Performance*. Also he worked as security adviser for Led Zeppelin but was sacked for starting most of the violence instead of stopping it. He was probably most famous for his affairs with Christine Keeler, Angie Bowie and allegedly Princess Margaret, whom he met in Mustique.

Anyway, after I threw him out we resumed in order to complete our business plan that was then presented to Bruno Sampson, who was delighted and keen to be involved. Our meeting was held at his office on Duke Street above a restaurant called JC's owned by Scouse light-heavyweight world champion boxer John Conteh. The restaurant lease actually belonged to Bruno and was yet another of his vast portfolio of properties that now included Kensington Market. It just so happened that John was there in the office that same day and I somehow got volunteered into accompanying him on a shopping spree down Bond Street acting as his minder, ha ha. After a tour of high-class clothing stores (say no more), we headed back to Bruno's headquarters to clinch the deal.

To celebrate the new venture, Bruno wanted to take us all out for the night, including boxer John, and we arranged to meet later at the Rainbow Room. This prestigious Art Deco venue was part of Derry and Tom's Spanish roof garden with its mock Moorish Alhambra and pink flamingos, but when we got there I was refused entry for being improperly dressed. Luckily, my new bezzy mate John Conteh, who was a megastar at the time, lent me his jacket before daring the doorman not to let us in. No contest and up we went. Brilliant. Anyway, after an unforgettable night out, Bruno agreed to sponsor all our requirements, and without further ado we started ordering all the screen-printing stuff we needed.

This is where we made a serious error of judgement. He offered us a basement on King's Road, the perfect location, but our 'technical expert' thought it was too small. Instead she convinced us that we needed more space and persuaded us to rent a much bigger room in Smithfield which she predicted as the new Covent Garden. This may eventually be true but not for years to come and King's Road was where it was at right now. Why we agreed, I shall never know. Our so-called 'expert' was the only one who knew about the screen-printing technology that she'd learnt at college and hardly got any work done at all. I don't think she produced more than a few metres of cloth all the time we were there.

King's Road would have been a far better bet on a smaller and more manageable scale, but it was now too late to change our minds. The girl, who shall remain nameless, suddenly bottled it and disappeared, leaving us to pick up the pieces. Neither myself nor Alice had the expertise or energy to carry on after this fiasco and poor old Bruno was left holding the baby. He was very gracious about it, rightly blaming the missing 'technician' and released us from our commitments.

My relationship with Alice seemed to falter soon afterwards but not before meeting up with Ossie Clark. We spent an evening with him and his son, but it was something of an anticlimax. He'd passed his peak as a designer, was almost bankrupt and into some weird drug shit by this point. He was later murdered by his former gay Italian lover.

Alice and I started to drift apart and after a couple of altercations we split up when she chucked all my stuff out the window in a fit of pique. Quite hilarious, really. Oh well, 'twas fun while it lasted. Gloriously eccentric but an amazing lady all the same. Last I heard was she'd opened up a vintage shop called 'Shake Rag' in San Diego's Gaslamp Quarter. I sincerely wish her well. All a bit sad, eh, but 'hey-ho'.

56

New York, New York

Shortly after my adventures with designer Alice Pollock abruptly ended, a timely message arrived from my punk friend Lisa, inviting me to visit her in New York.

A pilgrimage to the States was long overdue, so after obtaining a visa I was on my way, all bopped up in my Joe Strummer kecks and spiky new haircut. Upon arrival there was no way I was going to risk the New York subway, so I treated myself to a yellow cab from the airport. Driving in past Queens and all the other depressing suburbs didn't inspire confidence and I began to wonder what I'd let myself in for. However, having crossed over the East River into Manhattan with its magnificent skyline, it was like entering a different world. Seeing the lovely Lisa again was great and we spent a very pleasant afternoon getting reacquainted.

She was working at John Lennon's favourite restaurant but had taken time off to show me the town, so I could hardly contain myself. The next week was just a whirl of sights and sounds that blew my mind. We did the usual tourist trail that included the Statue of Liberty which nearly killed me. My knees turned to jelly about three quarters of the way up and I had to sit there on the stairs like a right Herbert whilst toddlers and little old grannies were zapping past me. I wasn't at all scared, but my legs completely seized up and I never did make it up to the torch at the top. Lucky for me there was a lift at the Empire State Building, which was the highlight of the visit. The Art Deco architecture was incredible and the view even more so. Pretty damn amazing and words can't do it justice.

After a couple of days' sightseeing I met up with my old bandmate Les Nicol from Distant Jim for a drink and he introduced me to a few of his favourite watering holes. He was now living in New York, New York (yeah, I heard you the first time) and played guitar with a quasi-glam rock outfit called Magnet after several years with Ray Owen's Moon and Leo Sayer's band. Then we bumped into singer Jess Roden and had few more libations before staggering back.

Lisa's apartment was conveniently located on Jane Street and, though bijou, was very stylish, not to mention wildly expensive. Lisa's sister was also in NY and now living with an Italian clothing manufacturer since breaking up with her Clash boyfriend back in London. We all got together for a Chinese feast and a few other memorable meals including one at the world-famous Ratner's Jewish Kosher restaurant by the Williamsburg Bridge, but mainly we just snacked at local bars.

Most days, hangovers would be worked off by jogging round Washington Square and jumping over the white chalk outlines of all the murder victims every few yards. Up until then I was having a great time but then my perception began to change. I started noticing that the sidewalks were filled with vagrants, hustlers and pimps, and the choked streets belched plumes of filthy smoke and steam. The noisy non-stop sound of wailing police sirens and alarm bells perpetually filled the air and I suddenly felt trapped. Sleep was nigh on impossible and it got to the point where I couldn't figure out if I was suffering culture shock or shell shock.

CBGB's rock club was on the agenda, but I was almost relieved that we never actually made it to the sleazy, graffiti-covered, smack-riddled hole. The pressure was rising and on 12 October 1978, Sid Vicious hit the headlines after stabbing and killing loopy Nancy Spungen at the city's Chelsea Hotel. The TV and newspapers were full of hysteria and the final straw was finding myself trapped in the middle of a supermarket hold-up. Definitely time to get out of this place.

After only a week I'd had enough, with claustrophobia and paranoia taking over. I think Lisa was feeling it too because it didn't take much persuasion to get her on a train down to New Orleans. I always loved rail travel, but this was something else. After booking a couple of overnight sleeper seats on the 'Crescent City' we set off from Penn Station, just off Madison Square Garden. Or was it Grand Central? Whichever it was, the station architecture was magnificent.

The 1,400-mile journey takes about twenty hours but was a sheer delight, with the route sounding like a set of Chuck Berry song lyrics. From New York to Newark, Philadelphia PA, Baltimore, Atlanta Georgia and Birmingham Alabama before finally rolling into Voodoo Central. The sky was dark when the train passed through Washington DC and we could see the White House all lit up in the distance. You could physically feel the heavy-duty power vibes, it was so strong. Truly awe-inspiring, as was the crossing of Lake Pontchartrain on a six-mile-long causeway, which created the illusion of being onboard a ship and totally surrounded by water.

We slept as best we could till daybreak, and then moved to the observation car for a sensational view of America as we traversed the ever-changing landscape. If we fancied a sneaky ciggy, we'd sit outside on the balcony right at the rear of the train and watch the tracks disappear slowly into the southern scenery behind us.

It was magical, just like you imagine in the movies. Surprisingly, for parts of the way it was single track as we trundled through countless little unspoilt backwoods towns. Every few miles the train would rattle over a level crossing with its warning bells ringing, accompanied by the continuous humming of the diesel and the mournful sound of its horn. By the time we arrived at the Big Easy we were knackered and had very sore arses (or should that be asses?), but boy, was it worth it. In a word: epic.

57

New Orleans / Cajun Country

So, after an exhausting twenty-hour train journey, Lisa and I arrived in the Big Easy and found a place to crash. Everywhere in America is crawling with cockroaches and New Orleans was no exception. The hotel where we stayed had giant bugs so brazen they didn't even bother scuttling out of sight when you switched on the lights. They lived mainly in toilets, kitchens and especially cutlery draws for some reason. The horrible critters were everywhere but you just got used to it.

As is the custom, we started out on Bourbon Street and the French Quarter taking in the jazz bars and blues clubs along the way. Regrettably we never managed to find our way to Tipitina's, the spiritual home of New Orleans music, which was very remiss of us. Tipitina is the title of a classic song by pianist Professor Longhair, otherwise known as Fess. Every year in tribute to the great man they have a jazz festival, called the 'Fess Jazztival', which I thought was very punny.

For your average mug punter, a river cruise on a paddle steamer is almost obligatory, so we dutifully clambered aboard the *Delta Queen* and moseyed on down the mighty Mississippi for a lazy, boozy afternoon. Surprisingly it was OK, with pleasant views of the colonial mansions along the riverbank and the madwoman who waves at every ship that sails by. Mind you, we all waved back, so what does that say about us?

Next we had a wander round the St Louis cemetery which is built on a huge stinking swamp. To stop the corpses floating about they're all buried aboveground in spooky crumbling crypts and mausoleums. This creepy old bone-yard has grown so huge it's now nicknamed 'City of the Dead' and is where the acid-trip scene from *Easy Rider* was filmed.

Food-wise we relished all the local cuisine – jambalaya, gumbo and French toast all smothered in maple syrup and then washed down with a jug of ice-cold mint julep. No wonder Yanks are so enormous. Then, after doing all the tourist stuff we rented a lumbering great jalopy and headed up the Gulf Coast to Biloxi, Mississippi.

Biloxi Mississippi is where Hollywood actress and alleged Satanist Jayne (lobsterisimus bummakisimus) Mansfield was supposedly decapitated in a horrific car accident. This typical brash, vulgar American seaside resort had all the usual trappings of high-rise hotels, casinos and theme parks, etc. At one of the amusement arcades there was a live chicken in a slot machine that played noughts and crosses, or tic-tac-toe, as it's called over there. For a giggle I stuck a coin into the slot and the chicken had first go. It was obviously rigged 'cos the crooked cockerel won. Suddenly a deafeningly loud bell started ringing and a huge flashing arrow began to point directly at me from the roof above, indicating to the whole world that I'd just had my ass whooped by a scabby old rooster. I wasn't really expecting such high-profile public humiliation but must admit it was rather funny.

After Biloxi we headed in the other direction towards the Bayou and Zydeco country. Back home I'd been listening to a fantastic Cajun album compiled by Charlie Gillett called *Another Saturday Night* featuring squeezebox rockers like Johnnie Allen, Belton Richard and Austin Pitre. It was a revelation at the time because virtually no one in Britain had heard this kind of stuff before. Even the names of the towns where these tracks were recorded held a certain mystique. Lake Charles, Ville Platt, Opelousas, Crowley, Beaumont and Eunice. The album had inspired me so much I was determined explore the swamplands and search out some of this amazing traditional Cajun music before it disappeared.

Ironically there was a massive revival shortly after my visit, but could I hell as find anybody who played it 'live' when I was actually there. We even went to Rockin' Dopsie's club in Lafayette, where I was convinced we'd strike lucky. The place itself was unlike any other venue I'd ever seen, with these amazing wooden walls that lifted up and propped open to let in the warm, or was it cool night air? Disappointingly, all they had on stage that night was the poor man's equivalent of a London 'pub rock' band that I could have seen any night of the week back home. All that way for nothing.

Finding a hotel or indeed anything else in Lafayette was a nightmare. It was just a sprawling mess that didn't seem to have any definitive town centre. In that respect it was like many other American towns. Just block after block of McDonald's, Taco Bells, gaudy neon-lit filling stations and all the rest of the usual rubbish.

After driving around for ages without success, I finally gave up and ventured into a rough-looking 'Roadhouse' bar to ask for directions. As soon as I stepped through the door it all went quiet, like the hick-town scene in a spaghetti western movie. As I stood there in my punk gear, all these huge biker guys and cowboy dudes closed in around me, toting pool cues, looking real mean and menacing. The atmosphere was electric, but I had nowhere to run so simply asked politely if there was a hotel nearby. As soon as they heard me speak and realised I was from England, they turned into pussy cats and couldn't have been more helpful. Thank fuck for that.

58

Los Angeles

Everywhere you go in America, people just love the British accent and want to hear you talk. Likewise, I love their graceful southern drawl and hep slang. On the other hand I can't stand those high-pitched, helium-voiced blonde bimbos and precocious brat kid actors that are in every shit Hollywood film and TV series these days. You can't understand a friggin' word that comes out of their stupid, luminous tooth-filled gobs and I hate them with a vengeance. Thank God for subtitles, not that any of that crap is worth watching anyway. Talk about dumbing us down. They are the pits. I always feel so much better after a quick *rant*.

Anyway, we were directed to what must have been the most wretched and seedy bug-infested motel in all of Louisiana and spent a hot, sweaty night without any aircon. Next day we headed for Baton Rouge State Fair, which was a massive event with all the big rides, music stages, livestock championships and even a freak circus. There were jars of pickled body parts, skellingtons, multi-headed creatures and everything grotesque under the sun. They also had plenty of hideous live exhibits too, though the one that sticks in my mind was a long wheelbase cow. What I mean is it had six legs, two normal at the front but four at the back with two sets of udders. That literally did freak me out so after a while we boogied on back to New Orleans to drop off the car and spend our last night together.

The following day we bid fond farewell at the airport then went our separate ways. A tearful Lisa was off back to the Big Apple and it was all a bit sad, but hey, I was off to pastures new and booked myself a Delta flight to the City of Lost Angels.

After quaffing complimentary champagne all the way, it was the middle of the night when the plane touched down in LA so I grabbed a cab into town. My old bass player mate Charlie Harrison from Poco was supposed to pick me up but never showed, so I had no option but to book into a hotel on Sunset Strip, which sounds very glamorous but was really just a flea-bitten knocking shop. At least I got my head down for a few hours until I eventually got hold of Charlie, who turned up impressively next day in an open-top Ford Mustang. After an introductory scenic drive around LA, we headed back to his gaff at a pleasant location in Poinsettia, Hollywood.

Tonight was party night and we'd been invited out to a fancy do at a former bootlegger's mansion somewhere in the Hollywood Hills. The party house was sumptuous with all original Art Deco features from the 1920s, with secret hidden compartments where they used to store the moonshine and machine guns. All the beautiful people seemed to be there and it wasn't long before I'd pulled. Shit, I'd only been in town five minutes and I was already on a promise with pretty young thing in a big floppy hippy hat.

It's amazing how drink and drugs can so drastically alter one's perception. By morning she didn't look anything near so young or pretty and I couldn't wait to get rid. She too seemed very glad to duck out so I guess there'd be no second date. Sometime later I saw her naked centre-fold picture in a mucky magazine, which didn't surprise me in the least, especially after I'd come down with a painful dose of a rather unpleasant social disease a few days after our little liaison.

Meanwhile, I went to stay for a few days with my old bandmate Steve Chapman at his pad. Because Steve and Charlie were both originally from the UK, their first Poco album was appropriately called *Cowboys and Englishmen* before getting a massive number-one hit with 'Legends'. It's interesting to note that Randy Meisner and Timothy B. Schmit from the Eagles were both former members of Poco. Anyway we spent a few nights hanging out at the Roxy and the Troubadour, although I was so out of it most of the time I haven't a clue what bands we saw at either of these illustrious clubs.

I enjoyed my few action-packed days in LA but the time had come to meet up with my long-term girlfriend Kate again. She loved travelling and we often didn't see each other for extended periods of time, so consequently it was something of an on/off relationship. Anyway, rather nervously I packed my bag and headed for the Greyhound bus depot. Destination, San Francisco.

59

San Francisco / Marin County

After an eleven-hour coast road drive riding the old grey dog, I arrived in San Francisco where Kate and her friend Sally were there to greet me. It was a bit weird at first, but we soon loosened up and were genuinely happy to be back together again after so long.

Before heading up to Marin County, where Sally lived, we had a quick guided tour of Shaky Town. Wow, what a place. The architecture, the fabulous wooden buildings, the bay, the harbour, Alcatraz, the open-sided trams that traverse seemingly impossible gradients up and down the steep hillsides are all just incredible.

After that we crossed the Golden Gate Bridge and made our way to Black Point, Novato, in Sally's trusty old Volvo. Marin County is the laid-back part of northern California and Black Point is even more so. Sally's hippy house was just beautiful with a fantastic view overlooking the Petaluma River and San Pablo Bay. The only problem was skunks living in the basement. Apparently they're OK if you don't provoke them and thankfully they never let rip when we were there. Don't know if they're regarded as a pest, but soulful Sally just let them be.

Seeing Kate again made me really horny, but the unfortunate social disease I'd contracted in LA had now kicked in so bad, it was no nooky for me. First job next morning was to find a clinic and get it sorted. The nearest one I could find was on Petaluma Boulevard, where they filmed the hot-rod scenes in *American Graffiti*, the greatest rock 'n' roll movie ever made. I suppose in some small way that made up for all the mess and misery I'd ignominiously suffered since my LA lay. What a martyr. Never mind, a week later the cure had worked a treat and the boy was back in business.

Marin County was relaxing after the hustle and bustle of all the cities and I started exploring the locale. Every day was sunshine and I'd jog around the hills and through the woods where one morning I found an old abandoned medieval village hidden away in the thicket. I thought I must be tripping as it was such a bizarre discovery and I couldn't wait to get back and tell the girls about it. As it turned out, the mysterious folly was just the hibernating remnants of the annual Renaissance, or Elephant Fair as the locals called it. Apparently it was a famous event where people came from all over the United States to see Tudor minstrels, Shakespearean re-enactments, troubadours, acrobats, dwarf-throwing and all manner of ridiculous hey-nonny-no. Obviously Sally knew all about it and laughed after I said I honestly thought I'd stumbled into a vortex and shot back in time five hundred years. Well, you never quite know with all the hallucinogenic drugs that were perpetually floating about that part of the world.

Every few days a couple of Sally's friends turned up with big bags of dope and started putting out lines of various substances on the kitchen table. Although I'd never chased the dragon before I thought I'd at least give it a go just to be sociable. It wasn't an entirely unpleasant way of spending the day, but I wouldn't ever want to be dependent on the stuff like these guys obviously were. I guess it was just their normal way of life. They seemed very happy and were obviously loaded in every sense of the word and I subsequently discovered why.

These dudes were seriously big-time dealers with armed guards and a ranch somewhere in the backwoods where they grew acres of the stuff. Having said that, they seemed like really decent, peace-loving ex-hippy types who were just doing their own thing. It's difficult to make any moral judgement when basically it's just a matter of supply and demand. And why should the CIA have a bloody dealership monopoly? Greedy, evil, hypocritical bastards. OK, these buddies of Sally's were probably addicts but with good reason. Essentially pacifists, they'd been drafted and sent to Vietnam and forced to commit terrible war crimes against their will. Thanks to Uncle Sam they came back all fucked up and trying in vain to make sense of an insane world. Good luck to them, I say. They're probably all dead or rotting in jail by now anyways… or billionaires.

60

Morroco / Marrakech / Agadir

Here in Marin County, California, where we were staying, our friend Sally had another car that she let Kate and I use during our vacation, so we took full advantage. It was a dinky little open-top Austin Healy Sprout which was cute but rather hairy to drive amongst the all the huge American gas guzzlers and massive trucks towering above us. It wasn't the most reliable of vehicles but we managed OK after a couple of minor breakdowns.

My most vivid recollection was going off in search of the San Andreas Fault and standing astride the fault line willing a huge tremor to erupt. It never happened, which is probably just as well, though I suppose it's inevitable one of these days. The weeks drifted by and I don't really remember anything very much apart from being stoned and having a really lovely relaxing time watching *Saturday Night Live* on TV. Oh yes, and the incessant 'chicky chack, chicky chack, chicky chack' – Jack in a Box adverts, which I quite liked, strangely enough!

Alas, my allotted six-week visa was nearly up and with money fast running out, it was almost time to head for home. Sally had been great putting us up for so long, but we hugged our goodbyes and spent the final couple of days in Frisco before flying back. By the way Frisco is the term guaranteed to annoy San Franciscans in the same way as Big Smoke deeply offends Londoners.

Speaking of which, London didn't seem very different from how we'd left it. Same old same old. Then along came the bad news that we had to vacate our World's End flat in Chelsea. The good news was that we were moving to a newly renovated garden flat in Cumberland Street, Pimlico. By the way, just in case you've never seen it, check out the fabulous 1949 Ealing comedy *Passport to Pimlico*. An absolute classic. It was a great pad in a great street in a great area and we couldn't have been happier. Also our new neighbour was a guy we already knew from Mick Taylor's band, so it was good to have someone next door with whom we were already acquainted. Having said that, I can't even remember his bloody name, ha ha. Anyway, all went well and we moved in according to plan.

To celebrate, Kate and I booked a week in Morocco and flew to Marrakech, where we spent a couple of days before going to Agadir. From the moment we stepped off the plane we were hustled by kids trying to flog us useless junk. It got really annoying until we finally gave in and hired one of the local guides to show us around. It was dirt cheap and at least got all the other hucksters off our backs. He was quite good actually and showed us things we'd have never otherwise found by ourselves.

We did all the usual shit like visiting the king's palace and riding round the city walls in a horse-drawn buggy. Also we spent some time in the huge Berber Market, or Souk, as it's called. That was a real buzz with whirling dervishes and snake charmers, fabulous food and anything you wanted to buy at rock-bottom prices if you knew how to haggle, which was all part of the experience. We bought a load of trinkets, a wall rug and a heavy, smelly old goat-hair 'zaytuna' cloak which completely filled our suitcases so we ended up buying more suitcases to carry it all in.

Then we hired a car and took off to a beach hut in faraway Agadir on some remote unspoilt coastline. For atmosphere we preferred Old Agadir rather than the new town, but we didn't really stray far from the beach, which had its own bars and restaurants. After a couple of days with nothing much to do we got bored and started squabbling about something inconsequential. This then turned into a full-scale row and before I knew what was happening Kate was threatening to catch the next plane home. She couldn't do that, of course, as we had pre-booked flights, but details like that didn't matter in the heat of the argument.

After she calmed down, we had a truce and just about made it through to the end of the week. Then disaster struck. As we drove to the airport I got distracted, causing me to knock a Moroccan cop off his motorbike. Though technically he ploughed into us, leaving a bloody great dent in the side of the hire car, it was entirely my fault for cutting him off. By now the cop was seething with anger, seeking vengeance and suddenly as a result I was facing a long stretch in some hell hole of a jail like the one in *Midnight Express*. Boy, was I crapping myself.

61

Putney / Incredible String Band

Fortunately the Moroccan cop wasn't badly injured so in the end they decided not to prosecute, which would presumably be bad for the tourist trade. Even so, until I got onto the plane and safely into the air I was terrified in case they changed their minds.

Once home, things were still very rocky between Kate and me. We briefly struggled on together, but the situation got steadily worse until we finally decided to call it a day. After all our years together, albeit in a slightly unorthodox relationship, it was extremely upsetting, traumatic even, but we both resigned ourselves to the inevitable. It wasn't a particularly acrimonious split and we basically remained friendly-ish, but it was obviously time for me to go. This effectively left me homeless. Kate suggested asking some friends from the Scottish Innerleithen crowd, now based in London, to see if any of them had any spare accommodation. Luckily they had plenty of contacts and turned me on to

Malcolm LeMaistre, a former member of The Incredible String Band, who had a spare room to let in Putney.

My new situation certainly felt rather depressing, but I guess one must take the rough with the smooth and remember that it's all part of life's rich pattern. Things do improve later, though, I promise. Malcolm LeMaistre was previously part of the Stone Monkey troupe of dancers and mime artists who joined The Incredible String Band to enhance the visual performance of the group. He and his 'wifey' girlfriend were living with his studious academic father in a dusty, book-filled apartment overlooking Putney Bridge.

So in I moved with just a few belongings, my guitar and an amazing little recording gizmo I'd recently acquired called the 'Tascam 144 Portastudio'. This brand-new 'pint-sized' four-track cassette-tape machine would soon revolutionise home recording and I managed to buy the very first one in the country. At the trade-show launch I was given a demonstration and the Portastudio surpassed my highest expectations. With cash in hand I paid the man, stuck the magic machine under my arm and rushed straight home to compose a masterpiece or three.

Back at the Putney pad I churned out song after song with a vengeance. For the first time ever, I got the music to sound how I wanted it to sound and not as some cloth-eared producer imagined it. Not only that, the awesome new gizmo literally saved my life during this very vulnerable time. It gave me something to focus on rather than the break-up with Kate and I channelled all my emotions into new songs. This was one of my most creative phases, obviously inspired by heartbreak, which is often the case amongst songwriters. Guess that's why they call it the blues.

It was a very sombre period indeed and for several weeks I hardly saw another living soul and just kept working away.

Malcolm was also in process of splitting up with his woman and always seemed quite depressed and morose. His father was even worse, so we all locked ourselves in our little rooms and got on with our own 'thing'. I was never really sure what their thing was, but after a while Malcolm opened up a bit and we got on quite well. He even started writing lyrics for some of my songs.

Then he told me a few stories about The Incredible String Band and their involvement with Scientology, which I had always regarded as something of an oddball cult. Apparently the whole band would wrap themselves up in silver foil for days on end and sweat the LSD and other drugs out of their systems. Although he never gave away any of their 'big secrets' he did open my eyes to the shadowy hidden workings of the CFR, Trilateral Commission and Bilderberg Group. Especially about how the power elite manipulates world affairs, media, major corporations and the arms industry amongst many other things. It had been many years since I studied Rosicrucianism and the works of Gurdjieff and Ouspensky, so this new information set me back on the righteous path of research into suppressed and occult mystical knowledge.

Putney was OK with a great view over the Thames at the starting point of the Oxford and Cambridge University boat race but was slightly inconvenient with hardly anywhere to park. The only place was in the Star and Garter pub car park over the road next to the river, where they often filmed *Minder*, but you had to be careful. There were only limited spaces and unless you got the highest one or two spots there was a good chance your car would end up underwater at high tide by next morning. I've seen many a distressed motorist over there that didn't know about the flooding and got badly caught out. After a while Malcolm decided he was moving back to Scotland and his dad wouldn't want me hanging around, so my only realistic option now was to doss at my sister's up north until I sorted myself out.

By now I was feeling pretty miserable when fortuitously one evening whilst out on a bender I bumped into Paul, an old mate of mine, at a wine bar. He was real decent guy and we always got on well ever since my old mum took him in after he once ran away from home. This was years ago after a falling-out with his folks, but he'd never forgotten the favour. He stayed with us till they'd sorted out their differences and always appreciated what we'd done. As we chatted, Paul told me that he was now living in Islington and had a couple of antique shops in Camden Passage, so he'd evidently done very well for himself. Right now he was on one of his regular buying trips where he'd scour the country for bargains and even go 'knocking' on doors in true 'Lovejoy' style to see what people would part with.

After hearing his success story I then related my current tale of woe and mentioned I was sick of Limbo Land and desperately wanted to move back to London. Amazingly, as fate would have it, he just happened to have a spare room and kindly said I could stay at his place for as long as I liked, which was brilliant. A few days later I arrived in Islington to find a luxurious balcony flat overlooking a large garden square near Highbury Corner. It was an absolute Aladdin's cave full of antique treasures and incredibly he let me have the accommodation rent-free. I could hardly believe my good fortune. At last things were looking up again.

62

Islington / Hope and Anchor / Pogues

So, after moving back to London I was finally getting over the break-up with my ex and things began to shape up nicely. At Paul's place it didn't take long to ensconce myself and assorted belongings, including my trusty vintage pre-CBS Stratocaster guitar and Tascam Portastudio. Paul's girlfriend Annette and her cat were also resident at the flat and we all soon settled into a pleasant routine. The place was really sumptuous and I quickly adjusted to a life of luxury in Islington, which was now the latest property hotspot with plenty happening around and about. Neighbourhood hangouts were the King's Head theatre pub, Screen on the Green, Tramshed jazz club plus stacks of restaurants and bars.

On Upper Street was the Hare and Hounds music pub as well as the acclaimed 'Hope and Anchor', or the 'Grope and Wanker', as we called it. I've forgotten the number of great bands I've seen there, but a couple of all-time favourites that spring to mind were Robyn Hitchcock's Soft Boys and Joe Ely's honky-tonk Texas rockers The Flatlanders. Joe Ely was doing a live recording there with guests Joe Strummer and Carlene Carter and was one of the best gigs I've been to. Another night at the 'Grope' I chatted up Pogues bass player Cait O'Riordan. We arranged a date, had a few drinks and went to the trendy La Cantina Mexican restaurant in Covent Garden but never really hit it off. She was still only a wild Irish kid and the age gap far too wide, so that's one that got away. I heard she married Elvis Costello a few years later.

As I continued writing more and more songs, my drummer mate Steve Holley from Wings turned me on to his publisher David Paramor, nephew of Norrie Paramor, who had produced hits for Cliff Richard and Helen Shapiro. David, who was formally with RCA, Columbia and EMI, had now set up on his own as Sunbury Music acting for Gary Numan and Rick Wakeman. As well as his own songs, Steve Holley owned all the rights to the Louis Jordan catalogue, which Sunbury Music also took care of. So upon his recommendation I went to see David with the new material recorded on the portastudio, and he put me in touch with Dick Polak, who ran Jam Studios in north London.

Dick was probably better known as a fashion photographer and for designing album sleeves for members of The Beatles. Also for being married to Edina Ronay, knitwear guru and daughter of restaurant guide writer Egon Ronay. It was Bonfire Night when Dick and Edina invited me to their home for drinks and to hear the new songs. To celebrate Guy Fawkes in the traditional manner I took along a box of bangers and after a few beverages started lobbing them insanely round the garden to the delight of their young daughter but the horror of Edina. I never could behave. Luckily I wasn't ejected and they loved the songs so we arranged a session at Jam Studios which was owned by a couple of pretty young Swedish boys we called Hansel and Gretel.

These two were very keen at first but ended up more interested in cocaine, which wasn't really my scene. To me it was just expensive speed that lasted ten minutes instead of ten hours so I couldn't see the point. Anyway, we weren't making a great deal of progress and the enthusiasm gradually wore off. We never actually finished the project, and next thing I knew, the studio wasn't there anymore, so I assume they'd buggered off back to Sweden.

At Paul's place, table football was a popular pastime, so we organised a house championship. There were always plenty of visitors and clients round buying antiques and such like, so everyone got involved in the game and things got very heated on occasions. Paul was ultra-competitive and was really into sports of every description, unlike me. The only sport I really like is boxing, which is strange as I'm a spineless wimp at heart. To keep in shape we began jogging and started running two or three miles every evening around the mean streets of Islington. Down Liverpool Road to the Angel, through Chapel Market and back up Caledonia Road past Pentonville Prison. It was always quite eerie in the dead of night, sprinting past the grim high walls of the jailhouse on the final stretch (pardon the pun).

Like I say, Paul was really competitive and physically fit, having been trained by Olympic athletic coach Frank Dick. At first it was a struggle for me to even make it past the first corner, but over the weeks I built up enough stamina to complete the course. No way could I keep up with Paul, but he kept encouraging me until I was reaching respectable lap times. Day by day I was getting faster and was soon managing to run alongside without too much struggle. Then he started getting worried as I began to get a little too good.

He always had plenty in reserve and could always pip me until one day I beat him fair and square. Yeeesssss! Poor old Paul, he didn't like it one bit. By now I was now fit as a fiddle and had dropped from thirteen stone down to below eleven, which was the target after years of bingeing.

63

Ranelagh Yacht Club

Annette decided to move out of Islington to her own place over in Barons Court after a bust-up with Paul, who I reckon had been seeing one of the girls from Bananarama on the quiet. Paul had quite a few celeb friends and regular visitors, including keyboard player Karl Wallinger who'd been musical director of *The Rocky Horror Show* before joining the Waterboys. We were both invited down to see him at the Secret Policeman's Ball for the debut performance of his new band 'World Party' just before he wrote Robbie Williams big smash hit 'she's the one'.

Then after a boozy night at Dingwall's we staggered back to his flat at three in the morning to record a load of old country and western standards in his home studio. Don't know what the neighbours thought as Karl knocked the hell out of his drum kit in the middle of the night while I screeched and a hollered Hank Williams hillbilly songs at the top of my voice. Karl had a few very successful years with

World Party before getting ill after a brain aneurism. As so often happens we lost contact but happily he seems to have recovered and is now back on the road again with a new CD out called *Arkeology*.

As well as antiques, Paul and I had another project on the go, running a rehearsal room in Putney that was situated very close to the illustrious Hurlingham Club. It had the deceptively impressive name of the 'Ranelagh Yacht Club' but in reality was a gangsters' after-hours drinking den under the railway arches, frequented by West London's most vicious psychopaths, hard nuts and felons. The guy who owned it was trying to diversify and go legit with three empty arches that he wanted to develop. We met through his girlfriend Maggie, whom I always remembered as a sweet, peace-loving hippy chick from my psychedelic Finchley days, but she was now helping run this dodgy dive. They both thought our rehearsal room idea sounded good, so asked us to come in and set it up as soon as possible.

The arches were empty shells so needed a fair amount of work to get them functioning. We planned six luxury studio units to be hired out to major record companies, many of whom were based close by in Fulham Road and Chelsea. The club owner was going to organise the building and materials whilst Paul and I would arrange finance by pulling in a couple of silent partners. The main club area was used by the bands until we got the first unit up and running and we soon had a steady stream of clients including Mick Taylor's band, The Boys, Gary Numan and punk band Mean Street.

At the same time we were busy knocking the other units into shape and all seemed to be going to plan. Then one day I arrived to find the arches crawling with 'Old Bill' turning the place over for hooky timber and other stolen items apparently supplied by an Essex pikey gang. I had to pretend to be an innocent punter just looking to hire a practice room before managing to skedaddle post-haste. Up to that point the project had been totally kosher, so when this crap suddenly hit the fan, Paul and I were extremely ticked off to say the least.

After this occurrence we began to regret our involvement and were trying hard to think of some face-saving way out when fate intervened. When previously mentioned thug John 'Biffo' Bindon (Vicky Hodge's boyfriend) supposedly owed drug debts to a rival South London mob, Johnny Darke and his Wild Bunch turned up one night at the club to get him. The place ended up knee-deep in claret after a massive fight broke out and John Darke was stabbed to death by Bindon, who claimed to be acting in self-defence.

Bindon himself had multiple stab wounds but managed to escape to Dublin by plane but was eventually caught and brought back to face a murder charge at the Old Bailey. At the trial he was found not guilty after character witness Bob Hoskins (yet another pal of Paul's) managed to sway the jury's verdict in his favour by humorously describing Biffo as, "Like a big gentle teddy bear, all lovely and cuddly." Immediately after this highly publicised incident, the Ranelagh Yacht Club was closed down for ever and that was the end of that.

Somewhere around this time I had an actress girlfriend called Eve who was just finishing a drama course in Ealing and about to present a play that was her end-of-term assessment. All her family and friends including myself were invited along to support this grand finale at the college. The audience section was just two long rows of seats and we were ushered in and placed alongside guest actors, tutors, adjudicators and various other dignitaries, all set to judge the quality of this farewell dramatic offering. It was only accessible through a door at one end, so once you were in and seated you were basically stuck and couldn't move till the finish of the performance. Eve was normally an outrageous show-off but was understandably nervous on this, her big night. I was also feeling nervous on her behalf and, to calm my nerves, had drunk several pints of beer just prior to the show.

The play began and everything was OK for fifteen minutes or so before I started feeling uncomfortable and needing to nip to the loo. Too late I suddenly realised I couldn't get out and tried putting it off for another ten minutes but by then I was bursting. A few more minutes went by and I couldn't hold it much longer. Would this damn play never end? By now I was sweating with panic and my mind had gone blank. I could think of nothing else but getting to a bloody urinal. Finally I could stand it no more and bowed to the inevitable. The only available exit strategy was to leap up and dash directly across centre stage as inconspicuously as possible and hope nobody noticed. The stupid grin and royal wave didn't help as I tripped and sent stage props flying en route. I don't know who was most mortified, me or Eve, but all I cared about at that moment was draining the main vein. Shamefully I hung around outside after relieving myself and waited to face the music.

When the play did finally finish I was expecting the worst, convinced that my dumb blunder had jeopardised all her future prospects. Well, to put it mildly she wasn't best pleased, but after hearing it was a huge success despite my worst efforts, I managed to squirm my way out it. All the audience members gave me filthy scowls or made tut-tutting noises as they left, but when you've gotta go, you've gotta go.

Eve had the knack of bringing out the prize plonker in me and this was just one of many embarrassing incidents we shared before our time was up. She was very funny and used to say I was mentally disturbed because my birth name was so hard and guttural. For instance, she would gleefully depict how as a baby, people would leer into my cot and shout 'CRAIGGER' at me in harsh, jarring tones that shaped the whole of my fucked-up personality for life. Whereas she was 'EEEEVE', which was soft and calm, all sugar and spice, thus making her perfect and harmonious. Makes sense to me.

Another embarrassing incident was when I met a very good friend of hers, Liverpool poet extraordinaire Brian Patten. The guy is brilliant and has the softest, most hypnotic speaking voice you ever heard. For anyone who says they don't like poetry I challenge them to listen to 'So Many Different Lengths of Time' and not shed a tear. Anyway, Brian and his lady invited us over to their swish Holland Park house for drinks. No common or garden Scouser is he. After a good tipple and some arty-farty conversation someone brought out the grass, which is the kiss of death for me after a few libations. I never learn and within seconds I was emptying the contents of my stomach over the balcony into the street below. God help any passers-by. Exactly the same thing happened another time at Pink Fairy Twink's house.

It wasn't long before a few choice acting roles came along and we had a trip up to the Edinburgh festival, where she appeared in Ibsen's *Hedda Gabler*. For two hours in the afternoon I had to sit and suffer this high-brow nonsense which to me was all complete Gablerdegook... Oh well, suit yourselves. Afterwards though, we'd be out on the town with her fellow thespians at the Assembly Rooms enjoying the rest of the 'Fringe' and some wild Auld Reekie nightlife.

Eve got her first big television acting role in a classic 1980s gangster series followed by countless other TV and film parts. She began working so much that we gradually lost contact, though I did see her singing with a band sometime later. Yeah, she was alright, was Eve.

64

Pepperdines Sarsaparilla

After our disastrous rehearsal room debacle at the Ranelagh Yacht Club, it was time to move on and start contemplating some more lucrative new project. As it happened I'd been thinking for a while about Sarsaparilla, a popular drink from the old Wild West Cowboy movies that everyone had heard of but which you couldn't buy in the UK for love nor money. There was obviously a huge gap in the market and I felt a sudden urge to do something about it. All at once it seemed the right time to get my fizzy pop-czar career up and running.

First job was to dig out the old chemistry set, don a white coat and head on down to my secret underground laboratory like a mad professor. However, after dabbling with various brews and potions for a while, I came to the conclusion it would be much easier and far more sensible just to contact a commercial flavour house and let the professionals do the donkey work.

Next, my former graphic design partners Baz and Caz came up with a selection of ideas for the label and we finally settled on the catchy brand name of 'Josiah Pepperdine's Olde English Sarsaparilla'. Pepperdine was in fact the family name of one of my great aunts somewhere down the line that sounded suitably hip and vaguely reminiscent of a Victorian temperance bar. In addition to actual labels for the bottles I also printed a load of sticky-backed advertising leaflets which were glued surreptitiously overnight to every lamppost in town. Predictably I was soon paid a visit by the council demanding their immediate removal or else face prosecution. It would have taken forever so to be honest I didn't bother and thankfully that was the last I heard of it.

There was a bottling plant in Pontefract that was willing to make trial pallets of one-litre plastic bottles at a decent price, so after collection I started selling them anywhere I could. After punting the drink round every newsagent, sweet shop and independent store within a five-mile radius, the stuff was flying out. Everyone paid cash and took a couple of dozen bottles at a time, so it was just a matter of waiting for repeat orders. I didn't plan on schlepping round individual shops for long so found a local 'cash and carry' to take over after providing them with a list of existing customers.

By this time it was about the mid-1980s and I'd moved from my mate Paul's apartment in Islington to a flat in Earls Court. Sales of 'Pepperdines Sarsaparilla' were well on target and everything was going to plan when a friend from Canada came to stay at my place for a couple of weeks. By a strange coincidence he was acting as UK sales manager for Coors beer, who were currently promoting a new range of natural-flavoured sodas. Although naturally flavoured, they were laced with sugar or corn syrup, but the 'natural' aspect immediately grabbed my attention and logically seemed to be the way forward. No one had ever done a completely one hundred percent natural, sugar-free, preservative and additive-free soft drink, so why shouldn't I be the pioneer? He who dares wins and all that.

After this revelation I was now inspired to take things to the next level. In order to raise sufficient finance and get the job done properly, I approached Bill Gibson, my old 1960s band buddy from The Imps. He now owned a successful engineering company in Sutton Coldfield called Zytek and was always looking to invest in lucrative projects. It sounds unusual but his daughter had a food additive allergy and couldn't drink any normal pop. He agreed if it was possible to develop a natural carbonated cola without any nasty e-numbers that would allow his little girl to enjoy soft drinks like all her pals, we were in business. No sooner said than done and we became partners. So to complete the range we added cola, lemonade, root beer, ginger and ginseng to the existing sarsaparilla flavour and changed the company name from Pepperdine's to 'FREE DRINKS'.

There were very few factories in the UK with pasteurisers necessary for this method of production, so the search was on. The first one we found was Devenish Brewers down in Cornwall and to check them out I travelled down by a Trathens 'Neoplan Skyliner' luxury double-decker coach from Victoria to Redruth. It was a long trek, but bizarrely, apart from the driver and conductress I was the only passenger on board for the whole journey.

The good thing was that it had a toilet compartment. The bad thing was that just as I was having a pee, the coach lurched and the bog seat lid fell down, causing me to accidentally slash all over the floor. Problem was, the wee trickled in a steady stream under the door into the bus and there was nowhere for me to hide. I couldn't blame it on any other passengers because there weren't any, so for the next few hours all I could do was avoid the conductress, who obviously knew it was me. Embarrassing or what? Thankfully I got a different driver and conductor for the return journey. After Devenish Brewery agreed to make the first batch I bought myself a smart new suit and set off round the UK on a major sales drive.

Pepperdine's Sarsaparilla.

65

Free Drinks

It was now the mid-1980s and, having created FREE DRINKS, the world's first one hundred percent natural range of soda-pops, we quickly set about promoting all the new flavours nationwide. However, just as we were starting out, we discovered that a very well-established health-food firm had a similar idea and were also making plans to launch a natural cola drink. Being so cocksure about being first to the market, they must have been quite surprised when FREE DRINKS appeared out of nowhere and pipped them at the post. I'd have loved to have seen their faces when they suddenly realised they'd been gazumped, especially later as we constantly out-performed and out-sold them at every turn.

FREE DRINKS was so revolutionary (and tasty) that it didn't take long to find plenty of wholesale customers within the health-food trade. Very soon we had all the biggest ones signed up and ordering significant quantities. Companies like Brewhurst, Goodness Foods, Suma and Holland &

Barrett. They were all taking multiple pallet-loads on a regular basis, but no matter how hard we tried, it seemed impossible to break into the mainstream supermarket chains. As always, they were dominated and controlled by the major corporations who don't like or want any competition.

In an attempt to remedy this we started doing trade shows and took on an agent in Manchester that specialised in networking events at major sporting venues. One of these was at Ascot races with a marquee in the Royal enclosure, where I was seated next to football commentator Kenneth (they think it's all over, it is now) Wolstenholme. Unfortunately I didn't manage to win anything on the gee-gees that day and we never did crack the supermarkets either. It didn't really seem to matter, though, and we found a much bigger bottling plant at Featherstone called Crystal Spring Drinks to deal with all the extra orders we were now taking in the health sector. Because business was so good I now had a regular salary plus a company car and all the perks that went with the job.

Soon FREE DRINKS was almost running itself, with administration and sales being taken care of at the Zytek office in Sutton

Free Drinks Flyer.

Coldfield. We had changed factories yet again to Robinsons in Manchester and also Cameron's historic brewery up in Hartlepool. This was now owned by boxer Billy Walker's brother George Walker of property company Brent Walker. Being contract bottlers, they were also making similar designer drinks to ours including Ame and Purdeys as well as their own famous Cameron's beer.

Seeing how well we were doing, James, the sales manager of our main rival, for whatever reason jumped ship and offered us his services. We were initially reluctant about taking him on, but he gave us all sorts of convincing spiel about his contacts and getting us into all the major supermarkets, especially as his girlfriend was a buyer for Sainsbury's. In fact he must have been a bloody brilliant salesman to persuade us to agree to his extortionate rates of commission. In reality he barely increased turnover at all, certainly not enough to justify employing him, but his contract was watertight.

By now my business partner Bill Gibson and I had also launched another company called 'Elixir Deluxe' selling two new stimulant designer drinks containing herbs and legal highs such as guarana. One was called Potion No. 9 and the other was Ginseng Sling. Next thing we knew, James had 'borrowed' the concept and brought out two almost identical products to sell in direct competition with Elixir Deluxe. Unbelievable. It was a step too far and Bill went berserk, threatening to sue and all sorts.

Anyway Jimbo relented and agreed to add his two drinks to our range. His new flavours were Guarana Gold and Lapaccho, which contained lots of other druggy stuff like prickly ash bitters, ginseng, damiana, royal jelly and guarana, of course. To be fair they were well packaged, tasted great and complemented Elixir Deluxe very nicely. Trouble was, they were all too expensive and didn't really sell that brilliantly. We figured a bigger bottle would make them more cost-effective and affordable, so we set about designing a larger size.

After searching round we found a sexy-shaped one-litre bottle that was then printed by an annealing process directly onto the glass. It looked amazing and Cameron's forged ahead with production. The first three flavours went through the hot pasteuriser without a hitch but then on the fourth catastrophe struck. Ten thousand bottles were already in the pipeline when one by one they started to explode. The whole factory ground to a halt and was evacuated as the place went up like an atom bomb. It took weeks to clear skips full of broken glass and assess the collateral damage. This multi-million-pound filling line was costing the brewery a fortune in lost production and someone was going to have to pay. What a bloody nightmare. Thus began the long process of investigation as to whose fault it was. Was it us, the brewery, the bottle suppliers, the bottle printers or anyone else who might in any way be involved?

After several agonising weeks the final verdict was that the bottle printer was more or less to blame. The guy was a huge ex-miner and right bruiser that hated my guts from day one. He claimed we didn't do enough research into how the inks would react, although we'd done everything we could and it was ultimately his responsibility anyway. He wasn't interested in any discussion but just wanted to kick my head in. He didn't like James either because he was a flash Porsche-driving southern softy.

It was only Bill's impressive negotiating skills that saved the day when he proposed a mutually acceptable solution or else he'd sue for the full amount. Luckily Cameron's were heavily insured for the bulk of the damage so we actually ended up getting off fairly lightly.

After that it was kind of the end of the road for Elixir Deluxe and although FREE sales were very respectable, it wasn't exactly setting the world on fire. If we could have cracked the supermarkets it might have been a different story, but basically we were getting bored and decided to sell the company. A health food company on the south coast wanted to buy us out so we worked out a reasonable deal and split the profits.

Surprisingly James also offered to buy our shares in Elixir Deluxe which we had figured was now worthless, so in a way that was a nice unexpected bonus. After the sale I kept the company car and was quite flush. With money and time on my hands, I decided to get involved once again with the music scene.

Elixir Deluxe Flyer.

66

Busking In London

After a spell living in Islington I'd eventually moved to a first-floor apartment in a pleasant tree-lined crescent in Earls Court, just off Old Brompton Road. However it wasn't long before I discovered that the woman in the flat above was a genuine certified lunatic, who once a month at full moon went through a lycanthropic transformation.

All through the night she'd drag heavy furniture across the floor, impersonating a herd of elephants or constantly leave bath-taps running to flood the place. The worst thing was that sometimes she didn't bother flushing her bog so that excrement overflowed and dripped unappealingly down my living-room wall. The mad cow was impossible and wouldn't listen to reason, so the only solution was to call the cops, who'd break down her door and haul her off to the laughing academy for a few days. Then she'd come back and start all over again.

For three weeks of the month it would be silent as the grave and you wouldn't even know she was there. Then at full moon she would go bonkers again, but at least it was a recognisable routine that I learned to cope with. This went on for quite a while before the situation finally resolved itself after she was forced by mental health services to have some sort of compulsorily treatment.

A good mate Geoff Marshall, who was a newly qualified architect, asked if he could doss at the gaff whilst looking for a job in London. He was also an excellent musician, so during his stay we started busking for fun and put a really good set of Hank Williams and 'Rusty and Doug Kershaw' Cajun hillbilly songs together for playing down tube stations, mainly Notting Hill Gate.

I'd already coined the name 'Jazzabilly' for some of the music I was writing when I spotted a wanted ad in Time Out for a jazzabilly guitarist. Intrigued, I arranged to meet up at Pyramid Arts in Hackney, where the band was auditioning. They were a fantastic young jump-jive outfit called 'Doo-Be-Wah' and as soon as they struck up I knew I was out of my depth. The arrangements were unfamiliar and complex, with chord changes every bar. Without knowing the songs inside out it was nigh on impossible to follow at the speed they were playing.

Slightly dismayed after struggling best I could, they ended up listening to a load of my ideas and surprisingly really liked what I was doing. As a result we instantly became buddies and started hanging out together, even though I never did actually join their band. They eventually found a new guitarist, changed the name to 'Bingo Pyjama' and started gigging and performing their own material at gigs around London.

Originally they hailed from the Manchester scene, with bassman Steve Harrison and sax player Paul O'Hara being the two main guys. They were managed by Paul's brother 'Bo', who was a street-smart wide boy, so I imagined they'd do really well commercially, but unfortunately there's no justice in the music game. Nothing happened and eventually Bo went off to live on a mountain top in India, lugging his grand piano with him, which always conjures up a very surreal Laurel and Hardy type image in my mind.

The guys were all totally skint and living in what must have been the slummiest squat in London. I went round there once and the only way in was through the basement via a load of rubble and some corrugated tin sheeting. There was no electric or gas, so in order to cook and keep warm, they'd burn floorboards and any old furniture lying about the house. The garden was a jungle, none of the plumbing worked, and the place was skank and crawling with vermin. No rubbish was ever thrown out and they literally lived amongst festering heaps of stinking refuse piled up to the ceiling. However, for a bunch of northern oiks this was the height of luxury.

To earn a crust, Steve came out busking with us and would push his big old double bass along the street balanced on a wheel which always looked very comical. It wasn't long before he joined a unique band of Irish lunatics called 'Sons of the Desert' whose first ever gig was at Brixton Academy on the live TV show 'Big World Café' presented by a young and stunningly gorgeous Mariella Frostrup. They were brilliant and for months were courted by Ensign Records, the hottest label around, with Sinead O'Connor, Boomtown Rats, Waterboys and World Party amongst their successful chart acts. However, instead of biting their hands off, the band got too greedy for a better deal and completely blew it. They could have been mega by now but instead drifted back into obscurity.

Steve was so pissed off with them for not signing; he left and moved to Paris, where he now plays in an assortment of different bands, orchestras and ensembles of many varying styles. It's very weird because poor little Stevie has a slight stutter in his native English tongue yet speaks perfect fluent French with no problems whatsoever. This stutter got him into trouble once when subbing at a pub gig with a gypsy jazz band called 'The Hot Club of Marylebone'. Although he was doing both the band and the pub a favour by standing in for the regular bass player, who was ill, the bar manager wouldn't serve him a drink. When he heard Steve's stutter he just assumed he was drunk and refused to listen to reason, so they started arguing. The more Steve tried to explain he wasn't drunk the worse the argument became until they ended up brawling outside in the street.

During the long hot summer days we'd go busking down tube stations or in Leicester Square, where we'd always draw a large and generous crowd. Later on we'd maybe do a circuit of local hostelries whilst usually avoiding the naff Aussie pubs and gay haunts of Earls Court. All the corny gay guys looked like Freddie Mercury clones with black banana moustaches and cowboy-style leather chaps. In fact the local gay bar on the corner was actually called 'Chaps', though we mainly headed to the 'Water Rat' or 'Roebuck' on King's Road. The best place was probably the 'Man in the Moon', which was an actor's pub with a theatre downstairs, run by the father of Row-land from Grange Hill. Tom Baker, the definitive 'Doctor Who' with a scarf, was always in there permanently inebriated.

There were some great parties and one celebrity shindig I went to with Stevie was at a flash house in Little Venice belonging to a songwriter called Scott English who'd written 'Bend Me Shape Me' for Amen Corner and also 'Hi Ho Silver Lining'. He found it quite amusing when I told him that my band The Dimples had been offered 'Hi Ho' before Jeff Beck but had turned it down.

By coincidence another guest there was our former producer Kenny Young who'd written 'Under the Board Walk', so it was almost like old times again. Boy George and his band were also mingling, as were lots of other famous names and faces. Steve had taken along his double bass, so I grabbed a guitar and we launched into our busking set which went down a storm. All the guys from Boy George's band joined in and we had a brilliant time. They absolutely loved it and everybody was asking us where we were gigging next so they could come down to support us. No one could believe it when we told them we were just mucking about busking for kicks.

67

Gigging In Munich

One day whilst busking, Steve and I were approached and offered a rather prestige gig in Germany by an international cultural organisation called the British Council. The fee was very generous, plus all our air fares, hotel and expenses were to be paid for, so we thought why the hell not?

Steve was on double bass with me on acoustic guitar and vocals. We also managed to recruit a lap steel player called Lonesome Tone who had a single out on Stiff Records called 'Mum, Dad, Love, Hate and Elvis'. He was a really amusing guy who talked exactly like Max Bygraves and in all seriousness kept saying, "I wanna tell you a story," but didn't even realise he was doing it. Well, it kept us in stitches anyway.

What happened was that some other act had dropped out and we were offered a last-minute replacement booking in Munich at the Culture Centrum (Kulturzentrum Gasteig) which was a gigantic-sized venue. Unfortunately we only had one small amplifier between us, so I had to use a huge plastic spoon instead of a normal-sized plectrum to get more volume. Even so, we still went down really well and managed to pull a few local frauleins into the bargain.

Lonesome Tone had previously lived in Munich and could fluently *'sprechende de Deutsch'*, which was really handy, plus he knew the best places to go. He showed us round all the interesting bits, including the Burgerbraukeller, where we supped a few steins of Germany's finest lager bier. This was the famous location of Hitler's failed Nazi Party coup attempt in 1923, now called the 'Beer Hall Putsch'. Hitler was shot and arrested for treason and served five years in Landsberg prison, where he wrote *Mein Kampf.*

Other than that I don't remember a great deal, apart from an angry old lady prodding me violently in the ribs with an umbrella for smoking on a tram. During our stay, a big pre-Christmas fair was being held in the Marienplatzt, which was the main city square. The place looked stunning with its beautiful glockenspiel tower, but it was absolutely freezing all the time we were there. In fact, straight after the final gig, we only just managed get out of Munich on the last plane before the airport became snowbound and was closed down. Echoes of the Busby Babes. Until we were safely in the air we couldn't help but dwell on the tragic Manchester United air disaster that had happened on that very spot thirty years previously. Then arriving back at Heathrow we had our own near-death experience after the worst, most God-awful landing ever and I honestly thought we were goners. As we disembarked in a state of shock, the hostess that Tone had been chatting up for the whole flight confided that it was the pilot's first solo touchdown. Bloody hell, now she tells us.

Apart from busking, Steve and I also went to quite a few memorable parties. One of these was at the home of actress

Antonia de Sancha, who'd been embroiled in a salacious newspaper scandal about an extramarital affair with the Secretary of State for Sport and National Heritage, David Mellor. Sleaze spread like wildfire throughout the gutter press after she did a kiss 'n' tell expose for creepy Max Clifford that subsequently damaged both their careers. At the party was an old black dude in the corner quietly tinkling the ivories when Steve decided to liven up the proceedings and inched the guy off the piano stool to take over. Steve was a very good boogie-woogie pianist but didn't realise whom he'd just nudged out the way. It was none other than the legendary Slim Gaillard, inventor of the original jive-talk and hipster slang dialect (slanguage) known as 'Vout' or Vout-O-Renee.

Slim was also an ex-boxer, mobster and rum-runner for the Purple Gang, Al Capone and bootlegger Joseph Kennedy, father of JFK. So all in all it was a very close shave for little Stevie. It was only when we got chatting to him that we actually discovered who this cool cat really was. Only the cult 'Daddy' of all time. The man who had inspired Kerouac and written such novelty jazz classics as 'Flat Foot Floogy (with a Floy Floy)', 'Dunkin' Bagels', 'Tutti Frutti' and 'Cement Mixer (Puttie Puttie)'. During the '40s, before we were even born, he'd starred in films like *Hellzapoppin'* as *Slim & Slam* and made records with Charlie Parker and Dizzy Gillespie. Boy, did we feel stoooopid.

Another one of the famous faces at the party was a former wrestler called 'Leon Arras the Man from Paris', better known as comedy actor Brian Glover who played the sadistic sports master in the film *Kes*. There was only one bog at the party and a bit of a queue was forming. By now, both myself and Brian were so desperate for a wee that we went in for a slash together. Hence my greatest claim to fame is having a piss sword-fence with the Tetley Tea Man.

68

Demon Records / Muswell Hill Murders

During the 1980s, I'd occasionally meet up with my old buddy Pete Macklin, who was now a big-time record company executive. He was co-director with Jake Riviera of Demon and Radar Records that managed Elvis Costello and Nick Lowe amongst many others. Later, Demon was sold to the Woolworths music chain and more recently Pete started Floating World Records. As a result we'd attend lots of band launches and new artist signings, which could be a lot of fun. At the Wembley Country Music Festival in 1989, I even got to meet rockabilly legend Sleepy LaBeef, which was a big thrill.

By now, Pete was quite affluent and decided to buy a house at 23 Cranley Gardens in Muswell Hill. It's an expensive area of North London but even so he still managed to bag himself an incredible bargain. How so? Well, the house in question only turned out to be the former home of notorious serial killer and necrophiliac Dennis 'the menace' Nilsen. As you can well imagine, there wasn't exactly a long queue of enthusiastic potential buyers apart from a few weirdoes like Pete.

Better known as The Muswell Hill Murderer, Nilsen had strangled and chopped up the bodies of at least twelve young men that he'd lured back to the house. He then boiled the corpses before flushing the remains down the toilet, which over time caused serious plumbing problems. Dyno-Rod were eventually called in and discovered it was lumps of rotting flesh and bits of bone that were blocking the drains at the rear of the building.

This is this very same spot where Pete held his regular BBQs. He obviously had a macabre sense of humour and invited me to one of these sinister soirees, together with a few of his friends, including Paul Riley from Chilli Willi and the Red Hot Peppers, and eccentric genius Viv Stanshall from Bonzo Dog Doo-Dah Band. Of course, after eating our chicken legs, it was obviously a big joke and riotously funny to pretend we'd just picked the bones out from the fabled drain of death which we were virtually sitting on top of. Gruesome or what?

Pete was always good for a laugh, but sometimes we'd maybe just have a quiet drink at one of our favourite pubs. The Flask in Highgate was always a popular choice and another was the trusty old Prince of Wales in Holland Park, where I bumped into an old girlfriend of mine. Her name was Gwen Earl, a ravishing redhead and girl about town who I'd not seen since my Kensington Market days. She still looked great and we immediately carried on from where we'd left off. Gwen had a colourful past to say the least, but that just made life more interesting. Amongst other things she'd run an antique shop in Portobello Road with her girlfriend and been a topless dancer with Zoot Money's psychedelic band

Dantalian's Chariot. She was married but separated from a Jamaican dope dealer and was also an ex-heroin addict.

Admirably, she was now a re-formed character, completely clean with a successful career at Saatchi's and her own house in Shepherd's Bush. Normally, a bird in the Strand is worth two in Shepherd's Bush, but not in Gwen's case. Even so, she still had a few dodgy connections in the Caribbean community and we'd occasionally live dangerously down the 'Mangrove' in Notting Hill, dancing to very loud dub in a dark cellar. I know: me dancing, there's a laugh.

Gwen bore a striking resemblance to the stunningly attractive actress and opera singer Julia Migenes, star of the film version of *Carmen*. It was quite funny when we went to see the *Carmen* movie premiere at the Curzon cinema in Bloomsbury, only to find the whole place full of Julia Migenes lookalikes. We always had a lovely time and were very happy living together, but then she got preggers with serious complications and had to get rid.

After that things kind of changed and we went our own separate ways, though I did write a song about her called 'Good While It Lasted Gwendoline'. Unfortunately we lost contact and she never did get to hear the song. Sadly I heard she later reverted to her old ways and died rather tragically a few years ago. RIP Gwen. An amazing lady and one of a kind.

69

Tex's Royal Connection

During this time I was also helping my sister Jane to research our family tree going back to Scottish roots on my mother's side and Lincolnshire roots on my father's. Going even further back revealed American Civil War and Irish Fenian connections, with one of my granddad's Irish forebears involved with the forming of Glasgow Celtic football club.

All very interesting, but even more interesting is something my dear little old Scottish granny had once said to us in the strictest confidence. She had told the family in hushed tones that we had close connections to Queen Victoria but was sworn to secrecy. That's all she would say and at first we just took it with a pinch of salt. However, she was a staunch church-goer and honest as the day is long, so not at all the type of person to exaggerate or tell tall tales.

After she died, this remarkable disclosure began to nag, urging us to look further into the assertion. Obviously everyone was curious and wondered what on earth could connect us to royalty, even though none of us were particularly keen monarchists. Perhaps someone had been a servant or worked in one of the palaces. Maybe we were somehow related, though it sounded too farfetched to be taken seriously. Whatever it might be, we decided to investigate further.

In Scotland it was traditional for a woman to take the family surname as her middle name, which in my gran's case was Brown, and we began to look more closely into this branch of the family. First job was to visit the graveyard where her ancestors were buried, which was in the small village of Stair in Ayrshire. There were several generations of Browns interred next to the ancient church with all the corresponding names and dates on the gravestones. It transpired that the men had all been blacksmiths in the area of Stair, Tarbolton and Mauchline, homeplace of Rabbie Burns.

Also it became clear they had all been high-ranking Freemasons affiliated with the local Lodge of St David (Tarbolton) Mauchline No. 133 and also Lodge Tarbolton (Kilwinning) St James No. 135. It's important to note that Kilwinning is reputed to be the oldest Lodge, not only in Scotland but in the world. This very historical fabled 'Mother Lodge of Scotland' attributes its origins to the twelfth century and is often called 'Mother Kilwinning'. Basically this place is Masonic Central.

Blacksmiths since ancient times through to the Victorian era were held in high esteem as an integral part of the economy and fabric of society. Not just for making horseshoes but more importantly in forging swords, weapons, gold and other precious metals, etc. In Freemasonic circles the blacksmith was especially revered and equated to the heroic Temple legend 'Tubal Cain', artificer in brass, bronze and iron. Known as 'Vulcan of the Pagans', Tubal Cain was also regarded as the first true chemist, architect and 'God of smithies and working tools'. So quite important then.

Some further digging into the Lodge archives revealed that most of the Browns had in fact been made Grand Masters in their day, as was the celebrated Scottish Bard himself in 1781. The Brown or Broun Clan claim descent from the ancient French royal line, with the Brouns of Colstoun near Edinburgh being heads of the family. The crest interestingly is a lion rampant holding in its paw three gold fleur-de-lys. This coat of arms is an emblem particularly associated with the French monarchy, though the fleur-de-lys also features prominently in British heraldry and the Crown Jewels.

No doubt the Browns and other civic dignitaries regularly rubbed shoulders with the local gentry and members of other secret societies. Especially as fellow Masons, they would always collude and stick together in times of crisis.

One such crisis occurred in 1868 when Queen Victoria mysteriously visited Switzerland after a dramatic increase in weight. After Prince Albert's death in 1861 it was widely rumoured that by 1864 her favourite gillie John Brown had become her lover. There was also speculation that they eventually married, though it was never officially confirmed. Whatever the truth, a steamy romantic letter was allegedly found addressed to 'Darling' Brown from Victoria, which confirmed that during a trip to Loch Ordie, 'Hochmagandy' (the old Scottish word for sexual intercourse) had taken place between them.

It was not long after the letter was discovered that Victoria's mystery trip to Switzerland took place and suggestions made that a child was born there. The insinuations were reinforced when she returned to Scotland having lost a huge amount of weight. If true, the whole scandalous affair would have been quickly and quietly hushed up and the resulting child farmed out to a suitable guardian. This would almost certainly be to the Brown side of the family: definitely not the Royal household of Saxe-Coburg and Gotha. This is when the whole Masonic network would have swung into action to find a trusted 'Brotherhood' member of the Brown Clan to covertly care for the child. An appropriate relative would be chosen in a secluded location such as Stair to allow the wee bairn to be brought up well out of the public eye, and here is the possible connection.

My granny's great-grandfather (the blacksmith) died in 1859, but his wife Sarah Barr Brown lived on for a further thirty-five years, and this is where it gets fascinating. Unaccountably, out of the blue in 1869 after being widowed for ten years, she puzzlingly 'adopted' a baby boy called John Brown (born 11/4/1869), so the dates match perfectly. Also because the Masonic fraternity is universally renowned for taking care of its own distressed widows and orphans, Sarah Brown is a perfect candidate as well as the perfect cover.

However, even with all this mounting evidence we suddenly hit a brick wall and the trail went cold. This wasn't helped by the fact that Victoria's journals were expurgated by her youngest daughter Princess Beatrice, the Queen's literary executor who thought her mother's diaries were too frank and so she destroyed them. Obviously without further definitive proof it remains speculation, even though the timing is spot on. So, for now at least, until such time as we've unearthed fresh new evidence, it must remain nothing more than a fanciful theory.

Finally it seems a strange coincidence that my granny's husband and most of their friends continued the metal-working tradition and were all involved in the steel industry as well as being Freemasons. It's quite mystifying how neatly everything ties up. Then again we might be barking completely up the wrong tree and the Queen Victoria connection is something else entirely.

70

Sooterkin

For the festive season many moons ago I went to stay at my sister Jane's country residence up in the north. A friend nearby was having a New Year's Eve bash so I went along to catch up with Bazzer and a few other old friends I'd not seen for years. I'm very glad I went because that's where I got it together with Josie, my girlfriend, missus, sweetheart, spouse, love of my life or whatever you want to call it. Actually it's high time somebody invented a sensible name for people that live together but who aren't married.

Girlfriend sounds ridiculous once you hit thirty. Partner sounds like we're in business together. Other half sounds like she's my Siamese twin and lady friend sounds like a feminine shaving product. Squaw or lodger are quite good, but the best one I've found so far is sooterkin, an old Scottish word for girlfriend. Curiously another meaning for sooterkin is a fabled small creature about the size of a mouse that certain women were believed to have given birth to. The origin of this was in the eighteenth century, when even eminent physicians of the day considered it factual.

Anyway, we'd always secretly fancied each other from afar since the 1960s, but she married young, had kids and disappeared swiftly from the scene. At the Hogmanay do I was mucking about as usual, setting my hair on fire and such like when we got flirting and hit it off. She told me she was recently divorced and we arranged to meet again and had a few dates. It then started getting a bit too serious and I wasn't really ready for commitment at that stage, so I backed off until a year or so later when I realised I couldn't get her out of my mind.

To cut a long story short I managed to get back in touch and was invited up to her newly acquired abode up in East Yorkshire. It's quite amusing that I only went up for a dirty weekend and never really went back home to London again. She had moved there to start a fresh new life with her daughter Katie and was renovating a quaint Victorian terrace cottage in Leven, a small village near Beverley. Her son Steven was away at Manchester University and Katie was still at school. To earn a living she was working for 'Warings' selling animal feed around local farms and had a little hatchback that came with the job. I did suggest she should trade it in for a big pink Cadillac with cow-horns on the bonnet and advertise herself as 'COWGIRL JOSIE LEE' down the side of the car, which would have been brilliant publicity, but no one ever listens to me.

Moving up to the Yorkshire countryside made a refreshing change as I was getting totally disillusioned with London. Tube trains were awful, crowded and unhygienic. Traffic was awful. Parking was awful and even the music scene was awful. Everything in the capital was getting worse not better. Anyway, whilst I was off cavorting, my mate Nigel was looking after my London flat and proved reliable.

After several years of chaos and turmoil I was actually enjoying a bit of normality and domestication again for a change. That is apart from housemaid's knee that I got from stoking the coal fires before gas was installed in the village. Eventually Josie left Warings to start her own telecommunications company based in Harrogate and for a while life was sweet. Things were going far too well and obviously something was bound foul up and it sure did, big time.

Up until now all this writing nonsense has just been a bit of a lark but I've really been dreading how to relate what happened next. In the summer of 1991 there was a fateful knock on the front door. Standing there were two uniformed police officers and somehow we both instinctively realised what horrific news they'd brought with them. In an instant our world was turned upside down when they told us that a few hours earlier, Josie's daughter Katie had been tragically killed in an accident whilst riding pillion on her boyfriend's motorbike. Josie immediately broke down and was inconsolable. Obviously I tried my best to comfort her, but there's not really a great deal one can do at such times.

After the initial shock, all concerned were informed and the funeral service took place at Leven Church soon after. Close family and friends walked behind hearse from the house to the church, and when we arrived I think most of the village was there. Katie had loads of mates, so the place was packed to the rafters. For her send-off they played one of her favourite songs, 'Shiny Happy People'. She was buried in the churchyard and 'Shiny Happy Person' was engraved on her headstone. It was obviously a difficult and sad time but very reassuring that so many people cared so much about her. As they say, "Only the good die young."

Time passed and slowly some sort of normality resumed. We eventually settled into our somewhat mundane but satisfying routines with dinner parties, BBQs and the occasional live gig. Our friends Chris and Jan even taught us how to play bridge.

There was also plenty of travelling and foreign holidays to Greece, Spain and other mainly European destinations. And let's not forget Italy, where we were given the old heave-ho from the much overrated and exceedingly dull 'Harry's Bar' in Venice for wearing shorts. Pardon silly old me, but it was only ninety-five in the shade and we forgot to pack our heavy tweeds. I'd really like to think that somewhere out there is a small but exclusive 'worldwide club' of fellow scantily and inappropriately clad misfits, who take perverse pride in also having been booted out of such a pretentious, glorified gargle-factory. Apart from that, Venice was amazing.

Another trip was to the Italian Riviera, where we stayed in a luxury villa with a private beach in Sorrento on the fabulous Amalfi Coast. We even had our own personal chef if we didn't want to bother going into the town after a hard day's sightseeing in Naples or the Isle of Capri. Whilst there we obviously had to see Pompeii and Mount Vesuvius so arranged a coach trip that unfortunately picked us up at 6.30 in the morning which was a real drag after a skinful the night before.

As well as a hangover I had a very gippy tummy that got worse and worse as we drove towards the volcano and by then I'd broken into a cold sweat. There was nowhere to stop on the long winding climb and I was seriously panicking about having to make an emergency call of nature halfway up a barren mountainside in front of a bus-load of passengers. Imagine the shame.

Then the coach driver announced on the tannoy that under no circumstances should anyone use the filthy, disease-ridden toilet in the gift shop once we got to the top. However, regardless of the warning, upon reaching the summit I was so desperate I didn't give a tinker's cuss whatever the state of loo and rushed straight to the forbidden bog for the best eruption I've ever had in my entire life. Very few people can claim to have pooped in Pompeii or evacuated their bowels on top of Vesuvius, so that's another exclusive club of which I'm now a proud member.

Tex and Josie.

71

Samoir Django Festival

Probably my favourite trip was to France after watching a fantastic TV documentary called *Django Legacy*. The programme was all about the Gypsy Jazz Festival held there every year, so we decided to check it out for ourselves. The festival site location was a small island on the river at Samoir Sur Seine, former home and last resting place of guitar genius Django Reinhardt. Everybody from Les Paul to Eric Clapton idolise Django, who is justifiably recognised as the most influential guitarist of all time. Almost unbelievably he developed his unique style after losing two fingers in a caravan fire.

We drove over with Stuart and my sister Jane and stayed at a hotel in Fontainebleau just a few miles from Samoir. Whilst there and not averse to a bit of 'effin' culture', we spent a day at nearby Monet's house and gardens at Giverny and also the village of Barbizon, home of realism and the romantic art movement. Another outing was a tour of the

Chateau de Fontainebleau and also a day trip to Paris, but the highlight without doubt was the three-day festival itself.

The line-up of guitarists and musicians included Bireli Lagrene, Martin Taylor, Stochelo and Jimmy Rosenberg, Babik Reinhart, and my favourite, Gary Potter from Liverpool. All over the island, everywhere you looked were amazing little duos and trios strumming away, entertaining passers-by and blowing a few minds in the process. The musicianship was staggering, the weather perfect and the setting idyllic. In fact the whole event was magical and could not have been bettered. Even after the official concert had finished, fretboard duels carried on into the night with all the players trying to out-do each other's licks and reaching a climactic and almost unbearable level of passion and intensity.

Also in Fontainebleau itself, the whole weekend was dedicated to music with bands playing in every bar and restaurant. All the streets were packed with buskers and huge crowds dancing right through the night. Back at the hotel bar, we were having a drink when in walked Scouser Gary Potter who was also staying there, as was Martin Taylor.

Anyway, I said to Gary, "How about a little tune?"

He said, "Sure," fetched his guitar and started playing especially just for us.

As well as gypsy jazz he can also play country-style pickin' better than just about anybody else on the planet. After a perfect rendition of Albert Lee's 'Country Boy' I jokingly asked him, "Don't you ever play a bum note?" at which point he launched into an hilarious Les Dawson routine with duff notes right, left and centre. I don't think his poor old guitar knew what had hit it and next thing we knew he'd bust a string. This I blagged for a keepsake and I've still got it stashed away in a drawer somewhere. Also for posterity I took a photograph of him taking a photograph of me. We had such a fabulous time that I would have loved to go back again, but alas it never seemed to happen.

There was a slightly strange holiday we had touring Scotland, which included a massive whisky-tasting blowout in Oban. Having worked our way through the menu to see which one we liked best, we got very confused and had to start right at the top of the list again. By the time we'd finished, Josie was so smashed that I had to physically restrain her from jumping aboard the last ferry of the day to Mull. Obviously she had some romantic notion of sailing off to a distant island but with absolutely no thought whatsoever of where she might sleep once she arrived in the middle of the night.

Having recovered next day we headed to the pretty little village of Plockton, up near the Isle of Skye. Plockton is on the Gulf Stream, with palm trees growing along the waterfront, and was the film location for the *Hamish Macbeth* TV series. We stayed at a fabulous B&B owned by Jane and Rod MacLeod that is reputed to have the most beautiful view in Scotland overlooking Loch Carron. Rod, it turned out, was born at Dunvegan Castle, the ancestral home of the Clan MacLeod on Skye and was something like third in line for the grand title of MacLeod of MacLeod.

The day after we arrived it was Princess Diana's funeral and we were invited to spend the day with our hosts, watching the service on television. Like most women, Josie and Jane were into the whole pomp and ceremony of it, and like most men, Rod and I couldn't have cared less so proceeded to get steadily kaylied instead. The stuff we were drinking was from his private stash of limited edition, individually numbered bottles of Dunvegan Whisky and it was lethal. I've no idea what the hell was in it, but it gave me hallucinations and the craziest dreams I've ever had in my life. All night long

I was seeing pixies, fairy rings, witches and demons plus all manner of weird Celtic symbols and mythological imagery. These visions were terrifying but also in a strange way agreeably soporific at the same time. This curious and almost supernatural experience obviously left a lasting impression, so just thought I'd mention it in passing.

Apart from once spending a horrendous wild, wet and windy weekend in Wales hanging on to a tent for dear life, most of these vacations were very enjoyable. Over time, though, with a few notable exceptions, all these foreign holidays, pleasant as they had been, seemed to merge into an almost indistinguishable amorphous blur.

After Josie sold her telecom business, she had plenty of time for hobbies such as walking club (she doesn't like it called rambling), where she completed both 'Coast to Coast' and 'The West Highland Way' amongst others. Also, being very creative, she loves painting, gardening, knitting, sewing, making tapestries and even belongs to the Women's Institute, none of which sounds very rock 'n' roll to me. In fact we are like opposite poles that attract. She likes coffee; I like tea. She likes brown bread; I like white. She likes pasta; I like rice. She watches trash TV; I don't. She listens to the Eagles whereas I listen to anything except the bloody Eagles, and so on and so forth. Even so, we still mostly rub along quite nicely despite our glaring disparities, though we both like Marmite. She also likes to think she keeps my feet on the ground, which is probably true, though I hate to admit it. Slowly but surely, it's almost as if my Blue Suede Shoes were turning into a pair of boring old Blue Suede Slippers.

72

Sam Miguels

Then in the early 1990s, DJ and promoter Steve Bird and I were offered some free quiet nights at a Leeds club called Sam Miguels by Julia, a mutual friend, so we decided to try our luck and put on a few live gigs.

Steve had previously been in Worcester for a while, where he ran his 'Birdsong Studio' recording ultra-heavy metal bands with daft names like Defecation, Pungent Stench and Doom. Also SOB from Japan and Napalm Death, who, according to the Guinness Book of Records, recorded the shortest song in the world called 'You Suffer' that was only 1.316 seconds long. He'd now moved back up north but retained his grind-core contacts from the Midlands and the plan at Sam Miguel's nightclub was to alternate rockabilly one week and death metal the next.

We kicked off by booking top rockabilly boys Restless together with local Wakefield outfit Darren and The Juvies as support. It proved a good start as both these bands were fantastic and it turned out a pretty successful night. Elkie Brooks' husband Pete Gage, who was Restless manager, also came along during the evening to keep an eye on his protégés. Pete was former guitarist with Vinegar Joe as well as iconic '60s groups The Zephyrs and Geno Washington's Ram Jam Band, so it was a privilege to meet him, even though for some reason he was now operating under the pseudonym Mickey Mutant. Perhaps he just wanted to distance himself from crazy King Kurt, a psychobilly band he was also managing at the time. Allegedly they used to crap live onstage, though it could be just an urban myth.

The following week we had Steve's choice, a shambolic crew called Extreme Noise Terror plus some obscure support act. The guys didn't have transport so they travelled to Leeds by train but turned up late, out of their heads with no equipment. We managed to cobble together some amplifiers and other gear, but it sounded totally shite. Or maybe that's how it was meant to sound, I don't know. Anyway it was all alien to me. Besides that, hardly anyone showed up so I can only assume death metal at the time was not as popular as Steve had led me to believe.

The following week we managed to book another hot rockabilly, or should I say psychobilly, band called Guana Batz supported again by The Juvies. This should have been a sell-out apart from the fact it clashed with another big psychobilly outfit Demented Are Go at a much more established Leeds venue. We gave it one more try, this time with a 'Mad'chester indie band called 'King of the Slums' and just about broke even. This was only because the Happy Mondays cancelled last minute at Leeds Poly and we managed to drag a load of their disappointed fans down to Sam Miguels. By now we were fed up losing money, or at least not making any, so gave it up as a bad job. Ah well, another good idea bites the dust.

My next brainwave was to set up 'Pigsty' recording studios at Catwick farm near Beverley in East Yorkshire, where I was now happily residing after leaving London for the country life. As the name suggests it whiffed somewhat but the rent was cheap. The costs were shared with another guy and I also occasionally hired it out as rehearsal space so the place just about paid its way.

After recording two of my own solo projects, 'Ripsnorter' and 'Jazzabilly Bopcats', my old mate Paul O'Hara from Doo-Be-Wah asked if I'd help him put down a few tracks, which I was thrilled to do. He came up from London to stay for a couple of weeks and the end result was a fabulous CD entitled *Nailed Together* containing some of my all-time favourite songs.

Another pal called 'Egg' played guitar in Buff Meaba, a band from Hull. They sounded brilliant and in a moment of madness I offered to be their manager. The idea was to secure a record deal and hit the big time, but of course the reality was a lot of hard slog and a big hole in my wallet. It's a drag the plan failed as they had massive talent, a great image and prodigious song-writing skills, but were simply in the wrong location.

Although the Buffs played a few dates round Camden and Islington, for any number of reasons they weren't prepared to move permanently to where the action was so their fate was sealed. Shame. Problem was that Hull doesn't get many passing A&R men, so in reality London or Manchester were the only places at that time to ensure success.

This is rather unfair as Hull has always had a thriving music scene, with the New Adelphi having been on the main national band circuit since 1984. The club owned by Paul Jackson had all the top names over the years as well as spawning home-grown artists such the Beautiful South, Housemartins and Fatboy Slim.

Another very good Hull venue was The Jailhouse run by guitarist Keith 'Ched' Cheesman, whose older brother John ('Big Ched') was a fan of my old band Gospel Garden back in the '60s. John would often act as unofficial minder whenever we gigged in the area and saved our skins on more than one occasion.

There have always been plenty of other music pubs and clubs in the city where local boys such as Mick Ronson's Rats and Spiders from Mars learnt their trade, so it's a pity that so few talent scouts ever got to visit, lazy sods.

While we're at it, let me just mention two great noble Hull institutions on Beverley Road (or Beverley Rerd in Hullspeak). The first one being 'Antones Guitars' owned by Tony Trotman-Beasty, a friend of mine and stalwart of the Hull scene. The other is Blakos 'Gig Shop' that's been supplying custom flight cases and PA sound systems for over fifty years. Oh, and lest I forget, one other notable place of worship that's also been operating for over fifty years is Keith Herds' iconic Fairview Studio. Everyone from Marty Wilde and Def Leppard to Heatwave, Paul Heaton and Shed 7 have recorded there over the years.

73

'60s Megabash

In 1999, Dimples drummer Stuart Smith appeared out of the woodwork suggesting we should reform the old band in order to celebrate the approaching Millennium and put on a charity reunion gig. Myself and guitarist Greg Tomlinson from the original Dimples 'Decca' line-up happily volunteered, but Gladwin and Wincott declined, miserable sods. Instead we recruited former Imps vocalist Fred Havercroft and Bill Gibson, who was now playing bass, so problem solved.

During that summer I had the use of my sister's garage and we began to practise in earnest, revamping old favourites from our former repertoire into a forty-five-minute set. Even after a thirty-five-year-layoff it actually started sounding pretty good, so we decided to record twelve of the best songs for a Dimples/Imps CD that is now on YouTube.

In the meantime, the reunion idea seemed to be catching on with a few other groups and a plan for a Millennium '60s 'MEGABASH' began to formulate. Smithy seemed to know everybody in town and generously offered to sponsor the event through his 'Smiths' and 'David Jason' fashion shops. Suddenly word of Megabash spread like wildfire amongst the local musicians. Spud Tate heard about it and re-formed the Badd Ladds, Steve Bird resurrected the Kraakens, Tony Borrell brought the Cadillacs out of retirement, and Tweedy and Andy Boyd revamped the Worrying Kind. All this was topped off with the Dimples, Aussie Pink Floyd psychedelic light show and Jill Firth's delightful Go-Go dancers 'People & Co'.

At the start we had absolutely no idea how it might work out but took the risk and booked the Baths ballroom, which was the biggest venue in town. Next, a vigorous promotional campaign thankfully caught the public's imagination and by the night of the big event, hundreds of old mods from the Jazz Workshop and Mojo all-nighters were flocking in from all corners of the globe. Everyone wanted to meet up again and catch up with the faces and bands they remembered from their pill-popping teenage raver days.

Even former Imps drummer Chris Ellerton and his family showed up from Canada, where they were now resident. With a great deal of help from Spud Tate and his missus Pat, the big charity night was a total sell-out and monster success, with all-time record attendance and bar takings. Local historian Don Ayris filmed the entire show and we sold the resulting video to bands and fans alike. Much of this Dimples footage can still be viewed on YouTube, together with several more Dimps CDs. It was indeed a fantastic event and so successful that Smithy and I continued to stage further '60s Megabashes for the next five years.

After Megabash, the Dimps carried on gigging until 2010, by which time I was also in a duo called the Beverley Brothers performing mainly Everlys covers. My partner in the Bev Bros was a great singer called John David Parker (otherwise known as JD), whom I'd known back the '60s. Bizarrely I discovered he'd been living in Catwick (where I had my Pigsty Studio) for several years without me even realising.

JD served his vocal apprenticeship in various Humberside Mod groups such as the Peighton Checks and the Hammer, during which time he'd been working with Rod Temperton from Heatwave who wrote *Boogie Nights* and most of *Thriller* for Michael Jackson. After a stint at the legendary Star Club in Hamburg he began writing his own dance material and carved out a solo career on the trashy but lucrative European disco scene.

In Germany he became a highly successful record producer, churning out a massive succession of worldwide hits, resulting in forty or more platinum, gold and silver albums and discs, including a song he wrote for Tom Jones. There were also two admittedly cheesy number-one hit singles by 'Goombay Dance Band' and 'Taco' with his 1983 rendition of the old standard 'Puttin' on the Ritz'. JD was even thanked personally in New York by its original composer Irving Berlin, but to be truthful the version was a real stinker. In fact the song was recently slated mercilessly on Graham Norton's 'I Can't Believe It's Not Better', who quipped, "Taco, tacky more like," and "What rhymes with Ritz?" Ouch. Vaguely amusing, though I'll wager it's Mr Parker that was laughing all the way to the Bradford and Bingley.

JD had returned in 1993 with his family to England to start a new venture producing meditation music for use in his hypnosis and complementary therapy practice. Though slightly sceptical initially about alternative medicine, I tried a few of his treatments to learn what it was all about. He had a group of fellow healers who did 'laying-on of hands' and I began to understand and appreciate the concept over time. Then after a horrific attack of gallstones I met one of their members who was a miracle worker, which finally convinced me there was something in this mumbo-jumbo after all.

The Beverley Brothers Duo.

For months I was in agony and waiting desperately to get into hospital for an operation when JD recommended Ray Brown, one of the top psychic healers in the country. He would go into a deep trance and be taken over by another entity Paul, who did the work. His voice, personality and whole demeanour instantly changed, which was very freaky, but he sorted me out in no time. After only a couple of sessions my symptoms had completely vanished and the hospital doctors could hardly believe the stones had gone without me having surgery.

The Bevs later did a gig at Sue and Tony Hewitt's 'Harmony Lodge' near Scarborough for healer Ray Brown and his wife Gillian on their wedding anniversary. Tony (who is three times world side-car champion) just happened to take a photo of them dancing together with us performing in the background. He sent us a copy of the photo and we were flabbergasted to see the room swimming in ethereal blue orbs (no, not balloons), so make of that what you will. Life is increasingly strange.

74

A Bonfire of The Vanities

'A bonfire of the vanities' was the burning of thousands of objects condemned by Italian religious authorities in fifteenth-century Florence. Anything regarded as sinful, such as books, musical instruments, playing cards, manuscripts of secular songs, works of art, paintings, sculptures, vanity items such as mirrors, cosmetics and fine dresses, were all destroyed. Similar acts of destruction were performed by Oliver Cromwell during the English Revolution and also by Thomas Cromwell who in Tudor times demolished countless monasteries. ISIS trashed and looted Mosul Museum and elsewhere after the Iraq War. It's so much easier for soulless scum to break rather than to make or create. Sadly the list of such appalling acts of vandalism is endless.

As you may have noticed I'm not a great fan of political correctness. Not sure if it's being overly melodramatic but by making some slightly iffy joke or frivolous comment, anyone these days can risk getting banned from social media and maybe even be accused by the thought police for some absurd hate 'non-crime'. So far there have been more than 120,000 such incidents in the UK when over-zealous cops started following unlawful 'College of Policing' guidelines (see Harry Miller court case). In Scotland now, kids are encouraged to snitch on their parents for saying the 'wrong' thing, even in the privacy of their own home. Plod has seriously lost the plot.

There are many others (the silent majority) who are increasingly frightened to speak their mind in public without the fear of censorship, cancelling, losing their job or worse. Most of these Stasi-style witch-hunts come courtesy of the rabid, perpetually offended Twitter mob who, it seems to me, are so intolerant they can't be reasoned with. Those pushing this pernicious culture war are like spoilt, petulant toddlers that can't even see the hypocrisy or irony of their spiteful behaviour and selective outrage. The best thing to do is just rip the piss. Being so dense and lily-livered they probably won't even realise.

So, beg pardon for stating the bleedin' obvious, but the scourge of this political correctness, jiggery-wokery and all the other fallacious variants have a great deal to answer for. Some of these deranged ideologies may well have started out with the best of intentions but have been hijacked and cynically perverted along the way. The road to hell and all that. Call me old-fashioned but here in Britain, as far as I'm concerned, respect, good manners and a sense of humour are all that should be needed for people to co-exist, not bogus-wokus, hocus-pocus.

Having said that, I might actually agree with some of their tenets, but herein lies the problem. With these vindictive, brainwashed fanatics it seems there's no nuance. Apart from being miserable, joyless simpletons, all their beliefs and dogmas are conflated, so it's all or nothing. Disagree with even one aspect and you are a branded a Nazi, fascist, racist, transphobic, gammon or any other random insult of the day. Because they keep shifting the goal posts and won't allow any reasonable debate, I believe it becomes impossible for any rational person to support their intolerant, radical extremism or malicious tactics in any way.

Very disturbing is the insidious way that academia and long-established institutions have now been infiltrated and infected by this mania. Museums, libraries and the National Trust, etc., are the very places that should be protecting our heritage, not revising or eradicating it. Go figure.

Of course we all want a better, fairer and more harmonious world, but in my opinion, their naïve, abstract, childlike, post-modern Utopian dreams are way beyond unrealistic. Remember, these are the narcissistic, uninformed, barbarian crackpots that topple statues, ban (effectively burn) books and actively promote cultural self-loathing. They manipulate language with Orwellian doublespeak and foolishly attempt to re-write history in accordance with questionable contemporary morals and criteria.

The whole phenomenon defies logic. It's almost inconceivable to me how much oppressive toxic twaddle can be promulgated and enforced by such a small but extremely noisy and hostile vocal minority. In so many ways this is the thin end of the slippery slope. Roll on the backlash and let's hope for a better and brighter future without any more of this profoundly irritating and vexatious nonsense.

Like most folk I believe in free speech and common sense and think that generally (with the obvious exceptions), it basically boils down to two simple rules. 'Live and let live' and 'treat others as you want to be treated'. Unless they deserve a good kicking, of course, ha ha.

There are clearly lots of other subjects to *rant* about, but this religious cult of woke, even though increasingly passé, still stubbornly manages to hang about like a bad smell. By all means let them believe what idiotic shite they like, but don't try and force it on the rest of us. With a bit of luck, woke will eventually eat itself and be irrelevant by the time anyone reads this… or God help us.

75

Conspiracy Theory Or Fact?

Other than music, my own various pastimes over the years have been collecting vintage American '40s and '50s clothing, reading, jogging (till the knees gave up), cooking curries, UFO-spotting (saw lots over East Yorkshire) and, as you may have suspected, conspiracy research. If only half of it's true, it still makes more sense than most mainstream horse feathers. Or even if a total pack of lies it produces far better fiction than most sci-fi thrillers. In any event it's seems sensible to at least keep an open mind and question everything.

So, let the scoffers scoff, but just read a few of the right books and you'll soon realise nothing is as you thought it was. If you don't believe it, check out Fritz Springmeier's distressing but vital work of unmasking MKUltra, trauma-based mind control, multiple personality disorder (MPD), dissociative identity disorder (DID), elite pedo rings, human sacrifice and satanic bloodlines. Some of this chilling subject matter was lightly touched upon in the 1962 film *Manchurian*

Candidate starring Frank Sinatra and Laurence Harvey, but it's been going on in various guises for centuries.

Probably sounds like bunkum to the uninformed, but do some digging and it soon becomes clear there's a secret and hidden occult world happening all around us. Modern science and quantum physics are now making such inroads that all the old, rigid, traditional disciplines look glaringly redundant. 'There are more things in heaven and earth, Horatio'… and all that.

Everybody knows history is written by the victors who want to perpetuate the status quo at all costs. Whether human or otherwise, these entities basically rule the planet and dictate most of all we think and do. We're just prawns in the game and they programme our hearts and minds from womb to tomb via the presstitute media, together with sophisticated social-engineering techniques courtesy of think-tanks and foundations like the Tavistock Institute, Brookings and even localised organisations such as Common Purpose.

Recently, for instance, 'The Great Reset' was suddenly foisted upon us with the stated aim of 'changing society' plus an intrepid plan to 'Save the Earth'. Call me an old sceptic but what it really amounts to is a coordinated assault on the populace that has conveniently compounded the pandemic, climate change, net zero, cashless society, digital ID, social credit scores, transhumanism and lots of other crazy stuff into one big menacing package of fear porn. So, how much of this bumph is actually genuine and how much is just a massively over-hyped con trick designed by the WEF grooming gang to scare the public into submission?

If that doesn't work and the peasants revolt, the outcome is protests, violent conflict and widespread civil unrest. This will eventually create so much 'Mad Max' chaos that the technocratic, corporate overlords then have the perfect excuse to crack down and take complete totalitarian control. Either way the sickos win. Or if all else fails they'll contrive a war. Divide and rule is always central to the global elite's devious plot for world domination. Farfetched? Perhaps, but there's definitely something deeply dippy going on down in Davos.

Thankfully an increasing number of people worldwide are now wising up and rejecting MSM fake news, misinformation and blatant lies. It's patently obvious there's an orchestrated campaign and outright harassment to discredit so-called conspiracy theorists and the alternative media. But just remember, the 'alternative' frequently becomes 'mainstream' once the general public eventually start to catch up months, years or decades down the line. Conspiracy theories are just spoiler alerts.

Another hypothesis, of course, is that there is no such thing as choice or free will. Everything is predestined by cause and effect, stretching back to infinity. We are all completely enmeshed in a fixed set of events with no control of the outcome whatsoever. Any pretence of self-determination is just delusion… Sounds like the perfect criminal mitigating defence plea to me.

Without casting nasturtiums, even Josie is something of a sceptic, though she did accompany me to the 2003 'Nexus' conference in Amsterdam. Amongst the many enlightened speakers there were Jim Marrs, Al Bielek, Laurence Gardner and Lloyd Pye during a three-day-long event. Most of these guys are probably dead by now, but go online and check them out anyway, together with the likes of Michael Tsarion, Jordan Maxwell, Peter Moon, Robert Anton Wilson, Bill Cooper, John Lear, Bob Lazar, Phil Schneider, Matthew Delooze and of course David Icke. Right then, that's the final mega *rant* now officially over.

Just one last thought. Perhaps the reason the planet is in such a mess is because we are all affected by the 'PETER PRINCIPLE' that states: "Sooner or later, everybody inevitably rises to their own level of incompetence." Yes, I can relate to that, ha ha.

76

Final Curtain

Anyway, back to the story. A couple of years after Katie's accident, Josie's mother died and it was decided that her dad Jack would sell his house in Lincolnshire and move next door to us in Leven. Jack was a really decent bloke, but like most of his generation he'd fought in the Second World War and then spent the rest of his life grafting for peanuts. He was now getting on a bit after retiring and becoming very forgetful. A wartime injury had left him deaf as a post and he often managed to fall asleep with the TV turned up full blast, keeping the poor neighbours awake half the night.

On a regular basis he'd put eggs on the stove to cook and then forget about them and nod off. Overnight the pan would boil dry and eventually melt, creating a blue fug and noxious stench that you could smell even through solid brick walls. I've lost count of the burnt and charred pans we've had to dispose of over the years. His electric bill must have been astronomical.

The old boy was becoming something of a liability, so we had to constantly keep our eye on him until eventually he had a heart attack followed by a stroke and finally ended up in Beverley Hospital. Despite his quirks he was a good old boy and Josie visited him every single day without fail for months until the end. She's totally loyal and brilliant like that.

My own parents also died shortly afterwards but guess they'd had a good innings. I was obviously upset but also partly relieved, especially as Mum had been ill for some time. They too had been caught up the Second World War like everybody else at that time. Eric, my dad (nicknamed Sneg), was an RAF radio operator on Halifax Bombers and by all accounts was fortunate enough to have had what they called 'a good war'.

According to his own memoirs, after basic training he was sent by convoy to India and stationed at Kodaikanal, known as the princess of hill stations. Being an accomplished pianist, much of his four years there was spent tinkling the ivories in various dance bands and playing football. Whilst there he also became very friendly with Dr Montessori, who created a revolutionary educational system that became known as Montessori Schools. He desperately missed Mum but apart from that said it was like heaven on earth. He always dreamt of returning there after the conflict but never did.

Janie, my mum, joined the WRNS (otherwise known as Wrens) together with her sister Alison and they both used to fly over enemy territory taking aerial reconnaissance photographs. Until her dying day my Auntie Alison wouldn't talk about it, having signed the official secrets act.

Lamentably, by the time you're old enough to want to know more about what they did during those dark days it's too late and they're gone. My mum was brilliant, but I didn't always get on with my old man. As a kid, though, we shared some happy times cycling out in the countryside and picking wild mushrooms or fishing with him and my granddad Wally on holiday in Bonnie Scotland. Thankfully our relationship did improve latterly but still remained somewhat fragile even to the end. Then all of a sudden we're all getting frighteningly ancient ourselves. Increasingly I'm not sure I actually believe in time anymore, just the eternal now. Or is it all a dream within a dream, where each day we merely wake up to a brand-new reality? Who knows?

As a result of all these family bereavements, Josie and I both received modest inheritances plus Jack's house, which became part of our vast property empire. Only kidding, though we did have five dwellings at one stage. Courtesy of Maggie Thatcher's 'Right to Buy' scheme, I'd bought and sold my London flat and with the proceeds renovated three nice village properties to rent out. Although I was never really convinced about the ethics or morality of 'Right to Buy', my conclusion was that you'd be mad not to take advantage of it. Eventually we sold both Leven houses and moved into the rural retreat, where we still reside to date. Josie in the east wing and me in the west wing, and I'm only half joking.

Apart from writing this drivel, I still enjoy playing guitar and doing occasional live recordings for YouTube and Facebook videos. By the way, that's why I started using the name Tex Austin, as there were hundreds of Craig Austins on Facebook. I even bought myself a big old double bass in order to lay down some authentic-sounding rockabilly. To get in some extra practice I joined a Pogues-style Irish band that rehearsed at a bar on Grimsby Marina, where the violinist had his yacht moored up. We had guitar, a fiddle, cajon drums and mandolin, with me on Doghouse bass and all of us chipping in with the vocals.

Then, just as everything was shaping up nicely, disaster struck as usual. Without going into the gory details, I got ill and ended up in hospital, which basically put the kybosh on any more gigging for the time being. Not only that, poor old Phil the mandolin man just dropped dead one day without warning. Rog the percussionist ended up in jail and the fiddle player was lost at sea for all I know. We might just as well have called ourselves The Jinxed.

Josie always enjoyed camping in tents with the kids when they were young but always fancied a motorhome. I kind of liked the idea too so decided to make a prototype campervan with a rear slide-out similar to the revolutionary VW 'Doubleback'. Mine was a much cheaper, more practical manually operated version that I called the 'Piggyback'. It worked brilliantly and could still be a real winner if I could find a suitable partner to help put it into production. In the end I reluctantly gave up on that idea and instead we treated ourselves to a Vee Dub T5 'gin palace'.

After fitting a pop-top roof I converted the van to our own spec with bunk beds, storage for the Brompton bikes and an emergency onboard bog which is essential when you reach a certain age. With that we drove off into the sunset to enjoy the rest of our lives as trailer trash. Livin' the dream, baby, livin' the dream. Well, maybe for a couple of weeks in July. Weather permitting... If we could be arsed, ha ha.

77

Appendicitis

It's totally irrelevant but just thought I'd just mention a little medical emergency that recently befell me. I was feeling right as rain and about to post a Halloween 'lockdown' horror video on Facebook, with me singing and holding a torch under my chin to make it look scary. OK, very silly and childish, I know. Almost immediately after doing this, I had an eerie sensation that, it being Walpurgis Night, I'd somehow provoked the devil and began to feel unwell with stomach ache and lack of energy. By Wednesday I felt no better but had a severe pain in my side so began to suspect it might be appendicitis. On the Thursday I rang the quacks for an appointment and was then immediately referred to A&E for hospital admission.

A scan confirmed my worst fears and I was pencilled in for an emergency operation next day on the Friday. I was all psyched up ready to go first thing but for some reason didn't get into theatre until seven o'clock that evening. It was a stressful day, but once there, they didn't hang about, and before I knew it, the anaesthetic kicked in and I was away with the fairies. Next thing I remember was coming to, not quite knowing where I was and spouting total gibberish, to the amusement of the surgical staff. Surprisingly they were nearly all young females with hardly a male surgeon in sight, so good on yer, gals.

It turned out that in my case, keyhole surgery was not an option and I was sliced open in the traditional old-fashioned way. They all said it was the worst and messiest appendix they'd ever seen and was literally on the verge of bursting. Basically, another eight hours and I'd have been a goner, so I was very lucky.

Back in the ward the morphine freak-show began in earnest as hostile biker gangs, football hooligans and all manner of ne'er-do-wells were out to get me. Leering monsters and demons with gaping six-foot-wide mouths kept leaping out of walls trying to eat me alive. This dystopian-type scenario carried on for a couple of days with me just about managing to control the hideous demonic visions and hallucinations. Why anyone in their right mind would want to get addicted to morphine is a mystery to me. Thankfully they put me on Tramadol and eventually just paracetamol and I started feeling slightly more human.

Sharing a ward with three or four grunting, farting, snoring blokes is not exactly my idea of fun, but after a while you do get a bit of banter going to relieve the boredom. Ultimately, however, this rapport is short-lived after you soon realise that you have absolutely nothing whatsoever in common with any of the other inmates apart from pain.

Also inevitably, there's always the nutter that manages to upset staff and vulnerable patients alike. In my case there were two. A wailing banshee that screamed and swore for hours on end, and a complete twat talking loudly on his mobile phone twenty-four seven, annoying everyone else around him to almost breaking point. After threatening suicide he was mercifully thrown out and taken away by social workers. Why on earth they don't have a separate ward for the real disruptive loonies I'll never know.

The hospital staff were simply amazing, especially considering how busy they were. From cleaners to the wonderful nurses who were angels, to the surgeons who essentially saved my life, I have nothing but the highest praise. Despite its many faults *thank goodness for the NHS*. Even the tea lady and caterers were friendly and courteous, although the food was truly disgusting. And it definitely wasn't Yorkshire Tea. Strangely enough some weirdoes actually seemed to really like the hospital food, but I managed to get a hamper delivered with some proper edible grub. I'd almost lost my appetite anyway and only thing I really fancied was fresh fruit, which for some stupid, inexplicable reason the hospital doesn't provide on the menu.

On the Wednesday I was discharged and back at home-sweet-home recuperating, feeling OK but still well spaced out. No doubt many of you have had a similar experience or worse, but what else can you do but just grin and bear it? Or is it bare it?

Yawn. Pardon me but I'm now starting to get as weary writing this bilge as you probably are reading it. In fact, congratulations if you've actually managed to get this far. Banging this crap out in dribs and drabs over the years has been an intermittent, long-drawn-out process, so please forgive me if I've lost the flow here and there.

So to quickly summarise, I'm seventy-five years old and not really sure if I'm any the wiser. I've never voted and think politics, banking, media, organised religion and wars, etc., are all a gigantic racket. I've no idea if I'm a good or bad person, and how could I possibly judge? As my dear old Scottish granny often used to say, "O wad some power the giftie gie us, to see oursels as ithers see us" (Robert Burns). Like most folk, I've done certain things I'm not proud of so hope I haven't unjustifiably pissed off too many people, and my sincere apologies to those I have. To this day, I haven't a clue who the Holy Ghost is and still think 'Hound Dog' is the best rock 'n' roll record ever made. Guess that just about sums it up.

Those, then, were the Rantings of the Loon Pant King.